THE GREAT RANGE WARS

Also by Harry Sinclair Drago

THE GREAT RANGE WARS

Violence on the Grasslands

Harry Sinclair Drago

Illustrated with photographs

DODD, MEAD & COMPANY
NEW YORK

ISBN 0-396-06242-3
Library of Congress Catalog Card Number: 70-128862

Printed in the United States of America
by The Cornwall Press, Inc., Cornwall, N.Y.

An Introduction and

Acknowledgment

It is not often that a writer is given the privilege of renewing acquaintance with men and events that at some time in the past—now a matter of nearly half a century—he had occasion to write about at some length. With such a vast amount of material available, it raised a question: could the story of range conflicts and rangemen, from Texas to Montana, including New Mexico and Arizona, be condensed into a single volume of average length? Now that it is finished, I trust that the casual reader, for whom it is intended, will find it a rewarding experience.

Of all the myths that refuse to die, the hardest are those woven about the so-called sheep-cattle wars, the frequency with which they occurred and the blood-letting that attended them. Actually, very few serious confrontations occurred, none, with the possible exception of the Pleasant Valley War, in Arizona, serious enough to deserve the name of war. In that instance the invasion of a band of sheep triggered the feud that followed in which a score of men died. Very few sheep were killed. The charge that sheep destroyed range—which they did when close-herded—was largely forgotten by some of the big outfits when they began running sheep as well as cattle, in the late 1880's. That didn't include the old-timers, who continued to regard the sheepman as an inferior. I had a father-in-law, a ranch-bred man who had become a very successful attorney, who was so prejudiced against sheep that he would not permit mutton to be served at his table.

In Colonial days swine were to be found on every homestead. Because they were easily raised and multiplied so rapidly, pork became the principal item of the American diet. It was not until after the conclusion of the War Between the States that America became a beef-eating nation. It was coincident with the development of what soon came to be called the range cattle business, which simply amounted to placing a great number of cattle on open range and raising them for beef. It began in Texas with its reservoir of millions of Longhorns. It was not, however, the beginning of the cattle business in what was to become the United States. In Virginia, long before the Revolution, cattle were being "walked" through Cumberland Gap from Kentucky to the Tidewater settlements. In New England drovers were buying cattle (Guernseys, Ayrshires and other English strains, in no sense range animals) as far out from Boston as the Connecticut River Valley and walking them to market over the well-defined Bay State Cowpath.

As early as 1828, thousands of cows, mules, turkeys and some horses were moving out of the Midwest into Pennsylvania over the Three Mountain Trail, which after crossing the Alleghenies, reached Harrisburg, the most important cattle market in America, where buyers from New York, Philadelphia and Baltimore were waiting to "dicker" with the herdsmen. Being a hard-cash market, it attracted thieves and cutthroats. It followed that homeward-bound men were often assaulted and relieved of their money.

The range cattle business began in Charles Goodnight's time and he saw it reach its peak. Of all the great plainsmen there were none to compare with him. Granville Stuart, the father of the Montana cattle trade, has been called "the Goodnight of the north." Both were men of outstanding character, but Stuart was not an Indian fighter nor a trailblazer, as Goodnight was. He saw it all: the killing off of the buffalo; the removal of the Indians to reservations; the upgrading of range cattle; the transformation of the Texas Panhandle from a silent, uninhabited wasteland to an ordered, thriving land of opportunity.

There was so much more I could have written about Goodnight which, due to the limitations of space, I had to forgo. Looking back, I particularly regret not having mentioned Bose Ikard, born a slave in Noxubee County, Mississippi. Of him Goodnight said:

"I have trusted him farther than any living man. He was my detective, banker and everything else in Colorado, New Mexico and any other wild country I was in. There was a dignity, a cleanliness, and a reliability about him that was wonderful.

"He was a good bronc rider, an exceptional night herder, and the most skilled and trustworthy man I had."

Long after old age forced Bose to retire, Goodnight kept in touch with him and saw to it that he did not want. When the ex-slave died, Goodnight buried him at Weatherford and erected a monument over his grave. "It was only fitting."

I wish to acknowledge my indebtedness to J. Evetts Haley for his masterful *Charles Goodnight, Cowman and Plainsman.* Many books have been written about Goodnight, but Mr. Haley is the authority on which all writers, including this one, must rely. I also want to thank William A. Keleher for his several books on New Mexico, especially for *Violence in Lincoln County,* which untangled for me the complex, often incredible relationship of Alexander McSween, John Chisum and William (the Kid) Bonney.

No one can attempt to tell the story of the Pleasant Valley War without leaning heavily on Earle R. Forrest's *Arizona's Dark and Bloody Ground.* Although I have not always agreed with him, measured against other available sources, he is the authority.

When the scene of range violence shifts to Wyoming, a mass of material confronts the commentator. In the past, in various articles and at least two books, I have ventured to tell the story of what transpired there. I have discovered nothing in the interim to cause me to change my mind about my earlier observations. That is especially true in regard to the Cattle Kate episode.

Numerous accounts of the Johnson County War and its causes have been written. Whether in defense of the powerful big cattle interests that had a stranglehold on Wyoming, or promoting the case of the "little fellers," the underdogs, all are biased. From the very nature of the conflict, that is inescapable. You either espouse the cause of the vested interests and accept their argument that they were being constantly harassed and begowked by the small farmer-stockman (nester) with his hundred cows, or, unable to close your eyes to the campaign of injustice piled on injustice directed at him, you are driven to his defense. During those years of conflict there was no neutral ground; you were either on one side or the other. Three quarters of a century later, that is still true. The best the historian can do is to tell it as it was and trust that bias stops short of prejudice.

I am especially grateful for Helena Huntington Smith's *The War on Powder River*. It is caustic, embittered and reflects my previously published condemnation of the Wyoming Stock Growers' Association.

Because the only photograph of Granville Stuart with which we are familiar was taken in 1909, when he was seventy-five, the image we have of him is that of an old man. But he was only forty-five when he brought his first herd into Fergus County, in 1879, and established the range cattle business in eastern Montana. In 1884, when he led the fight against the organized rustling ring in the so-called "Horsethief War," he had just turned fifty. His *Forty Years on the Frontier* has long since become a classic. If you would see him through cowboy eyes, read Teddy Blue Abbott's *We Pointed Them North* (put on paper by Helena Huntington Smith), the best of all books of cowboy reminiscences.

I have many people to thank for the material that has been made available to me. Particularly I must thank my friend Melvin J. Nichols for opening his library to me and placing in my hands some unpublished letters of Charles Goodnight to his friend Martin S. Garretson, historian and Secretary of the American Bison Society; and to Peter Decker, author, antiquarian and the most knowledgeable of all authorities on the West. Needless to say, I have received help from the historical societies of Wyoming, Montana and the University of Texas Library, the New York Public Library, and my own White Plains, New York, Public Library. Last but not least, I am grateful for the knowledge I have gleaned from the various Brand Books of the Westerners.

Harry Sinclair Drago

Contents

Illustrations

xi

WARRIORS OF
THE LLANO

I

Comanche Moon

On a June morning brilliant with sunshine, in 1881, five young riders loped into Tascosa, the cluster of unpainted buildings on the north bank of the Canadian, sixty miles up the river from the L X headquarters. The spring work over, they knew they would find others of their breed in town for a little hilarity.

Four of the five were seasoned men. Two of them, Jim East and Charley Siringo, the well-known L X wagon boss, had been over in New Mexico for a year, recovering drifted cattle and helping Pat Garrett round up Billy the Kid and his outlaw gang. The fifth man was young Fred Leigh, a new L X hand. He rode with them on their sufferance this morning. In the rough camaraderie of the range, he was one of them, but he had not cracked the inner circle of their acceptance.

To make sure that their coming was noticed, they raced down the main street, past the Widow Turner's boarding house, frightening the ducks that waddled about in a wire fence enclosure in her front yard, past Grabowski's general store, the cabin that was the post office, and the familiar old saloons, built of cedar pickets. They pulled up with a flourish that stood their broncs on their hind legs when they reached the hitch-rack in front of Jack Ryan's new establishment.

They agreed that Tascosa had surely changed since they were there last. With pride they saw that Ryan's emporium was built of dressed lumber that had been freighted all the way down from Dodge City, two hundred and twenty-five miles to the north.

They stepped inside to be confronted with other wonders—a back-bar mirror twenty feet long and chandeliers of oil-burning ormolu lamps suspended from the ceiling. These were physical things that they could understand, and they talked about them as they stood at the bar drinking Jack Ryan's red wheat whisky from Taos.

A shadow fell across the doorway and a man appeared, so tall and big that, unconsciously, he stooped a bit as he entered. They knew him at a glance. Here truly was a man cut to their own pattern. "Cape Willingham!" they cried, slapping him on the back. He tried to buy the drinks, but they wouldn't allow it. Charley Siringo, or maybe it was Jim East, noticed the star of polished nickel Cape wore on his vest, and his mouth fell open with surprise.

"Sheriff?" he questioned incredulously.

"That's right," the big man acknowledged a bit shamefacedly. "You're in Oldham County now. We organized a few months back and I was elected sheriff the same time Marion Armstrong was named justice of the peace. I don't like to bear down on you, boys, but you better hand your guns over to Jack until you're ready to leave. It's now against the law to pack a gun in Tascosa."

Four of them handed over their guns. They didn't like the idea, but if Oldham County wanted to play it that way, they would go along. Only Fred Leigh demurred. The liquor he had imbibed was gnawing at him. He said he had his rights and he'd be double damned if he was going to stand for anything like that. "I'm quitting this town right now and I ain't coming back."

He stormed out to his horse and left Tascosa in a smother of dust. Willingham stepped out and watched him leave, after which the sheriff walked up the street and sat down with Marion Armstrong in the cabin the justice of the peace shared with the U.S. post office.

Unknown to Cape, Fred Leigh had gone only a few miles, when his indignation boiled over. Obsessed with the feeling that he had suffered a great indignity, he turned back to town, determined to show the sheriff that he couldn't be pushed around.

The Widow Turner's ducks were still waddling about in their enclosure when he passed. His trigger finger itched with the thought that here was an opportunity to humiliate the sheriff. He brought his forty-five up and with luck, after several misses, knocked the heads off two of Widow Turner's ducks.

Young Leigh was standing at Ryan's bar, downing a drink, a few minutes later, when a man popped in and whispered to Charley Siringo that Cape was coming down the street carrying a double-barreled shotgun. Charley relayed the message to Jim East, and they tried to get Leigh's gun away from him. They were still struggling when Willingham walked in. A hush fell on the barroom.

"Hands up!" Cape barely had time to utter the words long reserved for such moments, when Leigh's pistol came up. The shotgun roared. Leigh pitched forward, dead before he hit the floor, "a senseless sacrifice on the altar of progress," as Fred Bechdolt observed half a century later.[1]

They buried Fred Leigh the following afternoon in what had been old man Rinehart's pasture, at the western edge of town, where other men who had expired in a flash of gunfire had been interred. But this was different; this was a legal killing and so ordained under the statutes of the State of Texas. The onlookers turned back to town, hoping that an alcoholic solvent would clear their minds and enable them to comprehend what had happened. It did. There was no question about it, they agreed: that indefinable thing called the law had come to Tascosa and the Panhandle.

But it was only a faint scratch; years were to pass before it acquired the authority to separate the sheep from the goats and draw the line between good men and bad. That year, 1881, the Texas Legislature had established the Thirty-fifth Judicial District, which embraced the present twenty-six counties of the Panhandle and the disputed part of Indian Territory known as Greer County. Or, in other words, all of that part of Texas west of the one hundredth meridian and north of an east-west line running from the southeast corner of present Childress County to Texico on the New Mexico boundary, a land mass larger than the combined area of several Eastern states. Most of the counties were still unorganized, and among the few that were, organization had not proceeded beyond haphazard machinery for the collection of taxes.

The legislators' belief that a lone prosecutor and a district judge, moving about that vast kingdom of grass and cattle by buggy, with their traveling court, could establish law and order, was due more to their niggardliness than their faith in their appointees, District Attorney J. N. Browning and Judge Frank Willis. In fact, some members of the august body were not sure that the Panhandle was, or should be, a part of the State of Texas.

A hint of which way the wind was blowing came when the cattlemen of the short grass country buried their differences and organized the Panhandle Stock Association. In earlier days some of them may have been a bit careless about whose cattle they slapped their brand on, but the buffalo and Indians were gone and cattlemen now had a vested interest in putting down the rustler and range thievery. Hence, they welcomed the law, in fact were responsible for its coming, for, among other things, they intended to manipulate it so as to give legality, or the color of legality, to whatever steps they might be compelled to take to protect their property rights in their cattle.

Many of them were tough-minded, slit-eyed old-timers who had helped to wrest this still savage land from the Comanches, the fierce, wild lords of the Llano Estacado, and the hardly less fearsome Kiowas. The proper place to begin the story of those thirty years of range warfare is back in the decade prior to the War Between the States. There were no white settlements then in north-central Texas west of the Cross Timbers, which, with little justification, were regarded as a protective barrier against attack. Comanche war parties seemed to raid through the Timbers almost at will, stealing horses and taking scalps.

The country at large, and many parts of Texas as well, knew little or nothing about the Cross Timbers until Congress ordered the publication of Captain (later General) Randolph B. Marcy's 300-page report of his successful military expedition in 1852 to locate the sources of Red River and its principal tributaries.

"On emerging from the timbered lands upon Red River into the great plains, we pass through a strip of forest called the Cross

Timbers. This extensive belt of woodland, which forms one of the most prominent and anomalous features upon the face of the country, is from five to thirty miles wide, and extends from the Arkansas River in a south-westerly direction to the Brazos, some four hundred miles.

"At six different points where I have passed through it, I have found it characterized by the same peculiarities: the trees, consisting principally of post-oak and black-jack, standing at such intervals that wagons can without difficulty pass between them in any direction."

While Marcy cites the ease with which he crossed the Timbers on various occasions and states that wagons could get through without difficulty, the evidence is all to the contrary. The Texan-Santa Fe pioneers encountered difficulties soon after the ill-fated expedition to open a trade route to New Mexico left the Brush Creek camp, fifteen miles north of Austin, in 1841 and began fighting its way through the Cross Timbers. Three hundred and twenty young men, strong of heart and muscle, chopping down creek banks, felling timber and clearing away brush to get their wagons through, unloading and reloading them when they tipped over, and all exhausted by the sultry air in the jungle of greenery, hardly suggests the "easy going" Marcy claimed to have found. In fact, to get their wagons through, the Texans began tossing away great quantities of their provisions to lighten the loads.

"The celebrated Cross Timbers," comments Josiah Gregg, always a reliable reporter, "entirely cut off communications betwixt the interior prairies and those of the great plains. They may be considered as the 'fringe' of the great prairies, being a continuous bushy strip, composed of various kinds of undergrowth; such as black-jacks, post-oaks, and in some places hickory, elm, etc., intermixed with a very diminutive dwarf oak, called by the hunters, 'shin-oak' [from which comes the Texan term shinnery]. The underwood is so matted in many places with grape vines, green briars, etc., as to form almost impenetrable 'roughs' which serve as hiding places for wild beasts, as well as for wild Indians; and [in] savage warfare, prove almost as formidable as the hammocks of Florida."

By 1845, Texas had won its independence from Mexico and, despite the violent opposition of the anti-slavery objectors in New

England, had been admitted into the Union as its twenty-eighth state. But its treasury was so bare that it could not provide the outlying ranches and settlements with protection against Indian attacks. As the Indian depredations increased, Governor Sam Houston established the Minute Men of Texas (not to be confused with the famous Texas Rangers), a volunteer organization of a thousand armed settlers gathered in small units stationed about a hundred miles from each other, in a line southwest from Preston, on Red River, to the Mexican border on the Rio Grande. This line more or less followed the route of the Southern (Butterfield) Overland Mail, which had the protection of the chain of forts that the federal government built across Texas from Colbert's Ferry on the Red to Dona Anna, on the border of New Mexico, for the safe passage of the thousands of gold seekers streaming to California. It was not until 1851, however, that the military posts, beginning with Fort Belknap, on the Brazos, sixty miles west of Fort Worth, and Camp Cooper, on the Clear Fork, were garrisoned.

The protection they offered attracted hundreds of immigrants, mostly from Tennessee, who were arriving by covered wagon to make Texas their new home. Often as many as two hundred wagons a day were reported moving down the so-called "Texas Road," through what is now eastern Oklahoma, and crossing Red River at Colbert's Ferry. The newcomers were sturdy, homespun, pioneer stock, cut from the same cloth that Houston was. The exalted position to which their fellow Tennessean had risen in the Lone Star State may have had something to do with turning them in that direction. But the compelling factor that kept them coming was the knowledge that a farmer could find free land in Texas.

There were none who arrived without some knowledge of the precariousness of life in north-central Texas. All had heard many times the story of the Indian attack on Parker's Fort, a lonely stockade far out on the Navasota River, in today's Parker County, in May, 1836, and of the massacre of the Parker family and the carrying off into captivity of Cynthia Ann Parker, a child of nine, and her younger brother John.

It was only one of many similiar accounts of Comanche and Kiowa attack and outrage. To move out beyond one's neighbors and the hope of assistance when danger threatened was foolhardy. But many did. They built their homes, double log houses, a fireplace at both ends, with a roofed-over passageway ten to twelve feet wide between them. The windows, if any, were made small enough to bar the entry of an intruder. Such double cabins were built for defensive purposes, rather than for convenience or comfort, and they often served their purpose.

The military road between Forth Worth and Fort Belknap came to be considered settled country. Men built their homes along it, although their farms, to which they went in the morning and returned before nightfall, might be four or five miles distant. The land was productive, but the farmer soon discovered that he had no market for what he produced. Of necessity, he became more a stockman than a tiller of the soil, which made him a target for Indian raiding. Indians were not much interested in running off cattle—the country was overflowing with them—but they were bold and expert horse thieves. Although still armed only with lances and arrows, they did not hesitate to swoop in and capture a band of horses in the face of gunfire.

In the days when north-central Texas was claimed by the Spanish and the French, it was the homeland of the once numerous Caddo nation and the lesser Tonkawas and Wacos. Remnants of those tribes were still there. They were "friendly," but they were Indians, and the feeling against all Indians was so high that they were gathered up and placed on a reserve on the Brazos above the town of Waco. They objected to being herded together there, and one night several hundred broke away, hoping to reach Mexico. A company of Minute Men cut their trail, and thinking it was a band of Comanches they had intercepted, opened fire and killed half a hundred before they discovered their mistake.

Although the black-land prairies along that part of the Texas frontier north of Austin continued to attract more and more settlers, no man could consider his life and property safe. The red warriors of the Llano continued to strike with increased boldness after the U.S. War Department, in 1857, abandoned Fort Belknap. The official reason given for withdrawal was the dwindling traffic to California and the shifting of the mail route to the northern Central Overland Trail across Kansas. While that was true, the deactivating of Belknap came when the military presence was needed most.

It was well known that the favorite route of the invaders was down Pease River to within a few miles above present Vernon, then south through the Timbers toward what was then Mesquite-ville and is today Jacksboro. From there they had the border open to them for hundreds of miles. The Quahada band of the Co-manches were the most persistent raiders. Sometimes they slipped through the Cross Timbers in parties of as many as fifty naked and greased bucks. Their presence in such numbers could usually be detected before they had time to strike. But big parties were the exception; it was the small parties of a dozen at most that chose their targets, struck and were able to make off with their plunder, sometimes without suffering any casualties. But not always. The savagery of the raiders, sparing no one regardless of age or sex, mutilating the dead and destroying and burning what they did not want or could not carry off, was not only for the pleasure they derived but, in the Indian tradition, calculated to instill terror in the hearts of the enemy.

No on can say how many Indians were killed in the years of frontier war in north-central Texas. Conservative estimates place the figure at three hundred, including the battle on Pease River, in December, 1860, in which Captain Jack Cureton and seventy volunteers, accompanied by Captain Sul Ross [2] with forty-seven rangers and twenty-three dragoons from Camp Cooper, annihilated a combined camp of Kiowas and Chief Peta Nocona's Wua-hadas.[3]

This battle was fought in Comanche country, in sight of the escarpments of the Plains, and well beyond where white men had previously ventured. Sul Ross always believed that in this engagement, in a hand-to-hand struggle, he killed Peta Nocona, Cynthia Ann Parker's Indian husband and the father of her two children. This contention has been doubted, however.[4]

In the Pease River fight, white men behaved like savages, killing squaws and children and driving over their piled-up dead bodies as they charged. If they needed an excuse for their conduct, they found it in the fact that within the past month twenty-three of their neighbors and relatives had been butchered by Nocona's raiders, who had got to within fifteen miles of Weatherford, the principal settlement west of Fort Worth. The settlers had joined the expedition up the Pease for the sole purpose of delivering a full measure of retaliation.

Although it was not apparent at once, the Comanche defeat at Pease River marked the beginning of the decline of their dominance; the white man began pushing the Indian back, cutting him down, sending military expeditions against him. Like waves running unimpeded over a sandy beach, thousands of Longhorns spread out over ranges that had once been his, until he had no place to which he could turn. Grudgingly he surrendered his weapons and suffered the indignity of becoming a ward of the nation and being herded with other Indians on the Fort Sill Reservation.

But government rations and handouts were a poor substitute for the freedom that had been the Comanche way of life for untold generations. It followed that large parties of them repeatedly broke away to taste again the wild, free life of the Llano.

II

The Battle in the Palo Duro

The Indians saw their first horses when Francisco Coronado and other Spanish explorers reached the Rio Grande in 1540. Until then horses were unknown in America. Imported from Spain, of Barb ancestry, they were the progenitors of the mustang. The Comanche and Apache, bitter enemies, had of necessity done their traveling and fighting on foot till then. At first, when they stole horses from the Spaniards, it was only to eat them, for they quickly acquired a taste for horseflesh, preferring it to buffalo meat. But they soon realized that, once they had acquired the skill to ride the animal, it would give them the same mobility the Spaniard enjoyed. The experiment was so successful that the Comanches became a mounted tribe, and were soon recognized as the most expert horsemen on the plains, the proud Cheyennes not excepted.

It followed as night follows day that they began raiding the *ranchos* of New Mexico, killing and plundering as they pleased. With distance no longer a problem, they extended their marauding across the Rio Grande into Old Mexico. Between the rewards of their thieving and the natural increase of their animals, their pony herd soon was numbered in the thousands. Horse stealing with its element of danger, became the most thrilling and exciting of all sports, and the individual counted his wealth by the number of ponies he had in his herd. Before they acquired the mobility the horse gave them, the Comanches were not able to follow the annual drift of the great buffalo herd from south to north and back again with the coming of cold weather. Now, with little effort, they could move as the shaggies moved, which solved the one recurring problem of sustenance.

It could not have been for many years that among the various tribes of Plains Indians, they were the exclusive users of the horse. The foundation stock of their neighbors, the Kiowas and Southern Cheyennes, certainly must have been stolen or lured away from the Comanches. The Pawnees were among the first to have them. As early as 1731, French explorers reported having seen Pawnee warriors riding off to battle with the chest and fore shoulders of their mounts protected against attack by a shield of flint-hard buffalo hide. A year later, when La Vérendrye made his historic discoveries in Manitoba, the Black Hills and Upper Missouri, he found the Indians on small, half-wild horses of *mestengo* (Spanish) strain.

The Comanches claimed all of the Llano for their own, and although they tolerated the presence of the Kiowas and Mescalero Apaches at certain seasons of the year, they made no alliances with them. There was room enough for all, for it was a kingdom larger than that over which many white sovereigns held sway.

To those readers who are unacquainted with Texas, a word or two about that vast tableland, as it was then, is overdue. It was a treeless, almost waterless plateau fanning out from the Pecos River and running north to south for 400 miles, from a point north of old Fort Sumner, New Mexico, down to the dry canyons which form the headwaters of the Colorado River (of Texas). It then sloped eastward for about 150 miles before it came down from the Cap Rock in rough, broken escarpments to the lower prairies, covering in all an area of some 60,000 square miles, its maximum altitude 5,000 feet, which occurs on its western border, and a minimum of 2,000 feet along its southern and eastern fringe.

On its northern front there are deep gashes in the Cap Rock. The most famous is Palo Duro Canyon, which is five to fifteen miles wide and has a depth of from three hundred to fifteen hundred feet. Its eroded walls are covered with trees and brush, and with its tributary canyons, each with a stream of clear, running water, free of gypsum, forms the headwaters of Red River.

For seventy-five miles the Palo Duro slashes into the Cap Rock. There, over the years, the Comanches made their winter camp. Well grassed and wooded, it offered a comfortable haven against the storms and freezing temperatures that swept the open plains. Once their immense horse herds had been driven in, they could safely be left unguarded.

When the Comanches were the landlords of the Palo Duro, and even after they were dispossessed, thousands of buffalo annually found shelter in its depths with the approach of winter. They became co-tenants with the Indians, providing what might be called a handy "serve yourself" commissary for them.

A whole literature has evolved about the perils white men encountered in crossing the Llano, of being lost and dying of thirst because they were unable to find palatable water. Much of it is fiction. Though the flat immensity of the country was distinguished by few landmarks to give a man a sense of direction, the ease with which the Comanches coursed it, seldom being reduced to the necessity of drinking gyp water, provides a true yardstick for measuring fanciful tales.

It could not have been much earlier than 1860 when the name Staked Plains began to be applied to the northern third of the Llano. Mexican and some renegade "white" traders of Las Vegas and Taos had developed a profitable, if hazardous, trade with the Comanches, to pursue which they moved out across the Llano to barter with the Indians at some established point. Usually the amount of merchandise was so limited that it was transported on a burro or two. Combinations of traders sometimes joined together and employed a *carreta,* the traditional Mexican two-wheeled cart, to move their goods. It was these *comancheros* who were supposed to have driven a line of stakes across that part of the Llano which they traversed, to prevent becoming lost. Hence, Staked Plains became a part of the geography of the region.

Of this trade, Josiah Gregg says it was "usually composed of the indigent and rude classes of the frontier villages . . . who launch upon the plains with a few trinkets and trumperies of all kinds, and perhaps a bag of bread and another of *pinole*, to barter for horses and mules."

He is speaking of the decade of 1830-1840. Twenty years later the *comancheros* were supplying the Indians with guns, lead, ammunition, knives, whisky, brandy and various kinds of bread, demanding fantastically high prices for their merchandise and puting a correspondingly low valuation on what the Indians had for sale. Cattle stolen east of the Cross Timbers were now a marketable commodity, and for a keg of whisky a small herd of animals was sometimes exchanged. Whenever the Indians brought their white captives to these meetings, the *comancheros* purchased them, not out of the goodness of their hearts, but to hold for ransom by relatives of the captives.

While this trade was conducted with the appearance of amity, neither side could trust the other. Sometimes when the *comanchero* drove too hard a bargain in trading for a herd of cattle, he did not get far with them on his return to the settlements before the Indians stampeded the animals and, after running them off, compelled the unhappy Mexican to purchase them a second time.

If whisky was the most irresistible item of the trade, it was also the most dangerous. The *comancheros* soon learned that to put a keg of whisky in the hands of a group of Indians gathered at a rendezvous could be fatal. To avoid facing a bunch of drunken savages, they secretly buried their whisky some miles from where the trading was to occur. Reluctantly the Indians were compelled to bargain for it sight unseen. But the practice proved to be satisfactory to both sides; when the traders began their journey back to the settlements, they were accompanied by two or three Indians. When they were well on their way, they disclosed the hiding place of the keg. It was always found at the indicated spot, which purchased for the *comanchero* the privilege to come again.

From the earliest days of which there is any record, Indians were in the habit of traveling whatever distance was required to reach a saline spring and there spend a month evaporating brine and making salt. When they first encountered sugar and coffee, they were ignored as unobtainable luxuries of the white man's world, but the red man no sooner acquired a taste for them than they became necessities. It is not surprising that by 1870 the nefarious trade had become a flourishing business for Mexicans. The thousands of stolen cattle, still wearing their Texas brands, that now grazed on New Mexican ranges were an indication of how profitable it was. Out on the plains, where the thievery occurred, the Comanches made constant warfare on the Texans.

Far from putting up stakes to guide them, the *comancheros* had hammered out a trail that was as clearly defined as a wagon road. It left Las Vegas, crossed the Pecos and went down the Canadian to Sanforn Springs, in the vicinity of today's Amarillo. Another route crossed the Pecos at Bosque Redondo and, pointing to the southeast, reached the neighborhood of present Lubbock, Texas.

Some of the traffickers, men like José Tafoya, a crafty old Mexican, became wealthy and powerful enough to defeat the efforts of Territorial officials to outlaw the trade. The State of Texas also wanted to put an end to it, but appeared to be impotent to do anything until help came from the War Department in 1872, when a military expedition, commanded by Colonel Ranald S. Mackenzie, and composed of cavalry and infantry, set out from Fort Concho with the double purpose of punishing the Indians and breaking up the *comanchero* trade.

Mackenzie, one of the ablest of frontier military commanders, chased the Indians for several months, inflicting some minor defeats but unable to force them into a decisive engagement. He had better luck with the *comancheros*. Catching old José Tafoya and his crew in their camp on the Qui-ta-que, he destroyed their trade goods and burned their wagons. Unable to draw from the Mexican such information as would enable him to destroy other *comanchero* camps, Mackenzie hanged him from an upraised wagon pole and kept him dangling there until he signified that he was ready to talk.

When let down, the old man talked "plenty," as the old saying has it. Thus armed, Mackenzie proceeded to smash the illicit trade. A second expedition led by him achieved a notable victory on the headwaters of the Brazos. But peace was farther away than ever, for now, wherever they looked, the Plains Indians beheld an outrage that turned their hearts to stone: the hide hunters had begun their ruthless slaughter of the buffalo. In every direction the Indians saw the plains littered with the rotting carcasses of the animals.

For generations the buffalo had supplied them with food, raiment, the covering for their lodges, even fuel when wood was not available. In return, they had woven the animal into their religion and culture. Exterminate the buffalo, and they were a lost people.

Comanche emissaries began visiting the Kiowa and Cheyenne camps. The war drum was soon sounding night and day. Red warriors numbering as many as a thousand gathered at an appointed rendezvous on the headwaters of the Washita. A violent explosion was inevitable. It came in the pre-dawn light of June 27, 1874, in the famous battle of Adobe Walls, on the South Fork of the Canadian.

When the Indians withdrew defeated that evening, carrying their dead and wounded with them, it was not without honor. Time after time throughout that long, hot day they had swept in close to the four buildings in which the twenty-eight besieged buffalo hunters had forted up and had their ranks thinned by the murderous fire of the booming Big Fifties. The chief who led the Quahada Comanches until he was wounded, was Quanah Parker, Cynthia Ann Parker's Indian son.[1]

Indians always minimized or concealed their losses, but many years later Quanah admitted that they had had eighty killed and twice as many wounded at Adobe Walls. Prior to that battle a number of hunters and their skinners had been killed, which, coupled with the confrontation at the Walls, temporarily halted the slaughtering of the shaggies. But with a flint hide bringing three dollars at Dodge City and it not being unusual for an experienced hunter to kill a hundred animals in a day, nothing could stop the carnage for long. By 1878, the great herds of the past were gone forever.

The disappearance of the buffalo had been accomplished with the assistance of the Federal Government and the U.S. Army. When General Phil Sheridan, then commander of the Department of the Southwest, voiced his dictum that the surest and quickest way to settle the vexing Indian problem was to destroy their commissary (the buffalo), it set the pattern for what followed. In the often-cited Medicine Lodge Creek treaty of 1867 with the five Plains

Tribes, the Apache, Arapaho, Kiowa, Cheyenne and Comanches, the government promised that white hunters would not be allowed to roam south of the Arkansas River, which cuts across southern Kansas. The chiefs who signed it apparently were not aware that it did not and could not apply to Texas lands, since Texas had retained her public lands when she entered the Union. The U.S. Commissioners did not enlighten them. They got the treaty signed and it became a dead letter before the Indians got home with their presents.

Seething with rage even as they mourned their dead, most of the Indians who had participated in the Adobe Walls fight had to be put back on their reservations by force. The military and reservation officials braced themselves for a fresh outbreak. It was not long in coming. On July 4, the Bull Foot Stage Station on the Chisholm Trail, in present Kingfisher County, Oklahoma, was attacked by a band of infuriated Cheyennes. Pat Hennessey, a popular boss freighter, and his three-man crew arrived at noon to find the station a smoking ruin. The station-tender and his assistant had heeded a warning and fled in time to save themselves.

Hennessey and his crew were attacked and killed. Their wagons, loaded with coffee and sugar for the Kiowa-Comanche Agency, were destroyed. Instead of being shot, as his companions were, Hennessey was tied to a wagon wheel and burned to death. An estimated two hundred Cheyennes left the reservation at once and headed up the Washita into the Texas Panhandle, carrying with them a sizable pony herd.

Colonel Nelson A. Miles, already a veteran Indian fighter, took after them with six companies of the Fifth Cavalry. When he had cut their trail, he kept them continually on the move, giving them no opportunity to hunt or recuperate their horses. After being kept constantly on the run for four weeks, the Cheyennes surrendered. They were starving and their animals in such pitiful condition that Miles had most of them shot.

No one was ever punished for killing Hennessey and his crew. But the town of Hennessey was named for him and a monument erected in his memory.

With Colonel Miles making his headquarters at Camp Supply on the North Canadian, Colonel John W. Davidson stationed on

Otter Creek with ten troops of cavalry and two companies of infantry, and the so-called Southern Column, under Colonel Ranald Mackenzie, amounting to 14 troops of cavalry and 7 companies of infantry, based at Fort Concho, the army believed it was positioned to prevent a major breakaway of the Indians from the Fort Sill Reservation, where, under the incitement of Chief Quanah Parker, widespread unrest was growing. The climax came when the Agent refused permission for Quanah and a number of his followers to leave the Reservation for a buffalo hunt. In open defiance, three hundred Quahadas pulled down their tepees, gathered up their pony herd of some twenty-five hundred head and, taking their women and children with them, left the reservation.

That a body of such size could slip past the troops patrolling the Otter Creek district without being discovered could have been due only to the immensity of the country. Once past Colonel Davidson's patrols, they were not seen again until September 27, three weeks later, when Mackenzie, who had climbed the escarpments and crossed the Llano to the northwest, looked down from the heights and saw the Indian camp fifteen hundred feet below in Palo Duro Canyon.

Realizing that they had been discovered, the Comanches charged out late in the afternoon and met Mackenzie's forces at the junction of Palo Duro and Canyon City Blanco creeks. After a brief engagement, lasting only a few minutes, the Indians began a swift retreat to the south. This was a feint by Quanah, undertaken in the hope that Mackenzie would follow them. He was confident that after a running fight of ten to fifteen miles, he and his warriors could shake off pursuit, return to the Palo Duro, evacuate their women and children and save their pony herd and a great quantity of dried and smoked meat.

Mackenzie was not fooled by this maneuver. He dropped back a mile or two and deployed his force in a strong defensive position. As he expected, the Indians made their way back to their camp during the night by way of a trail down a wall of the canyon, with which they were familiar.

Before dawn on September 28, the troops were at the rim of the canyon and began descending to the bottom by the same means the Indians had used. When they reached the floor, they found themselves between the big pony herd and the camp.

When their presence was discovered, panic seized the camp. Squaws and children ran screaming down the canyon for the mouth of the Palo Duro, which Mackenzie had purposely left wide open.

Most of the bucks had kept a horse tethered outside the tepee. They swung up at once and began firing their rifles, outmoded Enfields that had been purchased from the *comancheros* who had smuggled them into the United States from Mexico.

In the brief fight that followed, before the Indians broke and ran, a few were killed. Some historians have placed the number at thirty; others say as few as eight. Mackenzie's losses amounted to two men wounded.

If the victory he had won is measured by a body count of the dead, it does not appear impressive. Actually, it dealt the Comanches a stunning blow from which they never recovered. Mackenzie had burned their village in the Palo Duro, destroyed their cached food, and captured their immense pony herd. To make sure that the animals did not fall into their hands again, he drove them to Middle Tule Canyon, east of where the town of Tulia now stands, and after rewarding his Tonk scouts with a few head of the best, shot the rest. Until their bones were gathered up to be sold for fertilizer many years later, the spot was known as "Mackenzie's old boneyard."

There is a wide difference of opinion as to the number of horses that were shot, the figures ranging from 1,450 to 1,885, which is not important. Mackenzie had accomplished his mission, and "coupled with Miles' defeat of Chief Gray Beard and his Cheyennes at the mouth of McClellan Creek on September 8, it could be put down as the last major engagement between red men and white in the Texas Panhandle." [2]

Two years later, in 1876, cattlemen were beginning to move in. The first to put his roots into the ground was that celebrated scout, plainsman, Indian fighter and cowman, Charles Goodnight.

With no vestige of law to restrain them, their guns their only authority, the newcomers whacked up the great sea of grass without regard for their neighbors' rights. For ten years there was hell to pay. But Goodnight, a giant of a man, standing like a rock amid the violence that swirled about him, after a long and often discouraging fight, brought a sense of peace and cooperation to the Panhandle.

VIOLENCE ALONG THE PECOS

III

The Trailmakers

As the crow flies it is approximately seven hundred miles from Macoupin County, Illinois, to Waco, Texas. By the route the covered wagons followed in their day, it was nearer eight hundred. Many of those miles were rugged, up and down over rain-slashed hills, with countless creeks and fast-running streams to be crossed. And yet in 1845, a farm boy who still had his tenth birthday ahead of him rode all the way bareback on his blaze-faced pony, moving along ahead of or beside the covered wagon in which his stepfather, mother, brothers and sisters were migrating to Texas. "It was then," Charles Goodnight recalled in his latter years, "that I learned about the sting of horse sweat on my galled groin."

The foregoing sounds incredible. But, boy and man, he was usually incredible. Almost to the end of his ninety-three years he remained hale and hearty, his hunched, rounded shoulders seeming to be too heavy for even his giant frame. Right or wrong, he walked in no man's shadow.

Though born in Illinois, his father and mother had removed there from the Barren River in the Cumberland Mountains of Kentucky. Behind them were four generations of Kentuckians, frontiersmen and Indian fighters. For an adventurous lad of ten with such a background, Texas opened a land of wonders. He saw his first longhorned cattle, and after crossing the Trinity beheld his first buffalo. At old Nashville on the main Brazos, as the family moved about, unable to decide on where to make a permanent home, he saw the settlers forted up following a Comanche raid and gritted his teeth on beholding the hacked-up bodies of the men and women they had slain. That youthful experience made him an implacable foe of Indians.

This raw, new land was too much for Hiram Daugherty, his stepfather, and after a year or more of wandering about, starvation-poor, his mother and Daugherty parted and she resumed her name of Charlotte Goodnight. At the outlying settlement of Cameron, in Milam County, she rented a farm, the family income limited to the few dollars a month that Charlie and his elder brother Elijah were able to earn tending the herds of their neighbors and doing odd jobs.

Life became somewhat easier when Charlotte Goodnight married Adam Sheek, a country preacher and widower, with a family of his own. Charlie and his new stepbrother, Wes Sheek, three years his senior, were soon boon companions, hunting and fishing together and dreaming of taking off for California. It was one of many dreams that was not realized, although they once got as far west as the beautiful San Saba River. Charlie was twenty-one and Sheek twenty-four when the latter's brother-in-law, Clinton Varney, a prosperous businessman of Waco, persuaded them to take over his herd of some four hundred head, mostly cows, on shares. They were to graze the cattle wherever they pleased; "receiving every fourth calf for pay." [1]

Since she-stuff and calves were no sale and steers were not marketable until four or five years old, they could expect no early profits. But they were in the cattle business. They drove the herd north up the Brazos and into Palo Pinto County as soon as the grass came green, and made their permanent camp at Black Springs in the Keechi Valley, which lay within the Upper Cross Timbers. It placed them on one of the main invasion routes of the Comanche raiding parties. Small as their outfit was, it did not long go unnoticed. They lost some stock, but both were expert marksmen and when they got an Indian lined up in the sights of their rifles, they usually converted him into a "good" Indian the instant they squeezed a trigger finger.

Their prowess soon attracted the attention of other settlers in the Keechi Valley, and the deserted log cabin which they had appropriated and made their headquarters became a gathering point when word swept up the valley that Indians were in the neighborhood. Six years later they were but little better off financially than when they had formed their partnership. Goodnight, frontiersman as well as cowman, had acquired a knowledge of the country second to no man's, repeatedly scouting through the Timbers and the broken lands beyond to the north and west.

Although Goodnight hated Indians, he did not hold them cheaply. He studied them, hoping he could find the key to their way of thinking and be able to anticipate them. He had very little success, for they were as unpredictable as the flight of a swarm of mosquitoes. Several commentators have said that he was consciously preparing himself for the role he was to play in the expeditions against the Indians that were to follow. There is no reason to believe this.

When in December, 1860, Captain Jack Cureton called for volunteers to join his regiment of Minute Men gathering at Fort Belknap for the campaign against the Comanches and Kiowas, Charlies Goodnight reported along with some seventy other Texans. He was just one of many, neither getting nor expecting special treatment. It was not until Captain Sul Ross arrived with his Rangers and Dragoons that he was designated chief scout for the command.

As previously mentioned, Federal troops had been withdrawn from Fort Belknap in 1857. Cureton had simply moved in and taken possession of the substantial gray stone buildings. He was still there when Texas seceded from the Union in 1861. Without waiting for official orders, he ran up the stars and bars of the Confederacy, which were to fly from its flagpole for the duration of the War Between the States.

Goodnight joined the Texas Rangers a few months after the Pease River fight, and when in December, 1861, the Minute Men were officially disbanded and the ten companies of Rangers became the Frontier Regiment, he scouted with it. In addition to

Belknap, a company of militia was stationed at Camp Preston on Red River. But even with several thousand Texans crossing Red River to fight alongside their Cherokee and Choctaw allies in Indian Territory, there were settlements along the river that never saw official Confederate gray until the trail herds began going up the Chisholm Trail to Kansas in 1869. The cowboys wearing some part of their old wartime uniform were hailed as heroes.

Although no battle of great importance was fought on Texas soil, thousands of its men were off fighting and dying with the armies of the Confederacy east of the Mississippi. With Union gunboats patrolling the Gulf ports, shutting off trade in that direction, and no northern market open, the effect on the State's economy was disastrous. So many young men had left the range that on the plains and in the brush country of south Texas thousands of unbranded cattle and mustangs were running wild.

The shortage of rangemen was due in part to the fact that Texas was being called on to supply the Confederate armies with their beef. The cattle were trailed across East Texas to Shreveport and Alexandria, where they were loaded on steamboats and shipped across the Mississippi. The operation was so vital that men taking part in it enjoyed exemption from military duty.[2]

While Goodnight's duty with the Rangers often kept him away from the Keechi for weeks at a time, his stepbrother kept their little outfit together. But Wes Sheek must have sometimes wondered why, for the prospects were not encouraging. As the war dragged on, hard money went into hiding and Confederate currency was worth only what you could get for it.

Although the C-V herd now numbered upwards of eight hundred head, including the she-stuff and calves, title still rested with Clinton Varney, their silent partner, and its value was questionable. Determined to get a better deal or give up, Goodnight went to Waco and persuaded Varney to accept his long-term notes for his interest in the partnership. He then made a similar arrangement with Wes Sheek. No money had changed hands, but if he could hang on until war's end he would be ready for the day when, in his words, "all Texas would be heading north to trade its cattle for Yankee dollars."

Among those men who were qualified to express an opinion,

Oliver Loving was regarded as the most knowledgeable and experienced cowman on the Texas frontier. As a sideline, he ran a
country store on the Belknap road. In the years before the great
war his principal business was trailing beef cattle from north-
central Texas to the Louisiana river ports. In 1858, long before
there was a Chisholm or Western trail and the only route was over
the Texas Road (the white man's Osage Trace), he had driven the
first herd of Texas cattle up through the Nations to Baxter
Springs, Kansas, and on across Missouri into Iowa and Illinois,
fashioning his own route and swimming his big steers across a
score of rivers.

He was a quiet, mild-mannered man, somewhat over fifty,
when Charlie Goodnight first attracted his attention. Better-
educated, strongly religious, Loving admired the younger man,
who was no better than half his own age, for his drive and forth-
rightness, even though because of his incessant cursing and bull-
headedness he was regarded by many as a roughneck.

With the Colorado gold rush attracting thousands of people
and flourishing new towns and camps springing into existence
overnight, it was obvious that Colorado could not fail to become
an excellent market for Texas beef. By the time the snow went off
in the spring of 1860, Loving was convinced that by going up the
Texas Road to Baxter Springs and turning west there he could
reach Denver without too much difficulty. He let it be known
that he wanted a thousand four- and five-year-old steers and would
not pay less than ten dollars a head for them on his return. The
steers were to be driven to his bedground at Fort Belknap, where
he would shape up his herd and road-brand the cattle.

By late August he was ready to move. With his crew of eight,
he drove north, crossed the Red at Rock Bluff Crossing, near
Camp Preston, and four weeks later struck west across Kansas,
following the Arkansas River all the way to Pueblo, where he put
the herd on grass to recuperate. By spring of 1861 they were fat
and ready for market and he had no difficulty in disposing of them
at a handsome profit. Before he was ready to leave, war was declared, and being a Texan, he was rounded up with other Southern sympathizers. He had become acquainted with Lucien Maxwell and the influential Kit Carson. Through their intervention

he was permitted to leave Denver with his crew. They reached the Missouri River towns by stage, and four weeks later were home.

For twenty-five years following the return of peace among the states, Loving's successful venture was the cornerstone on which all trail driving from Texas was founded. He had proved the old truth that to be valuable, livestock had to find a market. It resulted in the greatest mass movement of livestock the world has ever seen, the hoofs of no fewer than two and a half million head of cattle, mustangs and mules carving indelible trails in the prairie sod as they were driven north.

No one was more impressed by Loving's success than Charlie Goodnight. Reconstruction and its army of scalawags had settled on the State like a swarm of greedy locusts. So, infuriated by the injustices he saw being committed on every hand, he contemplated leaving Texas. But he knew if he did he could not remain away long. An invisible chain in the person of Mary Ann Dyer, the young and pretty schoolteacher at Weatherford, would bring him back.

Mary Ann Dyer—Molly to all who knew her—was from Madison County, Tennessee, the only daughter of Joel Henry Dyer, a lawyer and man of some importance. His death after coming to Texas left her an orphan with five brothers, all of whom wore Confederate gray. Goodnight had become acquainted with her when she was teaching in the one-room Black Springs school.

He managed to get to Weatherford whenever the opportunity offered, which was never more than three or four times a year. It gave his rivals an advantage. But that gave him no concern. In fact, as a lover he was so improbable that those who were watching the budding romance were sure he was making no progress with Molly, who was much too good for him. And yet, she married him in 1870, and for half a century was revered by rangemen as "The Little Mother of the Panhandle."

In the spring of 1866, Goodnight, his eyes on distant Colorado, took the step that was to win him undying fame as the great trailblazer. His plans called for putting together a herd of a thousand head of mixed cattle, including all of the C-V steers and an equal number belonging to other ranchers and handled on shares. He knew the shortest way to Colorado, but that would take him through the heart of Comanche and Kiowa country, where he was likely to lose everything. In the past at least two drives had taken the old Butterfield Mail route and eventually got through to California with only moderate losses. Though such a roundabout course would add several hundred miles of driving, he decided that that was the way he would go.

When he was all set, he went to Oliver Loving and discussed his plans with him. That font of range wisdom approved the course Goodnight proposed taking: to the headwaters of the Middle Concho, where he planned to lay over and recruit his cattle before pushing on through Centralia Draw and crossing the Ninety-six Mile Desert to Horsehead Crossing on the Pecos. As a trail herd could not advance more than fifteen to sixteen miles from sunrise to sunset, it meant going without water for six days.

Years later Goodnight recalled that meeting in detail, regarding it as a turning point in his life. "He called me Charlie, but in my respect for him I always addressed him as Mr. Loving. I don't believe I ever called him Oliver. As we talked, he pointed out all the difficulties I was likely to face. I refused to be discouraged, and after we had talked for some time, he said to my surprise, 'If you will let me, I will go with you.'

" 'I will not only let you,' I told him eagerly, 'but it's the most desirable thing of my life. I not only need the assistance of you and your crew, I need your advice.' "

Goodnight had purchased a secondhand government wagon, stripped it down to the wheels and iron axles and had a wagonmaker who knew his business build him a new body and running gear of bois d'arc, the toughest wood there was. Instead of the usual tar bucket, he installed a can of tallow for greasing the axles. At the back end of the wagon he built a cabinet three feet high and the full width of the body. It was divided into sections for storing food and enclosed by a hinged lid, which when let down formed a table, supported by a hinged leg.

He coined a name for it, calling it a "chuck box," the first he or anyone else had ever seen. It was an invention for which every working cowboy and trail hand was to be eternally grateful. Of course, the wagon carrying the chuck box soon became the chuck wagon. Some minor refinements have taken place over the years, but basically it remains as Charlie Goodnight conceived it.

On June 6, 1866, some miles southwest of Belknap, he and
Loving threw their herds together, amounting to some two thousand head, and began their historic drive. Their combined crews
numbered eighteen men, among whom was the redoubtable One-
Armed Bill Wilson. A top hand in any company, he rode point
with Goodnight as the drive strung out.

When they camped for the second night beyond the Concho,
Goodnight and Loving knew they were in trouble. Through
clouds of biting alkali dust they had moved along under a pitiless
sun since daybreak, the body heat of the cattle adding to the agony
of man and beast. The hungry, thirsty cows refused to bed down
and milled around throughout the night. The weary crew remained in the saddle and got no sleep. Two hours before dawn
the herd was put back on the trail, the decision having been made
to drive right through without stopping again.

Under ordinary circumstances she-stuff cannot keep pace with
steers. Now, in their weakened condition, frantic for water, they
could not be hazed forward, and by noon the herd was strung out
for two miles. Goodnight and Wilson tried to hold back the leaders to give the drags a chance to catch up. But it was to no avail.
Loving, who was working the drag, was compelled to leave more
than three hundred cows behind, many of them with calf, to
perish where they dropped.

It was several hours after midnight when the leaders reached
the mouth of Castle Canyon, from which a cool, damp breeze was
blowing. Thinking they smelled water, the leaders broke away and
the rest followed them in a mad rush for the river. Nothing could
hold them back.

After gathering up a number of empty canteens the previous
afternoon, Goodnight had ridden ahead and reached the Pecos,
passing just before he came to it a large pond of stagnant water.
He tested it and found the water so impregnated with alkali that
it was poisonous. Now, with the herd in a mad breakaway, the
best that he, Wilson and the other head men could do was to turn
it slightly to the south to avoid the pond.

In those days the Pecos was swimming water. The trough of
the river was ten feet below the precipitate bank on its eastern

bank. When the cattle reached it, they plunged over, the pressure from the rear so great that the leaders could not have halted their wild flight if they had elected to do so. In a few minutes the channel was filled with a mass of crazed, struggling cattle. Many were pushed out on the low western bank without having had an opportunity to drink. They now turned back and the confusion became wilder than ever.

Above the crossing, there were unknown quicksands. The cows that turned in that direction to escape the crush were trapped and sucked under. Not until late that morning was what was left of the big herd put safely on grass that was found a few miles west of the Pecos. According to Goodnight's tally, half of the two thousand head with which he had left the Brazos had been lost.[3]

Charlie Goodnight summed up the disaster for all time in his much-quoted observation that Horsehead Crossing was "the graveyard of the cowman's hopes."

You are not likely to find Horsehead Crossing indicated on any modern map. It was on the principal Comanche trail to and from Chihuahua. According to Colonel Rip Ford, the old plainsman and stormy petrel of our war with Mexico, when the returning Indians reached the Pecos with their *caballados* of stolen horses, they paused at the crossing and killed the culls, which accounted for the great number of skulls that were left lying about. Hence the name Horsehead Crossing.

After recruiting horses and cattle for three days, the Texans recrossed the river, a reconnaissance by Goodnight having revealed that twenty miles up the Pecos on the eastern bank some grass was to be found. According to One-Armed Bill Wilson, what they found was "damn little grass and a million rattlesnakes."

Trailing northward through the most desolate country they had ever seen, they reached Pope's Crossing, several miles below the Texas–New Mexico line, where Captain John Pope had found the ford back in the 1850's while making a survey for a projected Pacific railroad. There, Goodnight and Loving recrossed the river to the west bank. Still pointing north, they found after they had put another hundred miles behind them that the country through which they were passing was changing perceptibly: the grass was better and the Pecos was losing some of its reddish-brown color and becoming palatable.

Every morning there were newborn calves on the bedgrounds that had to be shot. That was nasty business, but it was better than leaving them behind to be devoured by wolves.

Miraculously the drive had escaped Indian attack, although it was exposed to it by the Comanches to the east and the Mescalero Apaches who ranged the Guadalupe Mountains to the west. Future drives were not to be so fortunate; they would have to fight white outlaws and cattle thieves as well as Indians. The trail Goodnight and Loving were blazing was to become the battleground on which the bloody Lincoln County War was to be fought a few years hence.

Within a few miles of where the town of Roswell was to rise, the Texans came to the Rio Hondo, a stream of no importance as a river, but it ran cold and clear. It brought them to a little wooded valley that was green and verdant, called by the Mexicans Bosque Grande (the large timbers).

Goodnight explored a small tributary of the Hondo, which he named the South Spring. With its grass, water and wood the Bosque Grande would make an ideal place for a ranch. He meant to nail it down for his own, but before he got around to doing so, another Texan preempted his tenuous claim to the Bosque.

Short of the area of the Colorado mining towns, Charlie and his partner had no definite destination in mind until they were within forty miles of Fort Sumner. Here they learned that the Government had some eight thousand Navajos and Mescaleros confined there in the Bosque Redondo (Round Timbers) Reservation, whom it was finding difficult to feed. A few weeks back the situation had become so desperate that the Government contractors had paid as high as sixteen cents a pound for beef. Goodnight hurried to Fort Sumner to take advantage of this unexpected bonanza.

Fort Sumner, it may be injected, was only of secondary importance as a military post; but long after it was abandoned as such and the Indians in the Bosque Redondo dispersed to other reservations, it was to become famous as the place where on the night of July 14, 1881, Sheriff Pat Garrett killed William Bonney, the overpublicized outlaw, Billy the Kid.

Goodnight got eight cents a pound on the hoof for his beef, a fantastic price for cattle that in Texas were largely valuable only for their tallow and hide. But the Patterson brothers, the contractors at Fort Sumner, refused to buy the stock cattle, which left the partners with some seven to eight hundred head of cows and year-old calves. The partners drove twenty miles north to Las Carretas Creek to rest, celebrate, count their cash and make plans for the future.

Loving was well-to-do, but Charlie Goodnight had never had so much money in his life. Naturally he wanted more, and so he agreed to return to Texas at once, round up a herd of all beef cattle and retrace his trail to Horsehead Crossing. In the meantime Loving was to go on to Colorado, dispose of the cows and calves, after which he was to meet his partner at a designated spot on the lower Pecos, which is known today as Loving's Bend.

On July 7, Goodnight began the long, seven-hundred-mile return journey to Weatherford, accompanied by three of his most reliable men. They rode mules because of their staying power, and each man led a fast-stepping horse for a getaway if attacked. In Goodnight's saddlebags reposed the gold derived from the Fort Sumner sale. Riding by night until they were beyond the foothills of the Guadalupes, they proceeded without incident, and forty days later rode into Weatherford.

By early September, Goodnight had a herd of fifteen hundred steers, threes and fours, ready to move, but ten days were lost waiting for the wagon that was being rebuilt according to his specifications. At last they got away, and profiting by the lesson he had learned on the first trip, they laid over during the hot hours of the day and traveled by night.

At midday, between the North Concho and the Middle Concho, Indians caught the crew napping and ran off about a hundred head. After trailing them for fifteen miles, Goodnight called a halt and returned to camp. Time was now of the essence and he wrote off the loss as incidental to getting the herd through.

They reached Horsehead and crossed the Pecos without difficulty. As they turned north, Goodnight began wondering about his partner and if he would find Loving and his men at the appointed rendezvous.

He was relieved to find them waiting. It was now so late in the year that there was no hope of reaching Fort Sumner or Santa Fe before snow blocked the trail. Plodding on, they reached Bosque Grande, the spot Goodnight liked so well, and turned the cattle out for the winter, while the crew built dugouts and chopped wood to keep themselves comfortable in the months ahead.

The practicableness of the Goodnight Trail had been demonstrated. Over it thousands of cattle were to pass in the years to come. On some maps you will find it designated as the Goodnight-Loving Trail, and properly so, even as the Loving Trail from Fort Sumner to Denver is referred to as the Goodnight-Loving Trail.

In 1868, Goodnight drove the Goodnight-Loving Trail all the way to Wyoming, passing to the east of Cheyenne. As the empty ranges of that territory began to be stocked, the trail was extended up through Lusk to the Belle Fourche and on into Montana, and in local usage came to be called the "Texas Trail." It is so identified on the memorial monuments historical societies have set up to mark its course. But only north of Ogallala, Nebraska, was that name ever applied to the dusty trace over which half a million Longhorns and mustangs were trailed.

In 1875, just before he settled in Palo Duro Canyon, in the Texas Panhandle, Goodnight carved a trail from Fort Sumner to Granada, Colorado, on the Arkansas River. Even later he was to establish the important Palo Duro–Dodge City Trail.

By then he was famous, not only as a blazer of trails but as trail driver, stockman and breeder of cattle, known wherever there were rangemen. When asked for his opinion of Charlie Goodnight, John Chisum, no pygmy himself, summed it up in three words: "He knows cow."

I V

The Killing of Oliver Loving

Goodnight and Loving disposed of their cattle at Fort Sumner and Santa Fe at a handsome profit and were back on the trail with a second herd late in May. After they had passed Horsehead Crossing and proceeded a hundred miles up the Pecos, "It was decided," Goodnight wrote in his contribution to *The Trail Drivers of Texas,* the Bible of the Old Time Trail Drivers' Association, "that Mr. Loving should go ahead on horseback in order to reach New Mexico and Colorado in time to bid on the contracts which were to be let in July; to use the cattle we then had on trail, for we knew that there were no other cattle in the west to take their place.[1]

"Loving was a man of religious instincts and one of the coolest and bravest men I have ever known, but devoid of caution. Since the journey was to be made with a one-man escort I selected Bill Wilson [one-armed Bill Wilson], the clearest headed man in the outfit, as his companion.

"Knowing the dangers of traveling through an Indian infested country I endeavored to impress on these men the fact that only by traveling by night could they hope to make the trip in safety.

"The first two nights after the journey was begun they followed my instructions. But Loving, who detested night riding, persuaded

37

Wilson that I had been over-cautious and one fine morning they changed their tactics and proceeded by daylight. Nothing happened until 2 o'clock that afternoon, when Wilson, who had been keeping a lookout, sighted the Comanches heading toward them from the southeast. Apparently they were five or six hundred strong. The men left the trail and headed for the Pecos River, which was about 4 miles to the northwest and was the nearest place they could hope to find shelter. They were then on the plain which lies between the Pecos and Rio Sule, or Blue River. One hundred and fifty feet from the bank of the Pecos this bank drops abruptly some one hundred feet. The men scrambled down this bluff and dismounted. They hitched their horses (which the Indians captured at once) and crossed the river where they hid themselves among the sand dunes and brakes of the river. Meantime the Indians were hot on their tracks, some of them halted on the bluff and others crossed the river and surrounded the men. A brake of *carrca,* or Spanish cane, which grew in the bend of the river a short distance from the dunes was filled with them. Since this cane was from five to six feet tall these Indians were easily concealed from view of the men; they dared not advance on the men as they knew them to be armed. An Indian on the bluff, speaking Spanish, begged the men to come out for consultation. Wilson instructed Loving to watch the rear so they could not shoot him in the back, and he stepped out to see what he could do with them. Loving, attempting to guard the rear, was fired on from the cane. He sustained a broken arm and a bad wound in the side. The men then retreated to the shelter of the river bank and had much to do to keep the Indians off.

"Toward dawn of the next day Loving, deciding that he was going to die from the wound in his side, begged Wilson to leave him and go to me, so that if I made the trip home his family would know what had become of him. . . . He wished his family to know that rather than be captured and tortured by the Indians, he would kill himself. But in case he survived and was able to stand them off, we would find him two miles down the river. He gave him his Henry rifle which had metallic cartridges or waterproof cartridges, since in swimming the river any other kind would be useless. Wilson turned over to Loving all of the pistols—five—and his six-shooting rifle, and taking the Henry rifle departed. How he expected to cross the river with the gun, I have never comprehended, for Wilson was a one-armed man. But it shows what lengths a person will attempt in extreme emergencies.

"It happened that some one hundred feet from their place of concealment down the river, there was a shoal, the only one I know of within 100 miles of the place. On this shoal an Indian sentinel on horseback was on guard and Wilson knew this. The water was about four feet deep. When Wilson decided to start, he divested himself of clothing except underwear and hat. He hid his trousers in one place, his boots in another and his knife in another all under water. Then taking his gun, he attempted to cross the river. This he found to be impossible, so he floated downstream about seventy-five feet, where he struck bottom. He stuck down the muzzle of the gun in the sand until the breech came under water and floated noiselessly down the river. Though the Indians were all around him, he fearlessly began his 'get-away.' He climbed up a bank and crawled out through a cane brake which fringed the bank, and started out to find me, bare-footed and over ground that was covered with prickly pear, mesquite and other thorny plants. Of course he was obliged to travel by night at first, but fearing starvation used the day some, when he was out of sight of the Indians.

"Now Loving and Wilson had ridden ahead of the herd for two nights and the greater part of one day, and since the herd had lain over one day the gap between us must have been something like one hundred miles.

"The Pecos River passes down a country that might be termed a plain, and from one to two hundred miles there is not a tributary or break of any kind to mark its course until it reaches the mouth of the Concho." (An obvious error; the stream was the Rio Feliz, which comes up from the west, where the foothills, the Guadalupes, begin to jut in toward the river.)

In the first of the hills, that is, the southernmost, there was a cave that Wilson had discovered the previous year. It was twenty-five feet deep. Now, in his pitiful condition, realizing that he could go no farther, he crawled into it. Starving, his nearly naked body racked by the pitiless sun, his cut, swollen feet an endless agony, his only hope was that he might survive until the trail drive found him.

Having heard nothing from Loving or Bill Wilson since they left the drive, Goodnight, with the usual optimism of rangemen, hoped for the best.

Wilson had been hiding out in the cave for three days, looking for the herd, when he saw it coming. He stepped out, signaling with his arm. To conclude Goodnight's narrative: "His brother [Joe], who was 'pointing' the herd with me, and I saw him at the same time. At sight both of us thought it was an Indian, as we didn't suppose that any white man could be in that country. I ordered Wilson [Joe] to shape the herd for a fight, while I rode toward the man to reconnoiter, believing the Indians to be hidden behind the hill and planning to surprise us. I left the trail and jogged toward the hill as though I didn't suspect anything. I figured I could run to the top of the hill to look things over before they would have time to cut me off from the herd. When I came within a quarter of a mile of the cave, Bill gave me the frontier sign to come to him. He was between me and the declining sun, and since his underwear was saturated with red sediment from the river he made a queer looking object. But even when some distance away, I recognized him. How I did it under his changed appearance, I do not know. When I reached him I asked him many questions, too many in fact, for he was so broken and starved and shocked by knowing he was saved, I could get nothing satisfactory from him. I put him on the horse and took him to the herd at once. We immediately wrapped his feet in wet blankets. They were swollen out of all reason, and how he could walk on them is more than I can comprehend. Since he had starved for three days and nights, I could give him nothing but gruel."

By morning he was able to tell a coherent story of what had happened, describing in detail the place where Loving and he had made their stand against the Indians. Slim as the hope was that Loving was still alive, Goodnight took a dozen men and headed up the Pecos to find him after having Wilson placed in the wagon and ordering the drive to continue. He found the spot where the fight had occurred. He found Wilson's clothing and rifle, even the knife Wilson had buried. But there was no sign of Loving. Goodnight could only conclude that his partner had been killed and his body tossed into the river and swept away.

Without exposing his grief to those about him, Charlie Goodnight mourned the passing of gentle, kindly Oliver Loving as one strong man can mourn the death of another. The drive pressed on. One-armed Bill Wilson regained his vigor and took his place in the saddle. Two weeks later and again riding point with Goodnight, they were within ten miles of Sumner when they encountered Jim Burleson. He was a small-time gambler rather than a cowman. He had put a herd on the Goodnight Trail the previous fall, but at Horsehead Crossing he had turned south and crossed the Rio Grande. His herd was now on the way north in charge of Mexican cowboys. He had ridden south from Fort Sumner hoping to get some word of his cattle. Goodnight assured him that they were two or three days behind the Goodnight-Loving drive. Burleson was about to turn back for Sumner when he said something that shook Goodnight.

"Loving is anxious to see you, Charlie."

"Mr. Loving was killed by Indians two week ago far down the Pecos."

"No," Burleson contradicted, "he's poorly and under the Post doctor's care, but he's a long way from dead."

On hearing this, Goodnight changed to a fast horse, and taking Bill Wilson with him, set out at once for Sumner. The wound in Loving's side had not proved fatal, but the arm that a Comanche bullet had shattered just below the elbow was swollen to three times its natural size with infection.

"As soon as we beheld his condition," Bill Wilson said later in an article signed by him, "we realized the arm would have to be amputated. But the Post doctor had never amputated any limbs and did not want to undertake such work.[2]

"Mr. Loving told us how he had got to Fort Sumner. He said he had remained where I left him for two days, standing off the Indians. When he was sure they had gone, he made his way to the road and hid in the brush. He hadn't eaten in five days. He was so weak he was afraid he would be dead before the drive reached him. He had about given up hope when three Mexicans headed for Mexico in a wagon drawn by two yoke of oxen found him. They cooked him some *atole* [Mexican cornmeal mush] and fed him. He offered them two hundred and fifty dollars to take him to Fort Sumner.

"Without losing any more time Goodnight started a man for Santa Fe after a surgeon [a matter of a hundred and fifty miles] but before he [the doctor] could get to Sumner mortification [gangrene] set in, and we were satisfied that something had to be done at once. Goodnight persuaded the young doctor to cut off the affected limb. But too late. Mortification went into his body and killed him. Thus ended the career of one of the best men I ever knew." [3]

After half a century Bill Wilson's memory was excellent, but he erred in saying that Oliver Loving died a day or two after his arm was amputated. As a matter of fact, he lingered for over three weeks and died on September 25, 1867. During those weeks of waiting, as Loving grew weaker and weaker, Goodnight disposed of most of the cattle and sent the balance on to Colorado in charge of W. D. Reynolds, another Goodnight stalwart.

As the end neared, the dying man's twin regrets were for the financial condition in which he was leaving his family and his horror of being laid to rest in what he called "a foreign country." Goodnight promised to continue their partnership until there was enough money to leave Loving's family well provided for. And he assured his partner that he need have no fear of being buried far from home. "I will take your remains back to Weatherford, Mr. Loving."

Loving was interred temporarily at Fort Sumner, but several months later the body was exhumed and Goodnight set about fulfilling his promise to the man whom he always referred to throughout his long life as "my old partner."

"From about the fort the cowboys gathered scattered oil cans, beat them out, soldered them together, and made an immense tin casket. They placed the rough wooden one inside, packed several inches of powdered charcoal around it, sealed the tin lid, and crated the whole in lumber. They lifted a wagon bed from its bolsters and carefully loaded the casket in its place. Upon February 8, 1868, with six big mules strung out in the harness, and with rough-hewn but tenderly sympathetic cowmen from Texas riding

ahead and behind, the strangest and most touching funeral cavalcade in the history of the cow country took the Goodnight and
Loving Trail that led to Loving's home. . . . Down the relentless
Pecos and across the implacable Plains . . . reached the settlements
and at last delivered the body to the Masonic Lodge at Weatherford where it was buried with fraternal honors." [4]

The pioneer phase of the Goodnight-Loving Trail was over;
in central and south Texas cowmen began to respond to the tales
of the riches to which it had opened the way. Fort Griffin had been
established on the Clear Fork of the Brazos and Fort Concho on
the Middle Concho, which lessened the likelihood of a trail outfit
having its cattle run off by the Comanches. In north-central Texas
other men, mindful of the success Goodnight and Loving had
achieved, were encouraged to shape up herds and put them on the
trail the partners had pioneered.

Up in Colorado, miners were cursing the "damned black stuff"
they were bringing out of their tunnels and casting aside, not
knowing it was sulfurets of silver and that they were uncovering
a silver bonanza second only to the great Comstock Lode. On its
countless mountain streams an army of placer miners were wash-
ing fortunes out of the sands. Naturally the population of the
Territory was zooming. In New Mexico and Arizona the Federal
Government was establishing more military posts and putting
more and more Indians on reservations. The demand everywhere
was for beef and more beef. Far-seeing as usual, Goodnight established a ranch on the Arkansas a few miles above Pueblo in 1869.
With thousands of acres of virgin range and a long, sheltered valley to protect stock against the storms of winter, it was ideally
suited for a swing ranch where he could recruit cattle coming up
from Texas and New Mexico and hold stock that he was keeping
to take advantage of the ups and downs of the market.

His romance with Molly Dyer had progressed to the point that
they were engaged and planned to be married the following July.
He intended to make the ranch on the Arkansas their home, and
with Molly in mind he built a house on a style that would please
her.

We'll get back to Charlie Goodnight, still a young man whose
fabulous career was only beginning, after turning to another giant

who was moving in on him. He was that singular character John Simpson Chisum, unrelated to Jesse Chisholm of Chisholm Trail fame with whom he is often confused, and known to Texans as Jingle-Bob John.

Like Molly Dyer, Chisum was from Madison County, Tennessee, where was born in 1824. He was twelve years older than Goodnight and arrived in Texas in 1837 and settled with his family at the site of present Paris, in Lamar County. He blazed no trails, but in the most authentic use of the term, he was a cattle king.

That careful, authentic New Mexico historian William A. Keleher credits him with owning 60,000 head of cattle at the beginning of the Lincoln County War. Others place the number as high as 90,000. He branded his stock the Long Rail and earmarked his cattle with the famous Jingle-Bob, so-called because the knife left a piece of the ear dangling. It wasn't necessarily crueler than other ear markings, but screw flies often laid their eggs in the cut and infected it.

Chisum was a tall, angular man with a dour face. By his dress he could not be distinguished from the men who worked for him. Though he took to trouble as easily as a duck takes to water, he never carried a gun. His critics said that was for his own protection. In a country in which it was the almost universal practice for men to pack a gun, it was considered against the code to shoot an unarmed man.

At the opening of the War Between the States, John Chisum was ranching at Bolivar, in Denton County. He was one of the first to engage in the business of trailing cattle across northern Texas to Red River ports in Louisiana for the Confederacy. When the war was over, he seemed to have money while other Texans were penniless. It led to the unsubstantiated charge that he had violated the law against trading with the enemy and had delivered cattle to the Yankees at New Orleans. However that may have been, there is no denying that throughout his long career he always had his eye out for the dollar, and on occasion was not over-scrupulous about how he got it.

In August, 1867, having become convinced that Goodnight and Loving had opened a highway to prosperity, he put together a mixed herd of two thousand head, throwing into it his own cattle and getting the rest on credit, along with a power of attorney, which gave him authority to dispose of the stock as he chose. Then he began the long drive to the southwest, aiming to reach the Concho where new Fort Concho had just been commissioned. With him he had a large crew of eighteen young, reckless men on whose courage and loyalty he could depend. Throughout his long career he hired no other kind, and it is a matter of record that without exception they served him long and well.

West of Fort Concho, Indians got into the herd and ran off two hundred head. Chisum ordered the drive to continue, while he turned back with three of his men. In that day and the next they picked up approximately enough cattle to replace the ones that had been lost, of course without the knowledge or consent of the owners, but wearing brands on which he already held a power of attorney—a little legal nicety which he employed more than once. But in his climb to success trickery was only incidental. It was his drive, tireless energy and expert plainsmanship that carried him to the top.

When that first herd reached Bosque Grande, he looked about him and saw what Goodnight had seen. There, on the South Spring, a few miles to the west, he built his great South Spring Ranch, the headquarters house, more a fort than ranch house. But several years later, after his Mexican laborers had put the place under irrigation, from the front porch—144 feet long one looked out over flowering orchards and green fields of alfalfa.[5] His friends enjoyed its hospitality; other men who were to be his deadly enemies in the partisan war that was soon to tear Lincoln County asunder, swore that "they wouldn't be found dead in that hangout of cow thieves and outlaws." [6]

John S. Chisum could afford to smile at the barbs and epithets hurled at him. He had become the undisputed King of the Pecos. For a hundred and fifty miles up and down the river and from the Staked Plains to the El Capitan Mountains to the west—over millions of acres of grass—his vast herds of cattle roamed at will. He owed many thousands of dollars on cattle he had bought with notes and had not paid for. It didn't trouble him; the notes were in Texas and he was a resident of New Mexico. And there were other notes, given back in Arkansas in connection with a packing plant fiasco in which he was the principal investor.

Those old notes were about to catch up with him and hound him to his grave.

Seeds of Conflict

The borders of Lincoln County are wide even today, but when it was first established by the Congressional act of 1869 it was a vast land of thousands of acres of unsurveyed public domain. Great areas have since been chopped off to form other counties. In the original act it embraced the greater part of southeastern New Mexico, including "all that territory between the 34th parallel of latitude on the north, the Texas boundary line on the south, the 104° of longitude, or Pecos River, on the east, and the eastern slope of the San Andreas mountains on the west."

Most of it was excellent grazing country; in wet years the grama grew stirrup-high. The mountains to the west of the upper Pecos were clothed with virgin stands of pine and cedar. For a century or more Mexicans had been taking gold and silver out of its streams and hills. With such riches to tempt greedy men, and the simply ambitious, it followed that they would contest to make part or all of it their own.

Presumably the Territory of New Mexico was entitled to the equal rights and protection under law enjoyed by the several other territories under the jurisdiction of the United States. But being conquered territory, it was regarded by official Washington as having special status. As a consequence it got its officials by presi-

47

dential appointment. Since these appointments were almost invariably regarded as political sinecures that could be exploited for personal gain, they usually were.

Between its territorial officials and local officers (sheriffs, justices of the peace and tax collectors), New Mexico was the worst-governed place in the United States. Nowhere was that so apparent as in Lincoln town, the seat of Lincoln County. Those hard-headed, ruthless storekeepers from Ireland, Laurence G. Murphy and James J. Dolan, and their partner John H. Riley, were calling the shots, both figuratively and in life-and-death reality. Sheriff Brady did their bidding, and was ably supported by Thomas B. Catron, lawyer, banker and at the time attorney general of the Territory,[1] and District Attorney William L. Rynerson. In effect, Murphy, Dolan and Riley controlled the law, which, with very little subterfuge, they manipulated to serve their own ends.

In the long ago a group of Spanish Americans had settled on the Bonita River and named the village Placitas, which later was changed to Bonita. It was not until 1896, in the aftermath of the War Between the States, that Union sympathizers being in the majority, the name was changed a second time to Lincoln. Since then the town had grown. The newcomers were mostly farmers from the Middle West who settled on the various little streams in the country, which put them in conflict with cattlemen who did not propose to be shut off from the water they needed. Although it was a senseless argument, it ended in gunfire on more than one occasion. Both sides were trespassing, which neither would admit. There wasn't an acre of patented land in all of Lincoln County open to title.

But the influx of farmers did not stop the cattle from coming in. In 1872 it was reported that 9,000 had been tallied at Seven Rivers crossing on their way up the Goodnight-Loving Trail. From the same source a year later, 63,000 head were reported as having passed.

With that number of cattle being driven into the Pecos River country, range thievery on a scale never practiced anywhere else took place. The Santa Fe *New Mexican* reported in April, 1871, that an "estimated 30,000 head of stolen stock has been driven into New Mexico and that rustling has become an organized business in which a thousand men are engaged."

It should be said that most of that stock had been run off from Texas ranches by the Comanches and sold in New Mexico. Of course there were big stockmen in New Mexico who were buying stolen cattle and knew what they were buying. John Chisum's enemies accused him of buying thousands of cattle whose brands reflected no connection with the name and address of the sellers. Perhaps he did, for in that time and place a man didn't ask too many questions, so that later on, if it became necessary, he could claim that he had acted in ignorance, which was more or less excusable.

To the west of where Chisum's cattle ranged, beyond the flat lands of the White Sands and up among the forested peaks of the San Andreas Mountains, big, rawboned Pat Coghlan, the so-called Cattle King of Tularosa, didn't resort to subterfuge to explain his possession of his vast herds.

Known outlaws, wanted men on the scout, were always welcome at his headquarters ranch at Three Rivers. They occasionally repaid him by getting in among his cattle and running off several hundred head. Of course it sometimes happened that they stole previously stolen cattle that they had sold to him. It was said that after such a happening and if he had learned that the damage was minimal, the big Irishman would toss off a tumblerful of whisky at a gulp—he was a two-quart-a-day man—and laugh. But if the miscreants tried to sell him the same cattle twice, that was different; his rowdy humor didn't extend that far.

One of Pat Coghlan's frequent visitors was a beardless youth of nineteen. Whether on the prowl or just keeping ahead of the law (the Murphy-Dolan variety), it was his way to show up out of nowhere, remain a few days and then disappear as he had come. He was William Antrim before he became William Bonney. But the world was to know him as Billy the Kid, and New Mexico simply as the Kid. He was the principal actor in the ruthless, bloody conflict that has taken its place in history as the Lincoln County War.

If the reader is interested in the beginnings of the Kid, a library will provide him with at least a dozen accounts, most of them more or less accurate. We will pick up the threads in 1876, when he became acquainted with John H. Tunstall, the young Britisher who was, he said, "the only man I ever worked for who treated me fairly."

According to the evidence, the Kid killed eighteen men in his brief lifetime. And yet even today there are many people in New Mexico who treasure his memory and have a good word to say for him. They will point out that he never betrayed a friend; that good men and bad fought beside him.

Counting the Murphy-Dolan-Riley triumvirate as one faction, John Chisum as another, Pat Coghlan as a third, and Billy the Kid as the fourth, you have four of the five principals in the Lincoln County conflict. There was one other, Alexander Abraham McSween, the young Canadian-born lawyer who arrived in Lincoln town in 1875. Aroused by the infamy of the Murphy-Dolan crowd, he was naive enough to believe he could destroy it.

McSween was only thirty-two. He was not a gun fighter; not a man of violence. Had he been, the chances are he would have recognized the folly of trying to unseat the entrenched overlords of Lincoln County. Controlling the law, they controlled everything. Wherever McSween looked, he saw their greedy hands at work. They had a monopoly of the banking, general outfitting and grocery business, choking off by one means or another any possible competition. They operated the freighting business between Lincoln and Las Vegas and Santa Fe. Individually, Murphy and Dolan owned extensive hay and cattle ranches. Murphy had been the post sutler at Fort Stanton, a short ride west of town. By bribery or other fraudulent means, the firm now supplied the post with all its needs—beef, groceries and hay. It had a similar arrangement, similarly arrived at, with the Indian agent on the new Mescalero Reservation adjoining Fort Stanton.

McSween, the crusader, was not to be deterred. He sought help where he could and found it in John Chisum and Pat Coghlan, not that there was any love lost between those arch rivals. But they buried their differences in their mutual hatred of the Murphy-Dolan crowd.

By 1873 the old-fashioned cap-and-ball pistol and muzzle-loading rifle had been replaced by such new and improved weapons of destruction as Colt's .45 and the Winchester. As they came into general use throughout the Territory, death by gunfire became the prevailing method of settling a dispute. At the time it is doubtful if any political subdivision of the United States held within its borders, percentage wise, as many outlaws, criminals of different shades and cow thieves as were to be found in New Mexico. Killings occurred so frequently that they came to be accepted as a matter of course, until the night of December 20, when a group of men led by the four surviving Harrold brothers from the Ruidoso country assaulted a house in Lincoln in which a Mexican *baile* was in progress. They killed Isidro Patron, Isidro Padilla, Dario Balazar and José Candelaria, and wounded Apolonia Garcia and Pilar Candelaria.

The purpose of the raid was to avenge the killing of Ben Harrold in Lincoln by a deputy sheriff. The victims were in no way responsible for Ben Harrold's death. But that was beside the point; the Harrolds were declaring war on Murphy and Dolan, their friends, lawmen and hangers-on. One place to begin was as good as another. Following Ben's killing, Sam, Thomas, Martin and Merritt Harrold had hurried to Lincoln and demanded an investigation of their brother's death. This was refused on the ground that he had been killed while resisting arrest. The brothers had eyewitnesses present and ready to testify, but they were not permitted to be heard, which was typical of the Murphy-Dolan brand of "law."

Following the multiple slayings in Lincoln on the night of December 20, warrants charging Zachariah Crompton, F. Scott and the Harrold brothers with murder were issued. The identity of their other accomplices being unknown, "John Doe" warrants against them were handed down. The sheriff, accompanied by sixty hastily mobilized deputies, left Lincoln for the Ruidoso country within hours. No man in that large posse expected the warrants they carried to be served without bloodshed. But news of their coming got ahead of them, and when they reached the Harrolds' ranch they found it deserted. The brothers and their supporters had made a hasty departure for Texas, from which they had fled a year back, following the culmination of a long and bitter feud in Lampasas County.

Larry Murphy and Dolan had made a great show about organizing a vigilance committee. With the departure of the Harrolds and their followers, that seemed no longer necessary. But there was no peace in Lincoln County. Miraculously, Charlie Goodnight escaped becoming involved in the internecine strife that turned neighbor against neighbor. He was up and down the trail that bore his name almost constantly. According to his books, he handled at least 10,000 head of cattle a year from John Chisum for seven years running, charging him a dollar a head for driving them to Colorado, in addition to sharing the profits with him. It was a lucrative business for both. Once he refused to accept cattle Chisum offered him, knowing they were stolen. Both were hard men, and the incident did not end their partnership.

Fort Sumner had been abandoned by the army. Pete Maxwell, Lucien Maxwell's son, had purchased it and made his home there. Goodnight seldom stopped to spend an hour with Pete; the place had some painful memories for him. He was spreading out, getting rich. On the Apishapa River, twenty-five miles east of Walsenburg, Colorado, he established a second ranch to relieve the pressure on his other ranch above Pueblo. Ignoring in his prosperity the old truism that a shoemaker should stick to his last, he bought several thousand acres of irrigable land on the Arkansas River and put men to work digging ditches to bring water in from the river to convert the property into a rich irrigation project. It proved to be a costly dream. He made a much more costly mistake when he joined with several prominent Pueblo businessmen in organizing the Stock Growers' Bank. When the panic of 1873 swept the country, all he could save of his considerable fortune were sixteen hundred head of Longhorns.

John Chisum and Pat Coghlan were not similarly affected. They had stuck to cattle, and cattle multiplied in hard times as well as good. As the following year merged into 1875, the beginning of the so-called "years of violence," they had the muscle to hold their own in any showdown with the storekeepers of Lincoln town.

Judged strictly on the evidence, the Murphy-Dolan "crowd" was evil. It was the "establishment." Sheriff and Deputy U.S. Marshal William Brady served it openly. Others—Judge Warren H.

Bristol, associate justice of the New Mexico Supreme Court and Ex-officio Judge of the Third Judicial District, District Attorney William L. Rynerson, Attorney General Tom Catron (later U.S. Senator)—while never acknowledging any fealty to Murphy and Dolan were always in the right place at the right time to serve them, and to feather their own nests as well.

Robert Casey, who had come to the Territory from Mason County, Texas, in 1867, had established a ranch on the Rio Hondo a few miles from Picacho. He was in Lincoln attending a political convention, when he was killed on the main street on the afternoon of August 2, 1875, presumably because of charges he had made against county officials on the convention floor that morning. From behind an adobe wall William Wilson, a Murphy and Dolan hanger-on, and not to be confused with the Billy Wilson who rode with the Kid, fired the fatal shots into Casey as he passed.

Wilson was arrested and at his trial claimed that he and Casey had had a dispute over eight dollars in wages that the latter owed him. He was convicted and sentenced to be hanged. The sentence was carried out and it gave him the distinction of being the first man legally hanged in Lincoln County.

According to all accounts, Robert Casey was an honest, estimable young man. But killings occurred too frequently in Lincoln for his being taken off to cause any great stir. Sometimes, however, a relatively unimportant incident leads to another and another, until a major crisis develops. It was so with the killing of young Casey. He had some three hundred mature beef steers on his ranch on the Rio Hondo. Several persons were interested in acquiring the cattle, among them Larry Murphy, the titular head of Murphy and Dolan. He spoke to Alex McSween, who chanced to be Casey's attorney. McSween said no; that he had a much better offer. Murphy warned him that he better think twice before undercutting him.

McSween refused to take heed. Delighted at having an opportunity to take advantage of his adversary, he sold the cattle to John Tunstall, a young Englishman with money and a high sense of honor, who had recently arrived in New Mexico and was seeking a profitable investment. Trusting, without any experience in business or knowledge about the men among whom he was casting his lot, he appeared to be a lamb ready for the fleecing.

McSween had become acquainted with him in Santa Fe. In what appears to have been an unselfish gesture, he took the young Englishman under his wing to protect him from the wolves who were certain to tear him down. However, in light of what happened later, he has been accused of using Tunstall to serve his own ends. In any event, under his guidance Tunstall purchased a small ranch on the Rio Feliz and began to prosper, a happy circumstance that was not unrelated to the fact that he had Dick Brewer as a neighbor. "Young Dick," as they called him down on the Feliz, was wise in the ways of Lincoln County.

In June, 1877, Murphy sold his interest in the business he had founded to his partners, thereafter devoting his time to his ranches.[2] Not long after the new firm, known as Dolan, Riley & Co., took over, it was startled to discover that it was about to be faced with competition. When McSween began erecting a store building half a block up the street from the handsome two-story house he had recently built, the purpose to which it was to be put became obvious.

By mid-September the store was finished and a wagon train of merchandise to stock it began arriving. Over the entrance a sign was raised identifying the business as Tunsall and Company. It was no secret that the young Englishman's partners were Alex McSween and John Chisum.

Dolan and Riley viewed the arrival of competition with understandable misgiving. Prices might have to be cut and interest rates on loans lowered. The situation came at a bad time for the two partners. They had the notes they had given Murphy hanging over their heads and they would have to be met.

It was not to be expected that a fighter like Jim Dolan would take the Tunstall, Chisum, McSween challenge without striking back. The proprietors of the new store had hoped to garner the trade of the Mexican-Americans, who had been gouged outrageously for years by the old firm. The Mexicans were anxious to throw their business to McSween and his partners, but threats of reprisals that were spread among them by deputies from the sheriff's office kept them in line. So Tunstall and his partners waited for customers who did not come, and their groceries and assorted merchandise gathered dust on their shelves.

That was only part of the harassment Dolan dished out. With the assistance of Attorney General Catron, attachments were levied against Chisum. The old warrior fought back doggedly even after he had been pulled off a stage at Las Vegas and kept in jail for several days before he satisfied a minor judgment that had been taken against him. Things became more serious when McSween was charged with embezzlement and arrested. He was the administrator of the estate of the late Emil Fritz, a silent partner in the old firm of L. G. Murphy and Company. Fritz's estate had consisted largely of a ten-thousand-dollar life insurance policy. McSween had collected the insurance but refused to turn over the proceeds to the heirs until the books of Murphy and Company were opened to him and the amount of money owing Emil Fritz could be determined. Dolan refused to produce the company books. McSween was freed on bond and the case was never settled.[3]

Tom Catron persuaded Judge Bristol to issue attachments on all of McSween's property, "not only in Lincoln County but throughout the Territory, wherever it may be found, including his interest in the Tunstall ranch on the Feliz."

Judge Bristol would have been hard pressed to find anything in legal jurisprudence to warrant this high-handed act. But he was in the habit of interpreting the law to suit the occasion. Tunstall was not in debt; no one had taken judgment against him nor was there any reason to assume that the ranch and cattle on the Feliz were not exclusively his own. The fat was now in the fire, and later, after the smoke had blown away, it was to become unmistakably clear that the move against him was part of a larger plot to smash Alex McSween. Its author was none other than James J. Dolan.

At eight o'clock on the cold, blustery morning of February 18, 1878, a sheriff's posse numbering some thirty men—which was overly large to perform its announced business—rode out of Lincoln and struck off to the southwest on the fifty-mile ride to the Tunstall ranch on the Feliz. The delegated leader was Deputy Sheriff Jacob B. Matthews, a Dolan-Riley employee, not George

Peppin as some accounts have it, which is only one of many mis-
leading, contradictory statements made in explanation of what
occurred that day.

There were some good men in that posse who honestly believed they were on a lawful mission. There were some of doubtful
character as well as no fewer than six known outlaws on whom
warrants were out, charging them with rustling, horse stealing and
murder. They were by name: George Davis, Jesse Evans, Frank
Baker, Thomas Hill, George Hindman, William Morton and Andrew (Buckshot) Roberts. Deputy Matthews knew who he had
riding with him. Proof of this can be found in Sheriff William
Brady's letter of February 15, telling him: "You must not by any
means call on or allow to travel with your posse any person or
persons who are known to be outlaws. . . . Be firm and do your
duty according to law and I will be responsible for your acts."

"Why," asked the Las Vegas *Gazette* a week later, "did Sheriff
Brady find it necessary to instruct his deputy not to select 'known
outlaws' as a posse? Why did he permit a man to act as his deputy
to whom it was necessary to send such instructions? And how does
it come that notwithstanding the sheriff's written order, we find
these 'known outlaws' not only traveling and acting with the
posse, but brutally murdering Tunstall under cover of the deputy
sheriff's authority!"

As further evidence of Sheriff Brady's knowledge of and involvement in the raid on the Tunstall ranch on February 18, the
Gazette recalled that in the preceding December he had jailed
Baker, Evans, Hill and other desperadoes, charging them with
many deeds of outlawry.[4]

There are so many conflicting versions of what happened that
day of February 18 at the ranch on the Feliz that the reader may
accept the one he finds most believable. Because of his forthright-
ness, this narrative elects to tell it as Dick Brewer did.

The story of how Tunstall stepped out of his house and confronted the posse in the ranch yard has been told so often that it
has become widely believed. Supposedly he and his crew, among
whom were young Billy Bonney and Charlie Bowdre, whose
names were to become household words in New Mexico, were
there. Among others present, it is said, were Robert Widenmann,
for a time a deputy U.S. marshal, and John Middleton, a rancher

from over on the Ruidoso and a man-at-arms of the first order.

Tunstall surmised that Deputy Sheriff Matthews was there to levy on his horses and cattle. He said he would step out and talk to Matthews.

"You tell him to go ahead," the Kid spoke up. "But you warn him not to try to enter the house. Tell him there's ten of us and we'll start shooting if he does."

Matthews is said to have made his legal attachment of the livestock and ranch tools and then headed back to Lincoln.

The only trouble with this tale is that it is a blending of fact and fiction. Actually Tunstall was on his way to Lincoln to consult McSween. The previous evening McSween had learned about the move that was to be taken against Tunstall and had dispatched a messenger to warn him. The rider reached the ranch house by the Feliz some time after midnight.

"We listened to what he had to say," Brewer recalled. "There was seven or eight of us in the house. The Kid was there, and Charlie Bowdre, John Middleton, Bob Widenmann and the ranch hands. Tunstall did not get excited. He was sure his lawyer [McSween] could straighten out the matter.

" 'You and the Kid go out and get the horses as soon as it's daylight and we'll start for Lincoln,' he told me.

"He was so green he didn't know any better. I shook my head.

" 'There's thirty of them,' I said. 'I know what this means and you don't. If they catch us out in the hills, we won't stand a chance. The best thing we can do is to stick right here and fort up until we can get help.'

"The Kid and the others saw it as I did, but Tunstall wouldn't have it. He said it was a legal matter and that he would accept service from Sheriff Brady and there wouldn't be any fight. He couldn't get it through his head that a big posse like that wasn't making that long ride to attach a bunch of cattle; they were coming to get him and whoever stood by him."

They left for Lincoln early in the morning.

"Middleton and Widenmann rode with me and Tunstall. The Kid and Bowdre followed some distance behind as a rear guard. We were just coming through the hills to the Ruidoso when they spotted us. They were about a mile away. They pulled up for a moment and then came charging at us hell for leather. I waved to the Kid and Bowdre to come on fast. They did and the Kid said, 'We got to get out of here or they'll kill every man of us.' We turned away from the trail and headed up the slope for the timber. I thought Tunstall was with us, but I looked back and saw him sitting his horse and waiting. I yelled to him but he did not move. A minute later we heard shooting down there. We saw Tunstall lying in the road. He had been pulled out of the saddle and murdered.

"There was a brief exchange of shots between us and the posse. They went on then and I asked, 'Who did it?' 'There ain't no doubt about it,' said Middleton. 'Tom Hill shot him with his own gun and then bashed his head in.' "

Deputy Sheriff Matthews went on to attach Tunstall's property (which was later returned to Tunstall's estate) and handed Sheriff Brady a detailed inventory. Nothing could have been more meaningless, for the killing of John Tunstall had created a sensation. In little groups of twos and threes, men began riding into Lincoln with a rifle under their leg—farmers, small-time ranchers and footloose cowboys. The only question now was when the reprisals would begin.

John Newcomb, a Ruidoso rancher, brought Tunstall's body to town. A post-mortem was performed by the assistant surgeon from Fort Stanton. The result was not made public for weeks, and by then things had happened that made it meaningless.

Funeral services for Tunstall were held in Alex McSween's home. On the night before burial half a hundred grim-faced men crowded in to sit up with the dead. Dick Brewer was there and so was the Kid. The latter had a list of the men who had had a hand in killing Tunstall: Jesse Evans, Thomas Hill, Frank Baker, Bill Morton, George Davis and Buckshot Roberts. He knew them well. Before coming to Lincoln County, he had rustled cattle and caroused with them along the Mexican border. Brewer took the list and studied it for a minute.

"I don't know what Brady is going to do," he said. "I don't expect him to do anything. If he doesn't, I'm going to go after these fellows—with others if others are willing to go, but alone if necessary."

VI

Partisan Warfare

Days dragged by without any charges being filed against the men who had brutally killed Tunstall. Dick Brewer decided that he had waited long enough for Sheriff Brady to make a move. A number of the murdered man's friends, using the term loosely, had lingered in Lincoln. They felt as Brewer did about avenging the death of the young Englishman. He contacted ten of them and told them to slip quietly out of town and meet him at San Patricio, down on the Pecos, on March 4, 1878, two days later. They got away without incident and he met them as agreed.

Brewer had selected men he could trust. Among them were Frank Coe and his cousin George, Hendry Brown, John Middleton, Charlie Bowdre and others of the same ilk. The Kid was not one of them, but he and Tom O'Folliard, a young border cow thief, joined them at San Patricio. Brewer had had the great wisdom to have himself deputized a constable by Justice of the Peace John B. Wilson and had warrants in his hands for the men named by the coroner's jury as Tunstall's slayers. Wilson had been the foreman of that jury. Its recommendations had been ignored. His pique must have been great for him to send Dick Brewer forth with what amounted to letters of marque and reprisal against Sheriff Brady and the Dolan-Riley establishment. It was to cost him dearly. Governor Axtell removed him from office on the flimsy excuse that Wilson had not posted the nine-hundred-dollar bond required of him as ex-officio tax collector.

But it was much too late. Young Dick was off and riding to keep the rendezvous at San Patricio, armed with a piece of paper that gave the aura of legality to do whatever he did. It had never happened before and it was never to happen again.

He found his possemen waiting at the appointed place and welcomed the addition of the Kid and O'Folliard. Riding down the Pecos, he had received a tip from a source he refused to disclose (certainly it was from John Chisum) that down below Roswell at the last crossing of the Penasco he would find some of the men who had taken part in the killing of John Tunstall.

The posse rode hard for the Penasco, "keeping ahead of the news," as the old saying had it. As they turned toward the Pecos on March 9, they surprised Bill Morton and Frank Baker, who had holed up in one of those dugouts in which cowboys often wintered. There was a running fight that led up the river. There was some brisk shooting before Morton and Baker surrendered.

Brewer was in a quandary about what to do with the prisoners. The Kid, always practical, was for killing them on the spot.

"If we take them to Lincoln and turn them over to Brady, he'll turn 'em loose and we'll have it to do all over again. Why should we treat 'em any different than they treated Tunstall?"

It was a hard argument to answer, but Brewer held out for time to think it over. They were only seventeen miles from Chisum's South Spring Ranch. He said they would spend the night there, lock up the prisoners and decide in the morning what to do with them. Undoubtedly the fact that he was an officer of the law weighed on him and made him hesitant.[1]

At supper Chisum told them that he had received reliable word that Tom Hill, the man who had pulled the trigger on Tunstall, according to Middleton, had been shot and killed while attempting to rob a sheep camp near Alamo Springs, in Doña Ana County.

It was good news. The Kid counted up the score. When they had finished with Baker and Morton, that would be three of John Tunstall's killers who had been put under.

From Chisum's they circled around Roswell and turned westward in the direction of the county seat. After reaching the canyon of the Bonita, they made a detour toward Blackwater Springs. It was lonely, uninhabited country. Morton and Baker grew increasingly suspicious, fearing that here, where there were no witnesses, they were about to receive the same treatment they had given young Tunstall.

With the posse strung out in the canyon and the Kid and Charlie Bowdre leading the way, Baker made a move. Edging up close to William McCloskey, supposedly a loyal member of the posse, he managed to steal his revolver. As McCloskey fell mortally wounded by a bullet from his own gun, Baker and Morton lashed their ponies into a run. They didn't get far. The Kid's rifle flashed to his shoulder. Two quick shots followed and it was all over.

Brewer led his posse to Blazer's Mill and from there sent a Mexican out to bury the dead men. Blazer's Mill was a sawmill operated by Dr. Joseph Blazer, a dentist. It was located at the northeast corner of the Mescalero Reservation but was not a part of it, as some narratives claim. Mark the spot well, for it was to become one of the most often-heard place names in Lincoln County history.

As Constable Brewer and his possemen rested at Blazer's Mill, their principal concern was to pick up some clue to the whereabouts of Jesse Evans. With Hill, Morton and Baker dead, it left only Jesse Evans and Buckshot Roberts unaccounted for. Word reached them that Roberts had been seen far north in Mora County, and then again that he was around Las Vegas. Of Jesse Evans they heard nothing. And with good reason. Evans had returned to west Texas and was running wild with a gang of desperadoes robbing country banks. But he was back in Lincoln County several months later, where he was welcomed by the Dolan crowd. In the meantime, however, Lincoln had been rocked by a series of sensational killings.

On April 1, Sheriff William Brady and Deputy Sheriff Hindman were shot and killed in broad daylight on the main street of the town by a blast of gunfire that was directed at them from behind an adobe wall at the rear of the Tunstall store. Brady's chief deputy, J. B. Matthews, who had led the raid on Tunstall's ranch, was only a step or two behind them and escaped death by that narrow margin. Hindman had been a member of Matthew's posse. For that and without any evidence being presented to connect them with the crime, half a dozen men who were known to be riding with Dick Brewer were immediately accused of having fired the fatal shots.

Several eyewitnesses had seen the assassins run down the slope to the Bonita and disappear in the brush along the river bottom, but had been unable to recognize them. However, the Lincoln County grand jury promptly indicted John Middleton, Hendry Brown and the Kid.

The killing of Sheriff Brady and his deputy created a greater excitement than the killing of John Tunstall. At Dolan's urgent request Captain George Purington hurried into town with a company of soldiers and permitted George Peppin, who had been named acting sheriff, to make arrests and search houses without producing any warrants or authority. When McSween's brother-in-law protested that the Constitution of the United States guaranteed all citizens against search or seizure without warrant, Peppin told him Captain Purington had ordered him to search the town.

At a special meeting, the Commissioners of Lincoln County authorized a reward of $200 each for the arrest of the slayers of Brady and Hindman, to be "paid to the person who arrested and delivered any of the fugitives to officers of the law, dead or alive." News of the reward spread quickly and it brought a man to town who, under the circumstances, would not have been expected to risk claiming it. He was none other than Buckshot Roberts.[2]

Roberts knew the danger he ran in showing his face in Lincoln. The McSween crowd had him tagged as a member of the Matthews posse that killed John Tunstall, which made him a marked man. But he was a hard-bitten individual who played his cards as they were dealt him. He was in town to confirm the rumor that Lincoln County was offering a reward on the persons, dead or alive, who had assassinated Brady and Hindman. As soon as he was convinced that it was true, he left Lincoln astride the mule on which he had arrived. He was armed with a rifle in his saddle boot and a .45 caliber pistol. Although his shabby, colorless appearance did not suggest that he was a formidable bounty hunter, he was as deadly as any man who ever followed that ugly trade. You need pay no attention to the story that he rode a mule in a land where horses were cheap and plentiful to impress the Mexicans and poor whites whom he would be questioning that he was a poor, humble man on a peaceful mission. Actually a good mule could travel faster and farther than a horse. Goodnight's favorite mount was a mule. "I could trust her on the blackest night," he said. "She must have saved my life half a dozen times."

It was April 4, 1878, when Buckshot Roberts rode out of Lincoln. Several mysterious things happened that day which were never explained by the men who survived them. Why, when Roberts set out from town, did he ride directly to Blazer's Mill? Had he been tipped off that he would find the men he wanted there? If so, he knew the odds against him would be twelve or more to one. Is it reasonable to suppose that a man of his experience would have ridden boldly into Blazer's Mill as he did that afternoon? It passes belief. On the other hand, had young Dick Brewer and his riders received word that Roberts had been in Lincoln that morning asking questions about them? They had been searching for him. If they had learned that Roberts was in the country, what more likely than that they would have intercepted him before he ever reached Blazer's Mill?

When you are preparing to kill a man, it is usually deemed inconvenient to have witnesses present, no matter how richly deserved the victim's removal from this earth may be. There were witnesses at Blazer's Mill this particular afternoon. Doc Blazer was there; so was his clerk David Easton. Andrew Wilson (no relation to Justice of the Peace Wilson), who was farming down the valley on Blazer's Creek, had dropped in, and so had F. G. Godfroy, superintendent at the nearby Mescalero Agency. Clerk Easton and Andrew Wilson were neutrals in the struggle going on in Lincoln County. Dr. Blazer was very much anti-Dolan; Godfroy, on the other hand, had been rigging bids on reservation business with Jim Dolan for several years and of necessity was strongly committed to him.

But if Blazer and Godfroy were on opposite sides of the fence in the Dolan-McSween fight, they got along well enough personally. When he got bored with life on the reservation, Godfroy often rode over to Blazer's Mill, knowing he would get a better dinner or supper than he would get at home. Between them they had settled the vexing question of whether Blazer's Mill was on reservation territory and subject to Federal law, or on private land and under Territorial jurisdiction. Blazer had convinced him that years back the government had conceded that he was entitled to a patent on the millsite because of his occupancy prior to the Executive Order of May 20, 1873, creating the Mescalero Indian Reservation. And yet months later U.S. Attorney Catron was to insist that any crime committed there was a Federal matter and the Territorial courts had no jurisdiction.

In its day Blazer's Mill had been of some importance. Blazer had dammed the creek on which it stood to give him waterpower to operate his saw. Lumber cut there had been used in the construction of Fort Seldon and Fort Stanton, in New Mexico, and in the rebuilding of Fort Bliss and Fort Davis, Texas. But that was all in the past. The whining of the big saw was seldom heard now. Down the slope from the cluster of adobe buildings Blazer had built, a tangle of saw logs were strewn about, gathering moss.

While certain facts leading up to the confrontation that occurred at Blazer's Mill on the afternoon of April 4, 1878, must be left to conjecture, no doubt exists as to what happened. It was nearing five o'clock and Brewer and four or five of his posse were lounging about in the long adobe that was Blazer's dining room, when Frank Coe stuck his head in at the open door and said, "There's a rider coming up the trail, Dick."

"Go and see if he's the right man," Brewer told him.

It is obvious that they were expecting someone; that they had been tipped off; that the man for whom they were waiting was Buckshot Roberts. It goes without saying that the information they had received included the fact that Roberts had ridden out of Lincoln shortly after noon. Being familiar with the distance between town and Blazer's Mill, they knew how long it should take a rider to cover those up-and-down miles. If the man Frank Coe had seen was Roberts, he had been moving right along.

Frank Coe, the Ruidoso farmer, was well acquainted with Roberts. In the past they had been neighbors on the Ruidoso. He recognized his man this afternoon and wondered then, as all interested parties have wondered ever since, what such a hard-headed, tough-minded individual meant by riding single-handed into the enemy's camp, and how he hoped to turn the situation to his advantage.

Roberts reached a row of one-story, one-room adobes, each with a tiny window and a door that opened outward in the style common in the Southwest at that time. He came on deliberately, walking his mule and pretending that he was not aware that he was already covered by half a dozen guns. As he passed the open door of the room where Coe waited, the latter stepped out, rifle in hand, and ordered him to get down.

"Why, Frank!" Roberts answered good-naturedly. "What are you doing up here?"

"We've got a warrant charging you with the murder of John Tunstall," Coe told him.

"Oh, hell, that!" Roberts laughed. "I can explain that business. Let's sit down and talk it over."

He slid to the ground, rifle in hand. They had stood there talking for no more than a moment or two, when Charlie Bowdre stepped out from the corner of a building and ordered him to drop his rifle, which Buckshot Roberts had no thought of doing. He swung around to face Bowdre. Frank Coe could have shot him in the back if that had been his way, which it was not.

According to Dr. Blazer, an eyewitness, Roberts and Bowdre fired at the same split second. Roberts' bullet grazed Bowdre's belly and cut his belt in two; Bowdre's slug blasted its way through Roberts' abdomen, inflicting a mortal wound. In the brief flurry of shooting that followed, George Coe received a bullet wound in the hand; John Middleton was shot in the right lung. The wound did not prove to be fatal.

Roberts crawled into the little room out of which Coe had stepped. No one had the temerity to follow him. There was a mattress on the bed. He pulled it to the floor and propped himself up against it. Through the open door he could see the slope that fell away to the creek below. The shooting had brought the other members of the posse up on the run. He could hear them as they surrounded the adobe in which he lay, being careful not to get in his line of vision. His growing weakness and increasing agony told him he was dying. But with more grit than better men often display, he was resolved to hang on as long as he could and show Dick Brewer and his posse how a man should die.

The shadows were beginning to deepen along the creek when Dick Brewer said he was going to make his way down there and try to get Roberts with a lucky shot from behind the saw logs. It took him some time to get in position to fire a shot through the open door of the little room in which Roberts lay. But he finally was able to do it. He had pushed the barrel of his rifle over a log and was about to fire, when Roberts saw him. Steadying his shaking hands, he lined Brewer up in his sights and pressed the trigger. The slug caught young Dick squarely between the eyes.[3]

In many ways, that shot changed the tide of the Lincoln County War. Dick Brewer was an officer of the law, and when he died, his authority died with him. Never again, it was said, would Alex McSween be able to get one of his followers appointed a deputy sheriff. And that was important, for in a raw land, where the law was admittedly weak and corrupt and killings were an almost daily occurrence, the man who wore one of those metal emblems with which the law identified its hirelings had a decided edge.

Following the twin killings at Blazer's Mill, the Dolan-Riley crowd was in the driver's seat. They secured indictments against Charlie Bowdre for the murder of Buckshot Roberts and against William Bonney, alias the Kid, Hendry Brown and several others for the killing of Sheriff Brady and George Hindman.

The indicted men were not distressed when they learned that warrants had been sworn out against them. They lingered at Blazer's Mill for three or four days after Dick Brewer had been given a decent burial. They needed a new leader and they chose the Kid.

Why did hard men, twice his age, turn to the beardless, slovenly, buck-toothed youth to lead them? Historians, psychologists and social scientists have been asking that question for almost a hundred years and arriving at different answers. He is held by many to have been an illiterate moron and congenital paranoiac. This narrative is concerned with what he did, not with what motivated him. Prior to that April day at Blazer's Mill, when the warriors who had followed Dick Brewer turned to the Kid for leadership, he had done very little to distinguish himself as a partisan fighter, unless, as many believed, he had fired the shot that killed Sheriff Brady. But no one can say that he didn't possess that charisma, that unexplainable something that makes a man a leader, and with which he has to be born and cannot acquire.

Lincoln County became an armed camp as the number of killings multiplied. Dolan sent his partner Riley up to Santa Fe to hire a number of accomplished gunmen. When Riley returned with thirty mercenaries, mostly Texans, they were deputized at once.

Dolan was obsessed with the idea that John Chisum was his most important enemy; that if he could administer a stinging defeat to him, he could drive McSween out of the county. He was now ready for a showdown with the King of the Pecos. An army of not less than fifty Dolan adherents rode out of Lincoln and headed down the river. The Kid and his followers had got ahead of them and there was considerable fighting on the flat lands as they continued dropping back until they joined forces with Chisum's cowboys. Numerically the two sides were about even now. Thinking they had the advantage, the Texans were enticed into charging the house. Some say the scheme originated with the Kid. However that may be, the South Spring was put under attack. But it had been built for such emergencies, and after several days of fighting, in which the enemy received a number of casualties, the Texans withdrew.

When things had quieted down, Frank McNab, John Chisum's foreman, Frank Coe and Bud Saunders, believing the enemy had pulled out of the country, left the ranch for Lincoln. To make sure that they wouldn't be attacked, they turned away from the Pecos after a few miles and struck west across the big mesa and came down into the canyon of the Bonita. The first warning they had that they were not alone came when a rifle cracked and Frank Coe's horse dropped dead under him. The other ponies reared violently and threw their riders. Coe and Saunders were scrambling to their feet when a bullet fired from a clump of cottonwoods off to the left caught Saunders and felled him in his tracks. McNab darted into a little side canyon and dropped down behind some boulders. He saw Coe still trying to get control of his mount.

"For Christ's sake, let that horse go and get to cover!" he yelled. "They'll cut you to pieces out there!"

Coe found a sinkhole half-filled with water from a recent rain and rolled into it. He was safe there for the moment. McNab wasn't. Two of the Texans had climbed the slope. Once they were above him, they could see him crouching behind a nest of boulders. He tried to get out of their line of fire, but they picked him off before he could reach a protecting ledge.

Coe was in better shape and returning the fire of the two or three men who were shooting at him. A slug passed through his hat and carried it away. Warren Ollinger, the man on his right, recognized him as he peered over the rim of the sink. "Hell, that's Frank Coe!" he shouted. "Hold up, you fellows!"

Circumstances had put them on opposite sides of the fence. But they were old friends, neighbors on the Ruidoso. He spoke to Coe, told him if he'd throw away his guns they'd take him to Lincoln and no harm would come to him. Coe believed him.

Ollinger was as good as his word. He and the disarmed prisoner rode side by side, stirrup to stirrup the rest of the way up the Tonita to town. In Lincoln, Coe was placed in a second floor room in the old Murphy-Dolan store that had been converted into a combination courthouse and jail. The upper floor was reached by an outside stairway near the rear of the building. There was a row of cots in the room.

"Sit down," said Ollinger. "I'll go across the street and get my supper and bring back yours."

"No," Coe told him. "If you leave me alone, I won't have a chance up here if those fellows down below run up the stairs. They'll kill me, Warren."

"I know," Ollinger nodded. He unlocked a closet and brought out a needle gun and a belt of cartridges and laid them on the cot beside Coe. "Now," he said, "you just look out for yourself, Frank." [4]

Ollinger went down the stairs. At the bottom he pushed through a group of Dolan gunmen and crossed the street to the restaurant. Two of the Texans started up to have a look at the prisoner. Coe heard them coming. He opened the door a bit and thrust the barrel of his rifle through the opening.

"First man that comes another step, I'll kill him," he called out.

The two men stopped and then turned back. They saw that somehow Coe had secured a rifle. It called for an explanation. They were discussing it with their fellows when the sound of shooting from up the street at McSween's house interrupted their meditations. Rifle fire from that enemy stronghold meant that it was directed at some member of their faction. Hugging the buildings, they dodged up the street to succor him. They encountered John Kinney, the Doña Ana County outlaw, who had enlisted under the Dolan banner with his band and had taken part in the unsuccessful attack on Chisum's South Spring Ranch. Kinney's horse had been killed as he rode past McSween's house, and he had received a slug in his right leg.

In the confusion, Frank Coe ran down the stairs, made his way around the old Dolan store and hid in the brush along the Bonita. Biding his time, he reached McSween's house without being fired on. The ten or eleven men gathered there, including George Coe, greeted him with understandable warmth, for word had reached them that he had been killed down the Bonita with Bud Saunders and McNab that morning.

Among the men gathered with McSween that evening were some of his most important lieutenants, including Juan Patron, the county clerk and leader of the Mexican *gente*. They had double cause for being jubilant. Since the killing of William Brady, Lincoln County had been without a sheriff for twenty-seven days. McSween had been in Santa Fe putting pressure on Governor Axtell to order the County Commissioners to appoint Brady's successor and acquainting him with the deplorable conditions then existing in Lincoln County. The Governor had acceded to his request, and that morning the Board meeting in special session had named John N. Copeland sheriff.

The Dolan-Riley crowd was unprepared for such an unexpected turn of events. The naming of no other man could have aroused them as did the appointment of ex-judge Copeland. He was a McSween man, and they protested that he would be controlled in all his official acts by him. They did not propose to sit idly by and see that happen.

McSween beamed on his followers and was not disturbed by the threats of the other side. He had shown Jim Dolan that there was more than one way to skin a cat.

VII

Written in Gunfire

McSween's jubilation was short-lived. With his man Copeland installed as high sheriff of Lincoln County, he was in the best position he was ever to be in to smash the Murphy, Dolan, Riley establishment. He was unable to turn it to his advantage, for he lacked the audacity that was needed to wage successful war on an enemy as rapacious as Jim Dolan.

Copeland was a bitter disappointment to McSween. Instead of cracking down on the known outlaws who were enlisted under the Dolan banner, he did nothing. Whether his inactivity was due to threats he had received or because he had been bought off, the result was the same. The situation in Lincoln County deteriorated to the point where Las Vegas and Santa Fe newspapers called attention to the number of people who were leaving their farms and ranches and moving to Colorado.

Governor Axtell, who had had occasion to borrow $1,200 from Jim Dolan, was now in a position to repay the favor. He was only biding his time to remove Copeland from office and appoint in his stead, for the balance of Sheriff Brady's unexpired term, George W. Peppin, a long-time Murphy-Dolan stalwart. When Copeland had been in office for thirty days and had not posted bond as ex-officio tax collector, as required by law, Axtell summarily removed him. This was the same legal trickery by which Justice of the Peace Wilson had been set down in March, 1878. Jim Dolan's hand was discernible in this maneuver. He controlled two of the members of the Board of County Commissioners, and since no bond could be filed until they agreed on the amount of taxes to be collected, a delay of a few days in making their report made Copeland vulnerable.

George Peppin, Copeland's successor, was to play a leading role in the Lincoln County War. He was a stonemason by trade, fairly well educated and had Jim Dolan's complete confidence. He had worked off and on at Fort Stanton and was well acquainted with Colonel Edward Dudley, the commandant, and his officers. He knew that Dudley was strongly disposed in Dolan's favor, and from the time he became sheriff, Peppin tried repeatedly to win the active support of the military. That was the course Colonel Dudley wanted to pursue, and he was stopped from following it on the explicit orders of General Edward Hatch, Commander of the Military District of New Mexico, a correspondence that was flavored by the fact that the two men were bitter enemies. Hatch quoted to Dudley a Departmental ruling that troops could not be used even as part of a *posse comitatus* (a posse operating under local law). This was a direct rebuke of Captain Purington's conduct following the killing of Sheriff Brady.[1]

Although New Mexico was sparsely populated, it is doubtful if anywhere else in the United States so many men were indicted for murder. But a surprisingly large number of them were never brought to trial. Among those that were, few were found guilty. They had no reason to despair, for if their lawyer couldn't win a reversal, escape was always easy.

When George Peppin took over as high sheriff, it was with the obvious intention of smashing the McSween-Chisum combination and driving it out of Lincoln County. He put together a force of fifty hard-riding warriors, a sprinkling of whom were honest men. Included among the others were professional outlaws, such as the previously mentioned John Kinney. Providing wages and sustenance for so large a group was expensive. To relieve Jim Dolan of footing the bill, Peppin deputized every one of his men, which obliged the county to pay it.[2]

McSween had no difficulty in raising a force of almost equal strength. Men joined him without expecting to be paid. As for sustenance, they were used to living on a diet of beef, and that was always handy. Even so, some money was required. No doubt but what John Chisum supplied it, although he was having difficulties of his own. The old notes he had signed were showing up. They had been bought for a few cents on the dollar. Attorney General Catron had got his hands on some and was moving to collect. To short-cut him and others, Chisum "sold" to Colonel R. D. Hunter, the millionaire cattleman and banker of St. Louis, Missouri, his cattle, brand, range and practically everything he owned at Bosque Redondo. Nevertheless, judgments totaling more than $96,000 were taken against him.

During the months of May and June of 1868 there was incessant fighting in the mountains, on the flatlands and in many of the plazas of Lincoln County. Even in Lincoln town it was not safe for man, woman or child to be abroad. The "Sheriff's Party" and "McSween's Volunteers" chased each other back and forth across the county, hoping to take the other side by surprise and score a victory that would bring hostilities to an end. But although a tremendous amount of powder was burned, the result was a standoff.

Certainly as the fighting continued, McSween must have realized that the longer it lasted, the less likely he was to win. Many of the men who had aligned themselves on his side of the struggle were more anti-Dolan than pro-McSween. Having no control over them—men like the Kid, Bowdre, Middleton and a dozen others —he was held responsible for what they did. Beginning with the killing of his friend and partner, John Tunstall, a series of circumstances had thrust him into a position of leadership for which he was not fitted. Harassed by lawsuits, judgments, the constant sniping of Dolan's attorneys and the writs that were issued against him by Judge Bristol's court and District Attorney Rynerson, he realized early in July that he stood at the crossroads. His spirits at a low ebb, he turned to the only strong man on whom he could count for advice. Unaccompanied, he rode down the Pecos to John Chisum's South Spring Ranch.

No one knows what was said in their conversation of that day and the next, but when McSween set out on his return journey to

Lincoln on July 13, accompanied by a dozen of Chisum's most trusted cowboys, his indecision was gone. He was resolved to stand his ground and fight. "As he rode north along the Pecos River, and turned in the direction of San Patricio and Lincoln," says Keleher, "McSween was encouraged from time to time to note that men began to ride along with him, some from the Pecos, others from the Feliz, the Penasco, the Hondo, the Bonita, still others from far-off mountaintops and remote valleys of the upper country. . . . Some were ordinary farmers and ranchers; none hankering for a fight . . . some rode along in high spirits, as if bent on a crusade of righteousness, fearless and anxious for a showdown fight; others were silent and apprehensive of things to come." [3]

McSween and his followers reached Lincoln at sundown on the fifteenth. They had picked up more recruits and now numbered over forty. McSween deployed them so that they would be in an advantageous position to meet whatever the morrow might bring. He quartered ten men in his own home and placed others in the homes of Jose Montano and Isaac Ellis. A sizable party made camp on the Bonita, while others took up a position in the hills north of town.

Sheriff Peppin arrived with reinforcements during the evening. In all there were more than a hundred men under arms in Lincoln by midnight. There was some sporadic shooting. Apparently without effect.

In the morning Benjamin Robinson, a trooper from Fort Stanton, was nicked by a stray bullet as he got down from the saddle in front of the Dolan-Riley store. According to two eyewitnesses whom Peppin produced, the shot had been fired from the McSween house. Very likely it was. It was a blunder that was to turn the tide of battle against McSween. Peppin had several times appealed to Colonel Dudley for assistance but, under the instructions he had received, Dudley was compelled to refuse. But the wounding of a man in uniform put a different face on it. When Peppin dispatched an urgent letter requesting military help "to protect the helpless women and children of the town," Dudley called a meeting of his officers and they unanimously agreed that troops be sent into Lincoln at once.

At ten-thirty that morning, Colonel Dudley, a lieutenant colonel, three captains, two lieutenants and sixty troopers, with a Gatling gun and mountain howitzer, marched into Lincoln and set up camp in the center of the town.

There were three women and two children in McSween's house when Dudley ordered the Gatling gun and howitzer trained on it. At McSween's urging, Mrs. Shields, his sister-in-law, her two children, and Ruth Ealy, the wife of a medical missionary, left the house, but Susan McSween refused to go. In many ways she was a remarkable woman, and in the years to come Alex McSween's enemies were to fear her more than they had ever feared him.

Dudley persuaded Justice of the Peace J. B. Wilson to issue warrants against the men barricaded in the house. Peppin tried to serve the warrants, but he changed his mind when he found himself covered by a dozen rifles as he approached the entrance.

The presence of the troops had had a demoralizing effect on the Mexicans who had forted up along the Bonita. One or two slipped away, and in a few minutes all of them were gone. Up on the hills above town Felipe Chavez and his group, mostly Mexicans, could see what was taking place below. They had thrown up a stone barricade and were in no danger of being rushed. But the presence of the troops weighed on them too, and their unease grew when they saw a strong force of Peppin's deputies move into the recently vacated position along the river. They realized that the maneuver had put them out of the fight. No longer could they hope to charge down the slopes to help McSween without being cut to pieces. They hung on for an hour, exchanging random shots with an enemy they could not see, after which they went back to their horses and rode away. The care McSween had taken in deploying his forces had come to naught, and the fighting now had to swirl about the house in which he was forted up with no more than a dozen men.

As the morning wore on, Dudley and Peppin conferred repeatedly. Soldiers patrolled the main street. They moved in pairs, their belted carbines slung under the shoulder. Except for the troops, the seething town appeared to be deserted. No civilians were in view and the Peppin deputies who had not been ordered down to the river were gathered in the Dolan-Riley store and the Wortley Hotel, the latter a point of vantage from which any movement at the McSween house could be observed.

There was an interruption just before noon. Mrs. McSween had convinced her husband that something might be gained if she were permitted to speak to Colonel Dudley personally. With a hundred pairs of eyes watching, she stepped out of the front door. She stopped after taking a few steps for, looking back, she saw Bates and Washington, her Negro servants, at the woodpile in the rear chopping wood, with three of Peppin's armed deputies standing over them and telling them what to do.

"One of those men was Jack Long, a known outlaw," Susan McSween testified later. "I asked what they were doing. Long told me they were going to burn down my house. I begged him not to but got no satisfaction. I know they tried but the wood was green and wouldn't burn. I then started again for Col. Dudley's camp."

Dudley stepped out of his tent to meet her. An angry conversation followed to which the distant onlookers were not privy, but the following April, when testifying in the Court of Inquiry proceedings against Dudley, which General Lew Wallace, the new governor of the Territory, had instituted, she told her side.

"I demanded to know by what right he had seized control of the town. Colonel Dudley said he was there only to protect innocent women and children. I asked him why he had not protected me, my sister, Mrs. Ealy and my sister's children. He said a gang of murderers and outlaws were gathered beneath my roof and that we deserved no consideration. I asked what he proposed to do. He said that if a shot was fired from our house at or near his soldiers he would turn his cannon loose. That was the expression he used, and he said he would tear the house to the ground regardless of its inmates."

There is little reason to doubt the truthfulness of her statement. It was in effect a confirmation of the answer McSween had received earlier in the day in response to a note to Dudley. Despite his bellicose attitude, it appears that Colonel Dudley realized he had overstepped himself in interfering in the civil affairs of Lincoln County and that the best way to extricate himself from his difficulties was to maintain a position of neutrality and refrain from becoming more deeply involved in the conflict.

It became apparent as the long, hot afternoon merged into evening that his decision had produced a stalemate. Peppin's force was unwilling to risk an attack and the McSween men were content to remain where they were.

Since morning Sheriff Peppin had known that the attempt to burn McSween's house had fizzled. Now with night settling down and apparently fearful lest the men whom he had held at bay throughout the day would escape under cover of darkness, he called Marion Turner, Jack Long and other trusted deputies together and acquainted them with his decision to set fire to Mc-Sween's place and give the inmates the choice of marching out with their hands up or being mowed down as they attempted to flee. In a signed statement, not made under oath, Isaac Ellis, a friend and neighbor of the McSweens', declared:

"Peppin together with about nine men came in my house and ordered me to give them coal oil which they stated they intended to use in setting fire to the house of A. A. McSween. They further stated that they had him in the house and intended to burn him out. They took the coal oil with them and went back. When opposite the camp, Dudley came out and they, Dudley and Peppin, talked for some time. They (Peppin and his deputies) then went on towards the house of A. A. McSween and in a little while firing commenced around McSween's house, and we saw smoke arise from the house and the firing was kept up until about nine o'clock at night."

Ellis does not mention Marion Turner and Jack Long as being with Peppin, but from other sources the evidence is that they were. Also, Ellis and several so-called eyewitnesses later stated that they had seen a group of men approach the kitchen door of Mc-Sween's house, dump a bag of shavings against the door and pour coal oil over them, the flames leaping high as soon as a lighted match was applied.

There are various accounts of what transpired in the McSween house as the fire ate its way from room to room. The most fanciful has Susan McSween seated at her piano and playing as her home was being consumed. Actually she left the house sometime before the climax came. She and McSween spent a few minutes together in private before the front door was opened and she was permitted to leave. It was the last time they were to see each other. Her sister-in-law's home was not far away. There she found refuge.

Peppin had stationed himself at the Wortley Hotel with a number of his deputies, from where he had an unobstructed view of the flaming house, forty yards away. From that position, however, he could not observe what went on at the back of the building, and consequently was unaware that about nine o'clock that evening five or six men had run out through the burning kitchen and made good their escape.

In Sheriff Peppin's party were the three Beckwiths from the Seven Rivers country—Henry Beckwith and his sons John and Robert Beckwith. They had had trouble with Chisum and that was the only reason they had for allying themselves with the Sheriff's party. Bob, the younger brother, didn't like the way things were going. He didn't mind killing McSween and his friends, but he drew the line at roasting them alive like so many cornered rats.

"If we promise not to shoot them down if they walk out with their hands up, I reckon they will. You can arrest 'em and that will end this fight."

"All right," Peppin agreed. "If you want to walk up to the house and parley with them, go ahead."

Beckwith didn't get far. As he walked up the path to the front door of McSween's house, his hand raised in the sign for a parley, a fusillade raked him and he fell dead when a bullet struck him in the eye.

The Kid was with McSween's party when it reached Lincoln the previous evening and McSween had taken him into his house. He was still there when Bob Beckwith was killed. When he was called as a witness in the Dudley Court of Inquiry proceedings ten months later, he testified that he made his escape a few minutes after Bob Beckwith was killed. "We all tried to escape at the same time. Harvey Morris, a McSween man, was killed. In the getaway, Vicente Romero, Francisco Zamora and McSween were killed. I ran toward Tunstall's store, thirty or forty yards from McSween's house, but when a couple of soldiers fired at me, I swerved and ran toward the river. McSween wasn't armed. He said Mrs. McSween wouldn't be able to collect his insurance if he was found with a gun on him."

The Kid was asked if he knew who had killed McSween. He said no: "He barely got out of the door when he went down. 'Oh, my God!' he said. That was all."

VIII

Violence Is Its Own Undoing

On the morning following the battle, a coroner's jury held an inquest over the bodies of the five men who had been slain, noting the number of bullet wounds each had received. McSween topped the list with five. It was the verdict of the jury that he, Morris, Romero and Zamora "came to their deaths by rifle shots fired from the hands of the Sheriff's posse, while they, the above named persons, were resisting the posse with force of arms"; and that Beckwith "came to his death by two rifle shots from the hands of the above named McSween, Morris, Zamora and others, and while they were resisting the Sheriff's posse." As intended, it gave Peppin and Dudley a clean bill of health.

Believing that the fighting was over, Peppin removed most of his deputies from the payroll, which did not sit well with them. Waiting until Colonel Dudley marched out of Lincoln with his troops, they broke into the Tunstall store, which had been padlocked for several months, and looted it of an estimated $6,000 worth of blankets and other merchandise.[1]

That the events of the past forty-eight hours were not going to be regarded by Washington as merely the outgrowth of a local disturbance that would soon be forgotten became obvious when Governor Samuel Beach Axtell was given the choice of resigning or being removed. He resigned, and on September 30, 1878, he was succeeded by General Lew Wallace.

Wallace had had a brilliant military career and a short time later was to win world fame as the author of *Ben Hur* and other novels. He had expected more from the Republican party than appointment as the Territorial Governor of New Mexico. But he accepted it with good grace and settled down with Mrs. Wallace in the old Palace of the Governors in Santa Fe.

There are those who say he would have made a better governor if he had laid aside his literary endeavors temporarily and devoted all his time to the problems of the Territory. However that may be, there is no doubting that he was determined to put down the lawlessness that was terrorizing Lincoln County. Fortunately, General Edward Hatch, Military Commander of the Territory, was an old acquaintance. Hatch made his headquarters at nearby Fort Marcy, which enabled the two men to confer frequently and at short notice.

Colonel Dudley (properly Lt. Colonel) was often the subject of their conversations. Both were acquainted with the man's stormy military career. In 1871 he had been court-martialed at Camp McDowell, Arizona, on a number of charges, among them one alleging that he appeared before his command while intoxicated. Found guilty of some counts and not guilty of others, he had been suspended from rank and command for sixty days. Six years later, then commanding officer at Fort Union, New Mexico, he had been tried by a general court-martial and found guilty of drunkenness, disobeying orders of General John Pope, who commanded the Department of the Missouri, and of vilifying his fellow officers, among them, then Colonel Edward Hatch. He was deprived of command at Fort Union and put on half pay for three months.

Dudley had friends in high places in the War Department, among them General of the Army W. T. Sherman, and they were always ready to bail him out when he got into trouble. Both Governor Wallace and General Hatch were aware of this. Both were anxious to have Dudley removed from command at Fort Stanton, and they set out to accomplish it. Wallace got off a long letter to Secretary of the Interior Schurz, accusing Dudley of offenses against the citizens of New Mexico. "Troops are stationed at Fort

Stanton for the principal, if not only, reason, to control the Indians. Colonel Dudley's principal concern is to fight the battles of J. J. Dolan and Co. Without any justification he rode into Lincoln on July 19, with sixty troops and cannon and put the town under martial law. It was uncalled for and in the resulting fighting five men were killed." He spoke of the threats (alleged) that Dudley had made to destroy homes with his cannon, irrespective of who might be within at the time. He further accused Dudley of standing by and doing nothing to prevent the looting of the store of John Tunstall and Company, in which his men took a hand. "But for the presence of the troops there would have been no killing."

It was a bitter letter filled with truths and half truths. The Governor requested Secretary Schurz to ask the War Department to remove Colonel Dudley.

General Hatch received a copy of the Wallace letter and forwarded it to Washington through the regular channels. He got an answer, a stinging one from General Sherman; Wallace heard nothing at all. He had been in New Mexico without ever stirring out of Santa Fe. Newspapers that had been friendly at first began to take aim on him. Among the letters from readers that they printed, the sharpest came from Lincoln. "Let the Governor come down and see for himself how things are going," wrote Huston J. Chapman, one of the leading attorneys of Lincoln County, in the Santa Fe *New Mexican*. "The war may be over but it is a common occurrence for a bunch of Sheriff Peppin's drunken deputies to ride thundering into town, their revolvers cocked and sending honest men scurrying to cover."

Chapman found time to bombard the newspapers with letters demanding that Wallace appoint officials who could and would bring law and order to Lincoln County. Reckless in his charges, he excoriated James Dolan and those "murderers like Col. Dudley and Sheriff Peppin." And again: "There is not an honest man in Lincoln County who would believe Col. Dudley under oath." He not only trained his fire on Dudley but on his staff as well: "Fort Stanton is today and has been during all the troubles the rendezvous of the worst outlaws that have infested Lincoln County."

Wallace was not idle. To his monthly report to the Governor,

U.S. Marshal John Sherman, Jr. attached a long letter from Judge Warren Bristol giving his reasons for not holding the October term of court in Lincoln County. For once Judge Bristol seems to have thrown off the Dolan collar he usually wore. "The Sheriff it seems has either abandoned or been driven from office or duty, and taken refuge at Fort Stanton for protection. The prosecuting attorney is absent from the Territory. It is impossible at present to obtain fair juries whose findings and verdicts will not be tainted with gross partisanship. The court can meet only through such subordinate officials as are furnished by election or appointment, and juries taken directly from the people. When these utterly fail in their duties the holding of court . . . could be but a mockery . . . during the present state of public feeling and animosity the assemblage of a body of men by attempting to hold court unrestrained by the miltary or any adequate force . . . would do more harm than good."

When Governor Wallace had digested the two letters, he realized that they might unexpectedly enable him to seize control of the situation in Lincoln. Instead of communicating with Schurz by mail, he got off a fifteen-hundred-word telegram to the Secretary, quoting Judge Bristol in full and recommending that the President take drastic action.

The Governor's telegram produced almost immediate action in Washington. On October 7, President Rutherford B. Hayes issued a proclamation admonishing all persons in New Mexico, and especially in Lincoln County, who had been or were engaged in violation of the law, to "disperse and return peaceably to their respective homes, on or before noon of the thirteenth of October, instant."

That part of the proclamation might have been brushed aside as of little consequence, but not the unequivocal warning that when it shall become impractical to enforce by the ordinary course of judicial proceedings the laws of the United States, it shall be the duty of the President to call forth the militia and employ "such parts of the land and naval forces to enforce the faithful execution of the laws of the United States as may be necessary."

Wallace had hoped that Lincoln County would be put under martial law and the writ of habeas corpus suspended. But it was something. He was notified that the various Department Commanders had been instructed to be ready to move in troops.

The President's proclamation seemed to have had some effect. Thirty days after it had been posted, Wallace was able to write Schurz: "In Lincoln and Doña Ana counties there has been no report of violence or wrong in those localities."

Convinced by the success he was having, Governor Wallace issued his famous amnesty proclamation on November 13, 1878. It said in part "that the people of Lincoln County may be helped more speedily to the management of their civil affairs . . . and to induce them to lay aside forever the divisions and feuds [which] have been so prejudicial to their locality and the whole Territory, the undersigned, by virtue of the authority in him vested, further proclaims a general pardon for misdemeanors and offenses committed in the said County of Lincoln against the laws of the said Territory in connection with the aforesaid disorders, between the first day of February, 1878, and the date of this proclamation."

There were limitations: "It shall not apply except to officers of the United States Army stationed in the said County during the said disorders [aimed at Dudley and his staff, of course], and to persons who, at the time of the commission of the offense or misdemeanor of which they may be accused, were with good intent, resident citizens of said Territory, and who shall have hereafter kept the peace."

The amnesty proclamation created very little excitement in Lincoln County except at Fort Stanton, where it aroused a storm. Colonel Dudley angrily contended that in extending a general pardon to himself and his officers it in effect charged them with crimes they had not committed and about which they knew nothing. In a scathing letter to Wallace, signed by himself and endorsed by Lieutenants Smith, Goodwin and French of the 9th Cavalry (Negro) and Lieutenant Pogue of the 15th Infantry, he told the Governor: "Permit me to state that you have now been more than eight weeks in the Territory, and have never been during that period within nearly two hundred miles of the scene of the terrible death struggles that have been enacted in this county during this time. The occasional passing of troops over the public roads, has had the effect to give the poor, frightened settlers an

The entrance to Palo Duro Canyon.

Palo Duro Canyon, the scene of MacKenzie's battle with the Comanches.

Oliver Loving, "the most knowledgeable cowman on the Texas frontier."

Denver Public Library Western Collection

Colonel Charles Goodnight, the great plainsman, trail-blazer and cattleman.

The Trail Drivers of Texas

John Simpson Chisum, the Cattle King of the Pecos.

William (Billy the Kid) Bonney.

National Archives

Sheriff Pat Garrett, who shot and killed the Kid on July 14, 1881.

National Archives

John H. Tunstall, the young English rancher who was killed by a sheriff's posse.

James J. Dolan, one of the men who controlled the law in Lincoln County.

General Lew Wallace prior to his appointment as Governor of New Mexico.

Palace of the Governors, Santa Fe, 1881.

John Tewksbury, a ruthless participant in the Pleasant Valley War.

Edwin Tewksbury, the firebrand of
the Tewksbury faction.

John Graham, killed by Sheriff Mulvenon at Perkins' store.

Thomas Graham, leader of the Graham
clan.

Anne Graham, wife of the clan leader.

Headquarters of the JA ranch.

Granville Stuart, father of the Montana range cattle trade.

Montana Historical Association

Conrad Kohrs, "from butcher boy to cattle king."

Montana Historical Association

Huffman Photograph

Buffalo on the Big Dry, Montana.

Huffman Photograph

Oregon cattle crossing Monida Pass.

Bull train leaving Miles City, 1881.

Rocky Point on the Missouri, where Red Mike and Brocky Gallagher, notorious horse thieves, made their headquarters.

Argonaut Press

Mercaldo Archives

Left: John Clay, Jr., who brought stability to the range cattle business. *Right:* James Averell, who shared Ella Watson's fate.

Ella Watson, who was hanged by cattlemen on the Sweetwater, Wyoming.

Mercaldo Archives

Cheyenne, 1879.

Thomas Sturgis, powerful secretary of the Wyoming Stock
Growers' Association.

Moreton Frewen, who gave Wyoming its first taste of English culture.

The Cheyenne Club, 1885.

The Invaders under arrest at Fort D. A. Russell.

opportunity of a few hours of seeming security. Wherever the colored cavalry have made their appearance, doors that have for weeks been barred and barricaded, have been opened for a few hours, husbands and sons have enjoyed the luxury of a night's rest at their homes whenever troops have camped a single night near their ranches.

"Pardon me for saying, it is not to be wondered at that you have received erroneous views of the exact state of affairs here. I most respectfully ask you to come to Lincoln county, and see and judge for yourself, from personal observation of the facts."

Wallace heard from Huston Chapman again, this time in a letter mailed from Lincoln. "I am now preparing a statement of facts for publication, which I am sorry to say will reflect upon you for not coming here to get a correct idea of the outrages that have been committed here instead of quietly sitting in Santa Fe and depending on drunken officers for information. A decent respect for the people of this county would have caused you to come here in person and ascertain who was responsible for all the trouble."

Chapman was in Lincoln representing Mrs. McSween, who had been appointed executrix of her husband's estate.[2] His outspoken condemnation of James Dolan, Colonel Dudley and Sheriff Peppin resulted in tragedy. At midday on February 18, as he stood on the steps of the post office in Lincoln, he was shot and killed by two men, identified by eyewitnesses, of whom the Kid was one, as William Campbell and Jesse Evans, the same Jesse Evans who had had a hand in the slaying of John Tunstall. J. B. (Jake) Matthews, an off-and-on Dolan employee, was in their company at the time.

When news of the killing of Huston Chapman reached the Governor, he announced at once that he was leaving for Lincoln as soon as preparations could be made. It was not until March 2, however, that, accompanied by General Hatch, he rode out of Santa Fe with his little expedition, consisting of an escort of seventeen cavalrymen, sixty horses and mules, a Gatling gun and a supply train of ten wagons and three ambulances.

It was an imposing turnout and indicated that Governor Wallace was prepared to make an extended stay in Lincoln. Despite the fact that he considered his mission to be of the first impor-

tance, the road over which he traveled was in such wretched condition that he was four days reaching his destination. As soon as
he had established camp on the eastern edge of town, he sent for
George Kimball, who had succeeded Peppin as sheriff of Lincoln
County on February 1. Kimball had been trying to take the Kid
and Charlie Bowdre into custody for killing Shotgun Roberts at
Blazer's Mill in April, 1878. The Governor was more interested in
bringing to trial the killers of Lawyer Chapman. Kimball informed him that the wanted men, Campbell and Evans and Jake
Matthews, were at Dolan's Carrizozo ranch. Wallace at once requested General Hatch to send a sufficient force to the ranch to
arrest all three and take them to Fort Stanton "and hold them
securely until their cases can be investigated."

This was done, and Campbell, Evans and their alleged con-
spirator Jake Matthews were placed in the guardhouse at Fort
Stanton. The following day the Governor formally requested General Hatch to relieve Colonel Dudley of his command, charging
that "Lt. Colonel Dudley is responsible for the killing of several
people in Lincoln County. I have information also connecting
him with the recent murder of H. J. Chapman."

Acting on his own authority this time, Hatch suspended Dudley from active duty and ordered him to Fort Union, "there to
remain in readiness to face charges preferred by the Governor of
New Mexico."

The most dramatic meeting in the long history of the Lincoln
County troubles occurred on the night of March 17, 1879, when
Governor Wallace came face to face with William H. Bonney, the
Kid, in Squire (former Justice of the Peace) Wilson's house on
the south side of town. The Kid came to this secret meeting armed
with pistol and rifle and they were never far from his hands as he
and the Governor sat and talked.

The meeting had been arranged by Squire Wilson through
intermediaries. He had learned that the Kid, an eyewitness to the
slaying of Lawyer Chapman, was willing to come in and testify
against the killers, although under several indictments himself,
if the Governor extended his amnesty proclamation to include
him, and would guarantee his safety while in custody "so that I
will not be shot down like a dog."

Wallace agreed to the Kid's terms. The latter had only the Governor's word that measures would be taken to protect him. But he accepted it, indicating that in the short time he had been in Lincoln County, Lew Wallace had established his integrity.

But the Kid had some reservations as to where and when he would give himself up. He promised to come in, however, as soon as he was satisfied that the necessary precautions for his safety had been taken. When they parted, it was understood that they would keep in touch through Squire Wilson.

Two nights later Evans and Campbell escaped from Fort Stanton. That complicated matters for the Kid. He knew that Evans and Campbell would risk capture for an opportunity to kill him.

Matthews and Dolan had not attempted to flee with the others. In fact, Dolan had not been under technical arrest until a day or two before the escape. He had been brought to Lincoln under guard from his Carrizozo ranch a week back. Wallace had released him on his own recognizance when Dolan agreed to go to the Fort and remain there until the spring grand jury decided whether or not he should be held as an accessory both before and after the fact in the killing of Huston Chapman. Dolan had pledged his word, but a day or two later had violated his parole by appearing publicly in Lincoln. Properly indignant, the Governor put him under arrest and had him returned to Fort Stanton, with an order to Captain Carrol, the acting commander, to "keep him in close confinement."

Dolan must have realized that control of the county had passed out of his hands. Financially he was in a precarious position. The Lincoln County War had ruined his business. He had the Carrizozo ranch and not much else to show for the years of conflict.

Through Squire Wilson several missives passed between Governor Wallace and the Kid. The latter made good his promise to surrender and in a simulated arrest he was taken into custody by Sheriff Kimball at San Patricio on March 23. He was brought to Lincoln and lodged in the makeshift jail from which Frank Coe had made his escape back in March the previous year.

Governor Wallace was amazed by the reception the Kid received from the citizens of Lincoln. "I can't understand it," he wrote Secretary Schurz. "He seems to be the idol of the Spanish

Americans. At night, they gather about the jail and actually sere-
nade the young thug who is guilty of a score of crimes."

Against his wishes Judge Bristol convened the grand jury on
April 14. The Kid and scores of witnesses testified. When they
were finished, the grand jury had a field day, returning several
hundred indictments, most of which were nol-prossed by the amnesty proclamation. Two days later the Court of Inquiry into the
conduct of Colonel Dudley convened at Fort Stanton. The Kid
was put on the stand again. Most of the charges he and other witnesses made centered on the killing of Alex McSween and the
burning of his home. Wallace and his counsel, Ira Leonard, were
infuriated by the manner in which the proceedings were being
conducted. When the court ruled that the defense having closed
its case, its witnesses could not be recalled for cross examination,
it became obvious that the officers conducting the inquiry were
determined to whitewash Dudley. The Governor had returned
to Santa Fe temporarily. Leonard wrote him on June 11, "There
is nothing to be expected or hoped for from the tribunal. They
mean to whitewash and excuse his [Dudley's] glaring conduct. . . .
The evidence against him would hang a man in any country
where justice prevailed."

But the Court of Inquiry dragged on until July 5, its findings
being that "the charges preferred against Lt. Colonel N. A. M.
Dudley have not been sustained and that court-martial proceedings are therefore unnecessary."

The cost of the farce was said to have totaled $30,000.

The Kid had disappeared. Several weeks later he was reported
to have been seen around Portales, east of Fort Sumner, riding
with his old pals Charlie Bowdre and Tom O'Folliard and two
newcomers, Dave Rudabaugh and Billy Wilson. They were stealing horses and running them across the line into the Texas Panhandle. It is not necessary to follow the Kid through the dark days
of his outlawry and recount how one after another of his followers were rubbed out until, a hunted man, he stood alone when he
walked into Pete Maxwell's bedroom at Fort Sumner shortly after
midnight on July 14, 1881, and was shot and killed by Sheriff
Pat Garrett.

With better luck he might have survived another year or two.

But the days of unbridled outlawry and weak and corrupt local government were passing; the railroads were arriving, and in a few years their coming transformed New Mexican life. New towns sprang into existence; land values boomed; mining became an important industry; sheep and cattle ranching became a profitable, organized business.

Early in 1879 the first Atchison, Topeka and Santa Fe train came through the Raton Tunnel, and on July 4, the rails reached Las Vegas. Six months later an eighteen-mile spur from Lamy brought them into Santa Fe.[3] In another ten months, the Denver and Rio Grande Western Railroad, building down from Colorado, entered Santa Fe. Soon thereafter the Southern Pacific, driving eastward from the Colorado River, muscled its way across New Mexico.

Progress, so-called, was in the saddle and the old landmarks began to fade. For no good reason the county seat of Lincoln County was removed to Carrizozo, thirty miles to the west. Perhaps the old plaza held memories that the new breed preferred to forget.

ARIZONA'S
SHEEP-CATTLE
WAR

IX

The Pleasant Valley Feud

There was a time when Americans living along the Atlantic sea-board regarded everything beyond the Alleghenies as West. By 1860 that vast, vaguely bounded land had shrunk considerably. But it was still sizable enough to include those regions lying west of the Mississippi between the Canadian line and the Mexican border. In that wide empire of grass and the big sky there were regions where the law a man carried on his hip was considered the only effective law. Nowhere was that so true as in Territorial Arizona in the blazing decades of the seventies and eighties.

We can dismiss the super violence, gunplay and mayhem of a thousand western movies as picturing a West that never was, but some of their more incredible moments have a surprising similarity to unrelated events that occurred in Apache and outlaw-ravaged Arizona, with range thievery a recognized profession.

Cattle rustling as practiced on the northern ranges of Wyoming and Montana was a puny business compared with the mass theft of whole herds of Mexican Longhorns that were driven across the international boundary. Long before the first English-speaking Americans settled in what was to become Arizona, and cattle became a convenient medium of exchange among them, the Spaniards had explored that country and left the marks of their culture. They found the Indians—Indians as we know them, Pimas, Navajos, Apaches and a dozen other smaller tribes, not the ancient cliff dwellers who had long since disappeared into antiquity—in possession of that seemingly limitless expanse of mountain-desert. In the century and a half after the Spaniards withdrew, the Mexicans moved in. Although they opened a few mines, they mainly led a pastoral existence. Nothing seemed to change, and when the Americans began arriving in 1848, following the successful conclusion of the War with Mexico, Arizona was still largely a virgin land.

A majority of the newcomers were from Texas, and they brought with them their ingrained prejudices against all Mexicans, whom they regarded as peons. They killed a few, pushed the others aside and took over, not that there was much to take at first. The Indians were still there, and to control them the United States built and garrisoned a number of military posts and gathered the more peaceful tribes on reservations. That did not include the different Apache tribes, however, especially the Chiricahuas and Mimbres Apaches, who were violently opposed to being removed from the mountains and valleys that they regarded as their homeland. This vaguely defined region of mountain peaks, inaccessible canyons and spring-fed streams the late J. Frank Dobie named *Apacheria*.

Countless writers have collaborated in giving us the accepted picture of the cruel, vengeful Apache and his butcheries. Few have had the honesty to give him his due as a first-class fighting man. Such leaders as Mangas Colorada, Cochise Geronimo and Victorio gave no quarter and asked none. Is it possible that they were patriots fighting for the birthright of their people?

There is no record of what the population of Arizona was in 1863, when it was organized as a territory under the jurisdiction of the United States. According to the U.S. Census of 1870, it had a population of only 9,658. It had been formed by slicing off approximately the western half of the Territory of New Mexico. In size, with some straightening of its borders, Arizona was then, as it is today, rated seventh in land area among the states.

The reasons advanced for organizing Arizona as a territory separate and distinct from New Mexico were many, and they were all largely political. The nation was deeply involved in the War Between the States, and it was not going well for the North. In New Mexico, around Mesilla, Southern supporters were numerous. That was also true among the Texans who had settled in the Salt River Valley of Arizona. It was believed that by dividing New Mexico those groups could be weakened. Interested politicians further buttressed their case by claiming that New Mexico was so huge that it was impossible to govern it efficiently. Certainly its size alone was not responsible for the prevailing lawlessness, but it was a persuasive argument.

During the Gold Rush days to California an estimated fifty thousand men had crossed the almost uninhabited reaches of the projected Territory of Arizona. Few had remained. Thousands of them would be returning. Among them would be those who had failed to find their pot of gold in California. Hopefully with local government and some evidence of law and order, many of the discouraged could be induced to put their roots down and settle in the new territory. That hope must have been realized in some degree and been partly responsible for the fact that the population of Arizona zoomed to 40,440 in 1880.

It was widely known that under the direction of the padres, in the days of Spanish occupancy of the country, placering for gold at the mouth of the Gila and along the Colorado where Fort Yuma now stands, had produced rich rewards. Such tales do not dic. The old placers were reopened and new ones discovered at La Paz, Laguna and up the Colorado at Ehrenberg. By 1860, lode mining was opening bonanzas at Picacho, Wickenburg and other camps. All were so isolated that, in the absence of roads, the only way to reach them was by trail and pack train. Mining, rather than sheep and cattle ranching, became the leading industry of the Territory. To further it, a faster and cheaper means of transportation had to be found. The only possible solution was to move goods and treasure by water, via the Colorado River. That the Colorado could be navigated by steamboat north of Yuma was doubtful. But the Federal Government, mindful of the revenue the mines might produce, proved that it was not only feasible but immensely profitable.[1]

The lush days of Colorado steamboating ended a decade later

when the Iron Horse came stomping across Arizona, both from east and west, offering competition the steamboats could not meet.

Even in a country as thinly settled as Arizona, the growing prosperity of those regions adjacent to one or the other of the two trunk railroads, the Southern Pacific in the south and the Atlantic and Pacific (the Santa Fe) in the north, quickly became apparent. From sections of the Territory too remote to share in the windfall, there came a rash of demands for branch lines and a north-south railroad that would tie the mining camps and cow towns together.

A number of railroads were chartered. One or two actually did some work, the others never got off the paper. In Pima County, the Arizona Narrow Gauge Railroad actually succeeded in building ten miles of track over which no train ever ran. The fiasco cost Pima County $319,000. Several other counties subsidized railroad bonds and had to foot the bill when the promotions collapsed.

But those phantom railroads of the early 1880's became a reality before the turn of the century. The Santa Fe, Prescott and Phoenix (A.T. and S.F. subsidiary) building south from Ash Fork, reached Phoenix in 1895. It resulted in the Territorial capital being removed from Prescott for the second time and established permanently at Phoenix. Perhaps equally important was the effect it had on the sheep and cattle business of central and northern Arizona.

Vast as that region was, it was still wild and largely unknown, a land where the mountains were blackened with fringes of pine and crystal-clear streams wandered through the valleys. But even by the early 1880's, most of it had been overstocked and overgrazed. There were mountain meadows where the grama and other grasses still grew stirrup-high. And there were stretches of range that had been grazed down to the roots by bands of sheep, where even the soil had been cut up by the sharp hoofs of the close-herded animals. That had always been the basis of the classical feud between cowmen and sheepmen. It had led to violence and killing elsewhere. All the ingredients for such a blood-letting in Arizona were present, and there was little reason to believe that it could be avoided.

When it was to their interest to do so, the big outfits enforced such law as there was. They recruited their riders without regard for their known character, insisting only that they do their work and guard the property of the owners of the brand. This was asking considerable of men who were known rustlers and outlaws. But they were resourceful enough to find ways of stealing from the boss who paid them their wages. Although their character was devious, they were excellent range warriors who in a showdown were loyal to their outfit.

The great Aztec Land and Cattle Company whose headquarters were on the Little Colorado River, opposite the Mormon settlement of Saint Joseph, west of Holbrook, burned a replica of a hash knife for its brand on upwards of sixty thousand head of cattle. It was known from one end of Arizona to the other as the famous Hash Knife outfit. Such men as Tom Pickett, who had run with Billy the Kid, Tom Tucker, Billy Wilson, Buck Lancaster, John Paine, George Smith and half a dozen others, all known killers, were on its payroll.

Two other outfits employed men who had managed to reach Arizona ahead of the sheriff. They were the Mormon-owned Arizona Cattle Company, with its headquarters nine miles north of Flagstaff, in the foothills of the San Francisco Mountains, its A 1 Bar brand almost as famous as the Hash Knife, and Babbitt Brothers' C O Bar, also of Flagstaff.

These three big outfits—the Hash Knife, the A 1 Bar and C O Bar—dominated the range cattle business as far south as the great mesa of the Mogollons (safely pronounced Moy-ans) beyond the rim of which lies the Tonto Basin. What conflict there was between the big owners and the little outfits was only nominal. Perhaps that was because beneath their occasional bickerings they shared the common bond of being determined that sheep should never cross the Mogollon Rim.

If you will glance at a map, you will see how the Mogollons curve around the Tonto Basin, forming an almost impregnable barrier on the north, running from east to west, and leaving on the south a gateway across the mountains to the booming silver and copper camp of Globe, eighty miles away. Globe was the county seat of Gila County. It was only four years old and too lawless itself to give any thought to Tonto Basin, which up to then had shown a surprising ability to take care of itself. At different times Sheriff William Mulvenon, of Yavapai County, and Sheriff Commodore Owens, of Apache County, who were in the habit of ignoring the limits of their jurisdiction, had appeared in the Basin, looking for men on whom they carried warrants. Men who, for reasons best known to themselves, stuck to the back country, dropped in, but after a day or two disappeared as quietly as they had come.

If the reader has been told or has read about the so-called Tonto Basin War, he has been misled; properly speaking, there never was any Tonto Basin War. The bloody feud associated with that region was confined to the tiny valley along Cherry Creek which, in light of what occurred there later, was ironically named Pleasant Valley. After half a century and more it is still a beautiful, well-timbered valley, drowsing under the high, blue Arizona sky. In the long ago, when a score or more families dwelt there in peace, their ranches were scattered about instead of being huddled together, which reflected the independent spirit of the settlers who had carved out a home in Pleasant Valley. No one was interested in building a town; Charlie Perkins' store was as much "civilization" as they wanted.[2]

From choice they had gravitated to the rugged, pioneer life they led. No one among them was well-to-do. But they bent the knee to no man. They ran a few head of cattle and grew what they ate. If they needed meat, they could usually kill a deer from their doorway. In the pattern of men everywhere who lead isolated lives, they were strong-willed and violent in their likes and dislikes. Whenever they met at Perkins' store in late August and early September, 1886, a recurring topic of conversation was the rumor that had been passed on to them by friendly Hash Knife riders that the old Mogollon deadline against sheep, which had held for four years, was about to be broken.

According to those disturbing rumors, Daggs Brothers of Flagstaff, the biggest sheep outfit in Arizona, faced with the necessity of finding additional range, especially protected winter range, or of reducing the size of their bands, had decided to send their sheep over the Mogollon Rim, whatever the consequences. Even more disturbing was the whisper that the fighting Tewksbury clan, one of the most feared in Pleasant Valley, had hired out to Daggs Brothers and were to guard the sheep, once they had come in.

This talk, if true, meant war—the cruelest, most pitiless kind of war, turning neighbor against neighbor, costing the lives of good men and bad until it finally burned itself out. From the vantage point of hindsight, we know that the price of that bloody, internecine struggle was to be death to the last man.

In what is correctly known as the Pleasant Valley War, there were two factions. On one side of the coin were the Tewksburys— old John D., the father, and three grown, half-Indian sons: Edwin, John and James; on the other side, the Grahams, Tom and John, brothers, and William, a half brother. As soon as it was definitely established that the Tewksburys had hired out to guard the Daggs' sheep, the cattlemen of the valley turned to Tom Graham and made him their leader.

Due to much careless writing over the years, Tom Graham has been pictured as a bloodthirsty savage and held responsible for most of the violence and killing that distinguished the Pleasant Valley War. "Nothing could be further from the truth," says Earle R. Forrest, the feud's most reliable historian, "for he was a quiet, peaceful man and honest in all his dealings. Even after the invasion of sheep made war certain he refused to take human life; and his restraining hand held his followers in check until the first blood spilled by Tewksbury forces made further restraint impossible." [3]

Unquestionably there was bad blood between the Grahams and the Tewksburys by 1886. There is some evidence that at one time the Tewksbury boys and the Grahams had been on very friendly terms. Jim Stinson, a pioneer cattleman, and an early settler in Pleasant Valley, said when interviewed many years later, "I was there long before they came. The Grahams built a cabin on Cherry Creek about four miles from my ranch. I often saw them and the Tewksburys together. When I began losing cattle, I figured they got them, and pretty soon they were fighting over them. It was really my cattle that started the Pleasant Valley feud. Bringing the sheep was only incidental." [4]

Stinson was a colorful and knowledgeable man, but he is in error when he states that the invasion of the Daggs' sheep was only incidental to the violence that drenched Pleasant Valley with blood. Old court records of Yavapai County reveal that the Tewksburys brought the Grahams to trial in 1882, charging them with the theft of their cattle. A year later, the Grahams retaliated by filing a similiar charge against the Tewksburys. In both instances the cases were dismissed for lack of evidence. But they show what the situation between the feuding parties was when the Tewksburys made their deal with the sheep and mercantile firm of Daggs Brothers that was likely to cost them their lives.

No one knows what Peter P. Daggs offered the Tewksburys or what promises he made. Certainly they must have been of an extravagant nature, perhaps including the prospect of a future partnership.

Daggs must have had some reason for believing that the venture had a chance of succeeding or he would not have gone into it. He was a shrewd businessman. He and his brothers had come to Flagstaff from Ohio, opened their store and built up a large and profitable general trading operation before branching out into sheep and wool, which had made them wealthy. He was fully aware of the deadline beyond which cattlemen made it plain that sheep would not be tolerated. Several times there had been minor clashes with Hash Knife riders who had fired at Daggs' sheep and turned them back. Perhaps he believed—and this is only a conjecture—that if he could put his sheep south of the big mesa where they would have only small, unorganized outfits to face they could survive, especially if they had the guns of the Tewksbury clan to guard them. This is a sound argument and tends to explain why the deal with the Tewksburys was made.

That Peter Daggs had reservations about what he was doing is reflected in the fact that the first band of sheep he started across the big mesa was a small one, numbering not more than a thousand head. Moving slowly, grazing as they advanced, word that they were crossing the mesa ran ahead of them. In Pleasant Valley men stopped what they were doing and gathered at Perkins' store. Some of them still could not believe that sheep would be trailed over the Mogollon Rim.

"It's only a bluff to scare us," said Tom Graham. "We'll sit tight for a while."

Andy Blevans, one of the five sons of old Mark Blevans, was present. Rustler, gun fighter and killer, he had adopted the name of Andy Cooper to confuse a Texas sheriff or two who held felony warrants on him. Though a staunch Graham supporter, he was a firebrand, and he objected violently to sitting tight and waiting.

"We better git up there and turn 'em back while there's time," he argued. "If we don't, there won't be any grass in the valley, come spring."

Some of the men gathered in Perkins' store agreed with him. According to the word that had been received, the three *pastores* who were moving the sheep were young Navajos. Many accounts have it that it was decided then and there that if the herders refused to turn back across the mesa with their flock, that wholesale slaughter of the animals by gunfire would begin. Earle R. Forrest says otherwise. He states that Tom Graham carried the day; that there would be no resort to violence until after other methods had been tried and failed.

He was taking an untenable position, which he was compelled to acknowledge several months later. With others, he watched the sheep come over the Rim and pour down the trail into the valley unopposed on the last day of October, 1888. As though by pre-arrangement, for they were strangers to the country, the Navajos drove the band across Cherry Creek and put them on grass between that stream and Canyon Creek to the east. That placed the sheep on range claimed by the Tewksburys and within several miles of the Tewksbury house.

The deal the Tewksburys had made with Daggs Brothers included the service of William (Bill) Baker, a renegade cowboy with a fast gun. Baker had arrived in Pleasant Valley and was quartered on the Tewksbury ranch. It is doubtful if John D. Tewksbury, Sr., had legal title to the land he claimed. That was true of other Pleasant Valley cattlemen. In the back-country regions of Arizona in those days, just being in possession usually sufficed to give a man all the title he needed to guarantee his right to the range that he considered his own. This was an application of the old free-range rule that held if you saw it first and were strong enough to hold it, then the land was yours.

In the few weeks that remained before the first snows of winter fell, the herders were harassed, no matter where they bivouacked for the night. These raids usually lasted only half an hour or so, and while there was a lot of shooting and a number of sheep were killed, there were no human casualties.

Unquestionably Andy Cooper was the ringleader in these nightly forays, abetted by the other Blevans boys, Mark, Charlie, John and young Sam Houston Blevans. To their surprise, their rifle fire was returned in earnest one night. They cut off one of the opposing gunmen and chased him for several miles before they realized he was making for the Tewksbury house. When he dashed into the ranch yard, they recognized him. He was Ed Tewksbury. They drew the only inference possible: the Tewksburys had lined up with the Flagstaff sheepmen.

It had a cataclysmic effect. Both sides seemed to realize at once that any hope of peace was now gone. The two factions polarized, enlisted recruits, and were careful about where they rode. Meanwhile the band of sheep that had ignited the trouble had moved into the timbered side canyons above Cherry Creek, where they were seemingly forgotten. It proved to be only the lull before the storm. Mark Blevans and his sons had convinced the Graham faction that the first order of business was to get rid of the sheep either by driving them back over the Rim, even though it was winter, or killing them.

By now the Tewksburys were so openly supporting the Navajo herders and supplying their needs that the Graham faction began referring to them as "sheepmen." [5]

The Indian herders had established a more or less permanent camp in a rocky cavern above Cherry Creek. One night early in February one of them was killed as he stood revealed in the glow of the campfire. In the morning John, Jim and Ed Tewksbury picked up the trail of the sniper which led directly to the Blevans ranch. They were within sight of the house before they pulled up. Everything looked peaceful. But they were not deceived; they knew that the frosty air would be shattered by rifle fire if they attempted to cross the clearing between them and the house. Wisely, they turned back, convinced that the unknown sniper was Andy Cooper.

No one has ever thrown any light on what the arrangement

was or how it was made, but six weeks later, what was left of the Daggs herd toiled up the trail unmolested and disappeared over the Rim.

Their leaving changed nothing. Behind them they left a smoldering feud that was soon to burst into flame. Before it burned out, it was to take the lives of a score of men.

X

Death Stalks the Trails

In song and story the sanguinary feuding of the Hatfields and the McCoys in the mountains of West Virginia and Kentucky has been incorporated in the folklore of America. On the other hand, the violent, hate-ridden Pleasant Valley War, far more costly in the number of lives sacrificed to it, remains largely unknown. In some ways they were similar; both were fought against a mountain background in a wild, sparsely settled country. And both were waged by men of a singular sameness of character. Had the Grahams and the Tewksburys been whisked across the United States and set down in the feuding grounds of the Hatfields and the McCoys, they very likely would have been accepted as natives of that region.

John D. Tewksbury had been a wanderer in the West for thirty years before he settled in Pleasant Valley. He had left Boston in 1850, when the California gold excitement was at its height, and made the long trip around the Horn by sailing vessel. After several months of unsuccessful prospecting on the Mother Lode, he journeyed north, as many others were doing, to the new diggings on the south fork of the Klamath River, in Trinity County. There his luck improved, and he settled down and married a Klamath Indian woman. Whether this was a legal marriage or not, he remained faithful to her until her death. In the meantime, she had borne him three stalwart sons—John, Jr., James and Edwin.[1]

Tewksbury and his sons arrived in Globe in 1880, where he married a widow by the name of Lydia Crigler Shultes. By her he had two sons, Walter and Parker, neither of whom took part in the war. Accompanied by his sons and his new wife, Tewksbury journeyed across the mountains to Pleasant Valley, where he built a cabin and established a ranch. He had not been settled there more than a year, when the Grahams moved in.

The Graham brothers were from Boone, Iowa, where their father was a prosperous farmer. At first there were only two of them, Thomas the elder brother, and John Graham. They had been in California for six years prospecting, seemingly with some success, because when they located in Pleasant Valley they were well supplied with money. They were soon joined by William Graham, a much younger half brother born to the family by their father's second wife. With him William brought his nephew Louis Parker. Both were youths of only twenty-two, eager for adventure.

From the first, Tom Graham was the leader and spokesman for the family. He was a big, handsome man with an intelligent face, and despite the adventurous life he had led, had managed to acquire the rudiments of a good education. Ed Tewksbury, the youngest of the three boys, dominated his brothers. He had a driving, belligerent nature and a face that even in repose was cruel. In fact, he was said by his enemies to have been born mean. Being what they were, it was inevitable that he and Tom Graham should clash.

Ten miles northwest of the Tewksbury place Tom Graham built a substantial house and corrals. He was an affable man and as he rode about the valley, buying cattle with which to stock the ranch, he made friends. He said nothing about the rustling that plagued Tonto Basin. Perhaps that was just as well, because so many were engaged in it, one way or another. His avoidance of this ticklish subject has been used against him by his detractors. They would have it that he was a cattle thief in his early days in the valley, when he and the Tewksburys, acknowledged rustlers, were on good terms. This allegation may have been true, but no evidence has been found to support it. Nor can it be said with

certainty that the spark that ignited the bloody Graham-Tewks-
bury feud was touched off by a falling-out between the Graham
brothers and John Tewksbury's half-Indian sons. There is a
widely accepted and far more plausible explanation, the central
figure of which was "Old Man" Blevans.

Mark Blevans was one of the original settlers in Pleasant Valley.
He was a Texan, by way of New Mexico, fearless, an Indian fighter
and rangeman. Undeterred by its nearness to the western limits
of the White Mountain Apache Reservation, he located on Canyon Creek. In a surprisingly short time his Canyon Creek Ranch
was known by name throughout Tonto Basin.

As previously mentioned, he had five grown sons, and they were
as wild as the mustangs they rode and the Longhorns they herded.
Andy, the eldest, who went by the name of Andy Cooper, ruled
them as all five were ruled by the iron will of old Mark. He was a
hard man, as he had to be to exert any control over them. Honor-
able in his dealings himself, he knew his sons were stealing cattle,
both for amusement and gain. In his younger days he had used a
running iron himself. According to his code, pilfering cattle from
a big outfit was a sporting gamble. So he compromised by exempt-
ing his neighbors' herds from his sons' depredations and closing
his eyes to their running off Hash Knife yearlings.

The boys were agreeable. As a matter of fact, stealing from the
big spreads was safer and more profitable than raiding a small Pleasant Valley outfit. They had friends among Hash Knife and A 1
Bar riders who could be counted on to be cooperative for a share
of the loot. The Tewksburys were engaged in the same business,
and out of the rivalry developed a bitter hatred. It set the stage
for the violence that was to follow. History knows it as the Gra-
ham-Tewksbury feud, but it actually began between the Blevans
boys and the sons of John Tewksbury. There is no mystery about
how the family feud became a factional war.

Whether it was because old Mark Blevans genuinely admired
Tom Graham or because he saw trouble in the offing and needed
allies, no one can say, but it is an indisputable fact that he put
himself and his sons under the Graham banner at once. The next
move was up to Tom Graham. Since he could not hope to have
both of the feuding families on his side, he had to choose one or

the other. He chose the Blevans clan. It was a defeat for the Tewksburys. Left to go it alone, they reacted as might have been expected.

There are other explanations of the underlying cause of the Pleasant Valley War, but none so believable as the above. To that struggle old Mark Blevans was to sacrifice his own life and the lives of four of his sons.

Obviously he was a "character" or he would not have become known as Old Man Blevans rather than as Mark Blevans. He was still a vigorous man in his early sixties when he located his ranch on Canyon Creek. You might not believe it from the few times she was mentioned in newspaper accounts dealing with the trouble in Pleasant Valley, that Old Man Blevans had a wife, his second wife, in fact, and the mother of his youngest son. One local grass roots commentator refers to her as Mary Blevans. Whether or not Mary was her given name is immaterial.

Other women were living in Pleasant Valley in those years of turmoil and bloodshed; Lydia Tewksbury, to name one. But she is seldom mentioned by historians, undoubtedly because she and her husband John D. Tewksbury, Sr., although cast into the very heart of the conflict, miraculouly took no active part in it. On the other hand, a third woman, Mrs. Amanda Gladden, who was far removed from the conflagration, unfortunately became enmeshed in it through what can only be described as an act of kindness.

She was living on a homestead several miles below Canyon Creek Ranch when the trouble over the sheep began. Her husband had deserted her and she was trying as best she could to make a living for herself and several small children. If she had friends anywhere, it was Old Man Blevans and his wife. When a beef was butchered at Canyon Creek Ranch, they saw to it that a plentiful supply of meat went down the valley to Mrs. Gladden. Old Man Blevans drove up to the cabin one morning and told her to pack up. He and his wife had decided that it wasn't safe for her to live alone on the homestead with a range war brewing, and she and the children were to move into their Canyon Creek Ranch.

Such solicitude for a helpless neighbor was not uncommon on the frontier, where life was often precarious for all. Undoubtedly it revealed that beneath his flinty hide there was a streak of decency in Mark Blevans that he usually went to some pains to conceal.

On the night of August 1, 1887, several horses disappeared from Canyon Creek Ranch. Old Mark was of the opinion that the animals had been stolen by a group of Apaches from the White Mountain Reservation. Andy and his other sons were of a different opinion. According to them the horses had been run off by the Tewksburys. Against their advice, their father had a horse saddled, and armed with a rifle, set out to recover the animals. He rode out of the ranch yard in midmorning of August 2. It was the last time they were ever to see him.

When two days passed and he did not return, Andy and the others dismissed the thought that he was lost. They were convinced that he had been ambushed and either killed or so seriously wounded that he could not make his way back to the ranch.[2]

They searched for their father for two days without finding a clue to his fate. They could no longer doubt that he had been killed. They were in even less doubt as to who had done him in; the guilty men had to be Jim and Ed Tewksbury, accompanied very likely by such fast guns as Jim Roberts and Joe Boyer, who had aligned themselves with the Tewksbury faction.

Four Hash Knife cowboys came down from the north to join the posse the Blevans were organizing—the redoubtable Tom Tucker, John Paine, Bob Gillespie and Bob Carrington.

Andy Cooper (Blevans) did the planning. Instead of seeking help from Tom Graham, he deceived him into believing that the expedition he was organizing was going out for the sole purpose of finding his father's body and bringing it in for a decent burial.

When the "search" party left Canyon Creek Ranch on August 8, it numbered eight men. Hampton Blevans (known as Hank) was its nominal leader and the only one of the Blevans brothers to accompany it. The others were the four Hash Knife riders and three men whose names have been lost to history. Remaining behind were the other brothers and Al and Ed Rose, both dependable fighting men. They forted up and waited, hoping that the Tewksburys would attack it in the mistaken idea that Canyon Creek Ranch had been left undefended.

In light of what occurred two days later, such a move may have been contemplated by Ed Tewksbury and his followers who had taken to the hills. They had not been deceived by the talk about the posse going out to find old Mark Blevans' body; they knew its sole purpose was to hunt them down, catch them at a disadvantage and wipe them out. The outcome would depend on who surprised whom.

With Tom Tucker doing the tracking, the posse cut the fresh trail of seven or eight riders on August 9. After losing it several times, they found it again and followed it until nightfall. They camped on a branch of Canyon Creek, later named Wilson Creek. They were about fifteen miles east of the old Middleton ranch, one of the original holdings in Pleasant Valley and a landmark. In some narratives dealing with those dark and violent days the place is referred to as the Newton ranch. This is because George A. Newton, the Globe jeweler, bought the property prior to the beginning of hostilities and branched out into the cattle business with his son-in-law and a partner named Vosberg. Newton's reasons for espousing the cause of the Tewksburys remains unknown. But it was at his ranch that the first battle of the Pleasant Valley War took place.

It was nearing noon on August 10, when the trail the posse had been following since early morning turned back into the hills. Blevans and Tucker agreed that it was not leading them anywhere. Being within a few miles of the Middleton ranch, they decided to stop there for dinner.

Not being aware that Newton and his son-in-law had swung over to the Tewksbury faction, it seemingly never entered their heads that they might be refused the universal hospitality of the range that bade a passer-by to light and eat.

No one was in sight as they neared the house. In the brilliant noonday sunshine the place seemed to doze, not a leaf stirring and the silence broken only by the clattering of the cicadas in the sagebrush. They stopped at the fence momentarily, perhaps warned by some sixth sense that all was not well here. Tom Tucker got down and approached the door. Jim Tewksbury opened it. Instantly Tucker and the others realized what they had walked into. But Tucker had faced other situations when the chips were down.

"Can we get dinner?" he inquired.

"No, sir," came the curt answer. "We don't run a hotel here."

"Okay," Tucker told him. "We'll go down to Bob Sigsby's to eat."

He swung into the saddle and as he turned his back, several Winchesters spurted flame from the open doorway. Not only Jim Tewksbury but his brother Ed, Jim Roberts, John Rhodes and three or four other Tewksbury gunmen were in that room.

At the first blast, horses reared and collided with one another, unseating their riders. Hampton Blevans, a bullet through his brain, swayed limply in his saddle as his horse went down, then pitched lifeless to the ground, the first white man to die in the vendetta. John Paine snapped a shot at Jim Tewksbury. The slug plowed into the doorjamb a few inches from Tewksbury's head, leaving him untouched. Before Paine could fire again, his horse fell on him and he was caught beneath the dying animal. As he struggled to free himself, a blast from Jim Roberts' rifle clipped off his right ear. With blood streaming down his face, he started to run. He had taken only a few steps when Jim Tewksbury fired and stretched him out dead in the dust.

Tom Tucker was knocked from the saddle by a slug through the lungs that entered his body under the left arm and passed out through the other armpit. It was a terrible wound that would have killed most men then and there. But he was of that indomitable breed that dies hard. His horse had fallen on his rifle, but he managed to yank it out and fire at any man who appeared in the doorway.

Bob Gillespie received a bullet in his right hip and Bob Carrington was struck in his right arm and right leg. They and the unidentified other three men had recovered their wits and used their six-shooters to such advantage that the gunfire from the house was silenced. Tucker's mount got back on its feet and he managed to grab a stirrup and was dragged out of the line of fire.

It had been a costly three or four minutes for the Blevans posse: two men killed and three others wounded. That Tom Tucker could survive the grievous injury he had received appeared incredible. During the long, hot afternoon he crawled and dragged himself toward Bob Sigsby's ranch, several miles away, until he lapsed into unconsciousness. Blowflies attacked the wound as he lay there. By evening, maggots were at work. A cold rain and hailstorm revived him during the night and he was able to go on.

Tucker must have been near death when Sigsby saw him crawling toward his cabin. He ran out and carried him inside. He doused the double wound with creosote dip, the frontier's remedy for a score of different wounds, and fed him whisky, a spoonful at a time. Gradually Tucker began to revive. He had been there a day or more when Bob Gillespie hobbled into Sigsby's cabin. Sigsby nursed the two of them back to health. When they were able to ride, he supplied them with horses and they made their way north to the Hash Knife line camp at Big Dry Lake. They had had enough of the Pleasant Valley War.[3]

The Tewksbury version of the battle at the Middleton ranch was that it resulted from a move by the Graham faction to drive them out of Pleasant Valley. It sounds incredible, and no evidence to substantiate the story has ever been produced.

News of the killing of Hampton Blevans and John Paine spread quickly. Two days later a burial party led by Charles Perkins, the storekeeper, and John Meadows went to the Middleton ranch and without ceremony interred the dead men. On their return they did not report that they found the ranch buildings in ashes. If the place had been burned following the fight, there is no known reason why the Perkins party shouldn't have said so. But such a conclusion contradicts several widely believed tales. In 1927, forty years after the event, Jim Roberts, then in his seventies, who had participated in the Middleton ranch fight, said that shortly after what was left of the Blevans posse had withdrawn, he and several others had gone out into the yard to bury the dead men and remove the slain horses, when they saw a large group of riders top a distant hill. Believing at first that it was a force of Graham-Blevans warriors returning to avenge their fallen comrades, he and the others retreated to the house and forted up again for another attack, only to discover that the oncoming riders were Apaches.

As Roberts told it, the Indians came on until they saw the dead men in the yard, when they wheeled their ponies and fled. Knowing that the Indians would return as soon as they had overcome their momentary panic, he, Jim and Ed Tewksbury and the others got into the saddle and disappeared in the hills. Looking back, they saw the Indians set fire to the buildings.

Without justification, it seems to the present writer, Earle Forrest accepts this tale as factual. When Jim Roberts told his story, he was in no danger of being contradicted. He was by then the sole remaining survivor of those bloody days in Pleasant Valley.

Equally unbelievable is the account of how Andy Cooper, the fighting head of the Blevans clan, thirsting to avenge the killing of his brother, as well as the loss of his father, and a large party of Graham supporters chased the Tewksbury brothers and a few followers into the hills and brought them to bay in a rocky mountain canyon from which there was no escape. After settling down to starve the enemy out, Andy Cooper and several of his followers are said to have returned to the Middleton ranch and made a bonfire of the buildings. How the Tewksburys escaped from their predicament is not clear.

That such tales were given credence was undoubtedly due to the fact that in Pleasant Valley the incredible had become a commonplace. Bushwhacking and sniping became an almost daily occurrence. Any turn of the trail might hold an ambush where death awaited the passer-by. Two wandering prospectors, without cause or reason, were found murdered.

Hatred had to have something to feed on, and nothing was so flammable as the fear that if the Tewksbury faction prevailed sheep would be brought into the valley again, not by the hundreds but by the thousands. It was charged by the cattlemen who looked to Tom Graham for leadership that the Tewksburys were still in the pay of the Flagstaff sheepmen. Undoubtedly they were. Proof of it is found in a statement made by P. P. Daggs some years later concerning the cost of the Pleasant Valley War to Daggs Brothers. No greater stigma could be hurled at the followers of Ed and Jim Tewksbury than to label them "sheepmen."

As the vendetta tightened its grip on Pleasant Valley, Perkins' store, because of its proximity to the Graham ranch, became the political as well as the trading center for the so-called "cattlemen." The Tewksbury faction gave it a wide berth and got their supplies by the trail north through the mountains to Holbrook. Perkins' store provided Tom Graham with a convenient place to meet his partisans. It can be taken for granted that he was often there, but in the two weeks following the battle at the Middleton ranch there is nothing in the evidence to connect him with the daily sniping and the killing of the two prospectors and an unidentified cowboy on Tonto Creek. Beyond question, fire-eating Andy Cooper was usurping Graham's position and spearheading the violence.

When news of the situation existing in Pleasant Valley reached Prescott, townspeople demanded that the lawlessness be put down and the suspected killers brought to trial. Sheriff William Mulvenon, of sprawling Yavapai County, armed himself with warrants for the arrest of those members of the Tewksbury faction known to have participated in the killing of John Paine and Hampton Blevans at the Middleton ranch. All were charged with murder. In addition to organizing his own posse, he telegraphed Deputy Sheriff Francis at Flagstaff (then a part of Yavapai County) to meet him at Payson, a crossroads settlement in Tonto Basin, with half a dozen deputies.[4] Francis met him at Payson as planned, and when the posse rode into Pleasant Valley it numbered twenty men.

They found the Tewksbury ranch deserted. After a week of trying to find the men he wanted, Mulvenon decided that they had fled the valley temporarily and forted up in some impregnable spot in the mountains and that it "would be endangering the lives of his men to follow them." So the posse toiled back across Tonto Basin, a dismal failure, having accomplished nothing.

The posse had scarcely left the valley when young Billy Graham, the half brother of Tom and John Graham, was shot and fatally wounded on the Payson trail, two and a half miles west of the Graham ranch, where he died the following day.

The bushwhacker who put the boy in his grave was Jim Houck, a one-time sheepman from Apache County. He was a loner who had entered Pleasant Valley to fight for the Tewksburys. He had been commissioned a deputy by Sheriff Commodore P. Owens, of Apache County. His commission had long since been revoked, but he still wore a law badge and passed himself off as an officer, claiming he held a warrant for the arrest of John Graham, issued at Saint Johns. This is contrary to the facts. On the day that he shot Billy Graham, he had stopped at the Haigler ranch and got dinner. Not wanting to become involved in the feud, Haigler asked him to leave as soon as he had eaten.

Houck obliged, but he did not go far. Half a mile east of the Haigler place, he concealed his horse and himself in the brush and waited for one of the Grahams to come riding by, a not unlikely circumstance, since they often used the Payson trail.

How long Houck remained hidden in the brush, high enough above the trail to command a view of it in both directions, before he saw a rider approaching from the west, we can't be sure. In the course of a statement made to a reporter for the Saint Johns *Herald*—he had lost no time getting out of Pleasant Valley after the shooting—Houck said it was the middle of the afternoon when he saw the horseman approaching. "I thought at first that it was John Graham. As he was passing, I saw it was young Billy. I called to him to stop. Instead of pulling up, he drew his six-shooter and fired at me. In self-defense, I fired back."

When his story got back to Pleasant Valley a few days later, it was branded a damnable lie by the Graham partisans. Which it surely was, for after Billy was lifted unconscious from the saddle and carried into the house, his gun had been examined and found to be clean—indisputable evidence that it had not been fired recently.

The killing of his youngest brother changed the course of the conflict, and it changed Tom Graham from a man of peace, opposed to violence, into an enraged lion, thirsting for vengeance. No longer could he view the struggle as a conflict between sheep and cattle interests. Graham blood had been spilled and only the spilling of Tewksbury blood could atone for it.

Andy Cooper welcomed the turn of events. He and Tom Graham buried their differences. Both had lost a brother and Andy his father as well. He had a ready-made plan for wiping out the entire Tewksbury family in one decisive stroke. That Tom Graham was won over to Cooper's projected raid on the Tewksbury ranches and actually took part in it, along with his brother John, cannot be doubted.

But they made no move for a week or more. With tension in the valley growing from day to day, armed men riding the trails, prepared to kill a suspected enemy on sight, some settlers packed up and left, determined not to return until the trouble was over.

During the late evening of September 1, a number of riders gathered at the Graham ranch. Each was heavily armed and fully acquainted with what they were about to do, so there was little need for last-minute consultation. It could not have been much later than midnight when they struck off for the south, their destination the Tewksbury ranches on Cherry Creek, twelve miles away. (The term "ranches" came into use when John Tewksbury moved out of his father's house and built his own a few yards away, where he was living with his wife and baby daughter.) By two o'clock in the morning of September 2, the forces of Tom Graham and Andy Cooper had the houses surrounded. Taking advantage of every bit of cover they could find, they moved down through the brush-covered hillsides until they reached the edge of the ranch yard.

The attackers held their fire and their presence was not discovered until dawn was breaking, when two horsemen were seen approaching the elder Tewksbury's log house. They were permitted to cross the yard. After pulling up, they yanked the saddles off their broncs and turned the animals loose. As they stepped toward the door, they were literally blasted into eternity by a dozen or more rifles.

And now gunfire flashed from every window and the interstices left in the log walls for just such an emergency. The besiegers did not attempt to rush the house, knowing that the men who were trying to pick them off were dead shots and would fight until they could no longer work a rifle bolt.

Andy Cooper crawled along a small ravine and got close enough to the house to recognize the two men sprawled out in death near the door. "We ain't had our work for nothing," he chortled when he got back to Tom Graham. "It's John Tewksbury and Bill Jacobs."

In most of the published accounts dealing with the Pleasant Valley War, an incident is reported to have occurred in the Tewksbury yard just before noon. When the tale first got into circulation, men who were in a position to know denounced it as never having happened. Among them was Jim Roberts, who was in the Tewksbury house at the time. Others, men such as Justice of the

Peace John Meadows, of Payson, who held an inquest over the bodies of John Tewksbury and Bill Jacobs and helped to bury them, insisted that the bodies were in a gnawed, mutilated condition when he examined them.

According to the often-told tale, John Tewksbury's wife ran screaming out of the house with a shovel as a drift of Tewksbury hogs began devouring the bodies. Driving them off, she covered the remains of her husband and Jacobs with mounds of earth. The attacking men held their fire while she worked, but as soon as she returned to the house, the battle was resumed.

A gloomy foreboding of their fate settled on the cabin as the afternoon wore on. Unless reinforcements reached them, and there was no hope that they would, for their partisans were scattered out in the mountains, the attackers would set the building on fire after darkness fell and shoot them down as they ran out. When hope was almost gone, a man astride a mule rode out of the brush and came across the ranch yard. Thinking it was a trick of some sort, Ed Tewksbury lined him up in his rifle sights and was about to squeeze the trigger, when he recognized Judge Meadows.

The Judge wasn't there alone. Word of the fighting had reached him in Payson. He had hurriedly organized a posse and they had put twenty-five miles of riding behind them and reached the scene of the battle in time to stop it.

To Tom Graham, John Meadows represented the law, and he was not yet ready to tangle with it. Reluctantly he ordered his followers to withdraw.

No one was ever indicted for the slaying of John Tewksbury and Bill Jacobs, although Andy Cooper boasted in Holbrook two days later that he had killed them, which may or may not have been true. It doesn't matter, for he was cut down by Sheriff Commodore Owens in the battle of Holbrook on September 4.

XI

Trigger Gospel

Following their father's disappearance and prior to the fight at the Middleton ranch, Andy Cooper and his brothers removed their mother, Eva Blevans, John's wife, and Mrs. Gladden from Canyon Creek Ranch to Holbrook for their safety. The record does not show what became of Mrs. Gladden's children, but no mention is made of their being with their mother in the cottage at Holbrook, which the Blevans boys had either rented or purchased.

In those days the tracks of the Santa Fe Railroad divided Holbrook into what were known as the north side and the south side. The street that paralleled the tracks on the south side was the main business street of the town. The Blevans' cottage faced the tracks on the north side. It stood far enough back from the street line to afford it a small front yard. Old photographs show it to have been a comfortable, rather attractive-looking building, time and place considered. Next door to the east stood the Armbruster blacksmith shop, which played an important role in the events that occurred on September 4, 1887. To the west there was an old stone house and beyond it, across an alley, Brown and Kinder's livery stable. The livery, stone house and blacksmith shop stood flush with the street line, so that a full view of the cottage could be gained only when one was in front of it.

On the morning of September 4, Andy Cooper, his brothers John and Sam Houston Blevans and his brother-in-law Mose Roberts rode into Holbrook. It was Sunday, which was no different from any other day in Holbrook. So far as is known, no special business brought them to town. After visiting with his mother, Andy strolled across the tracks to renew acquaintance with friends in the saloons that lined what is now Central Avenue. There was a warrant out on him, issued the past July, for stealing a number of Navajo ponies. To date no Apache County lawman had shown any interest in serving it, Andy's reputation for having a fast gun being what it was. So it is not likely that the warrant rested heavily on his mind that day, even though Apache County had a new sheriff who was reputed to be tough.

You may read that a little group of Holbrook businessmen, working through the County Democratic Committee, were responsible for the election of C. P. Owens to the exalted position of Sheriff of Apache County, for the express purpose of putting down the rustling that was "endangering the growth and prosperity of Apache County." You should not believe it, for Saint Johns, fifty miles to the southeast, was the county seat, and there, with the help of the weekly Saint Johns *Herald,* the big Aztec Land and Cattle Company and the Defiance Cattle Company dominated county politics. Since it was their cattle that were being rustled, it is reasonable to surmise that they, and not the Holbrook storekeepers, were responsible for the election to office of a gun-fighting sheriff whose credentials had convinced them he was the man to put down the wholesale range thievery.

The author has tried without success to discover what reason the big owners had for believing that the new man could give Apache County at least a semblance of law and order. He had not come to Arizona with a reputation of having subdued other lawless communities, nor did he claim to have done so. In fact the only information he volunteered about his past was that he had spent ten years driving Texas cattle up the Western Trail to Dodge City. If so, he had graduated from a rough, tough school. But he had no fearsome reputation with which to impress range outlaws. At first, they refused to take him seriously and wrote him off as a picturesque tinhorn who would make them no trouble. They were soon to discover, however, that they were grievously mistaken. Old photographs of Perry Owens suggest that it was an excusable error. In his dress and accouterments he was an incredible figure, as unbelievable as the most bizarre "sheriff" ever seen in an early western movie.

In eastern Tennessee, on July 29, 1852, a son was born to what must have been a super-patriotic couple who burdened him for life with the horrific name of Commodore Perry Owens. He was named, of course, for the hero of the Battle of Lake Erie. Sometime after the conclusion of the War Between the States, the boy drifted westward to Texas, where, according to his word, he spent ten or twelve years cowboying and trail-driving to the Kansas cattle markets. After coming to Arizona, he had put in two years as foreman with a cow outfit at Navajo Springs.[1] During the course of those two years he had killed two (or three) Indian rustlers, which may have led to his being installed as sheriff of Apache County. He was thirty-five.

Owens was less than six feet tall, blue-eyed, of fair complexion, with an unwrinkled, rather effeminate face. He wore his blond hair long—not only to his shoulders, but halfway down his back. In his photographs it appears scraggly and unkempt. Cowpunchers seldom wore their chaps, warm, heavy and clumsy, when in town; Perry Owens never appeared without them. That was not his only break with tradition; he wore his six-gun on his left hip, butt forward, which any seasoned Westerner could tell you was the sure sign of a tenderfoot. To use a gun worn on the left side, it was necessary to make what was known as the "across-the-belly draw," which took a fraction of a second longer than simply dropping your hand to a gun worn on the right side and drawing in the same motion.

Even his hat differed from the usual run of cowboy headgear, being a flat-crowned, stiff-brimmed sombrero. It was habitual with him never to get down from his horse without drawing his Winchester from the saddle scabbard and cradling it on his arm wherever he went. With six-gun and rifle on his person, he was a walking arsenal, for his reflexes were instantaneous and his aim deadly.

This may seem to be getting far away from the Pleasant Valley War, but not too far. Perry Owens played a part in it and the men he dueled with that Sunday afternoon in Holbrook were among its principal actors. Very likely that battle changed the outcome of the war.

It was perhaps an hour past midday when druggist Frank Wattrous, one of the men who claimed credit for having elected Sheriff Owens, hailed Andy Cooper as he was passing his shop and informed him that Owens had just ridden into town.

"So I understand," said Andy. "He knows I'm here, too. He's got that warrant that was issued back in the summer. He says he's going to serve it. You better advise him not to try it. I won't give myself up to any sheriff, but if I live through the trouble down in the valley, I'll go to Saint Johns and stand trial at the spring term of court."

From the known facts it does not appear that Wattrous had an opportunity to convey Cooper's message to the sheriff.

Andy recrossed the railroad tracks and as he was passing Brown and Kinder's livery stable, his brother John stepped out to tell him Sheriff Owens was inside.

"He's in the office cleaning his pistol and talking with Brown. He says he's going to arrest you."

"You bring my horse to the house," Andy told him. "I'm leaving for the ranch."

Obviously the "ranch" was the Canyon Creek Ranch—so John Blevans understood him to mean, and he testified to that effect at the inquest on September 6. Beyond question Andy Cooper had decided to run rather than face a showdown with Sheriff Owens. John Blevans put it another way, saying that his brother wanted to avoid trouble, which amounts to the same thing. But Andy had waited too long.

John Blevans got his brother's horse out of the barn without attracting the attention of the two men in the livery barn office. When he reached the little yard in front of the Blevans cottage, Andy came out and began saddling up. At this juncture one of Sam Brown's hostlers stepped into the office with the two bits he had collected from John Blevans for use of the stable.

"The sheriff was still fiddling with his .45," Brown testified later. "I told him his man was getting ready to leave town. He put the pistol together, grabbed his rifle and stepped out into the street."

Fifty yards away Owens saw Cooper hurriedly saddling his mount. As he took a step toward his man, Andy turned back to the house, crossing the porch and closing the door behind him. The cottage had two doors opening on the porch.

"I went up to the door through which he disappeared," Owens testified at the hearing. "As I did, the other door opened a crack and I saw Cooper standing there, a six-gun in his right hand. He asked me what I wanted. I told him I wanted him; that I had a warrant for him. He said I'd have to wait; that he wanted time to think it over. I told him I wanted him now; that I wouldn't wait. The other door opened a crack and I saw John Blevans standing there, his gun leveled at me."

No one will ever explain why, with Perry Owens caught between them, the Blevans brothers hesitated for even a fraction of a second about cutting him down. A few heartbeats later Andy Cooper's .45 and Owens' Winchester roared simultaneously, the two shots coming so close together that men who heard them said they sounded as one. A split second later John Blevans fired from the other door, his slug missing the sheriff and wounding Andy's horse that was still standing out in the yard. Owens swung halfway around and still firing from the hip, his deadly Winchester roared again. John Blevans staggered back from the door, shot through the right shoulder. At the other door, Mrs. Blevans caught Andy as he was collapsing and laid him on an empty trunk. He was mortally wounded, but he fought off death until the following morning.

After shooting John Blevans, the sheriff ran back into the street from where he had a view of both sides of the cottage. He was in time to see Mose Roberts leap through a window on its rear northeast corner, gun in hand. A snap shot from Owens' rifle dropped him fatally wounded. It is remarkable that throughout the fight Perry Owens never used his six-gun; every shot he fired came from his Winchester and without raising it to his shoulder, the accepted position for using a long gun. To this day, rifle experts insist that the havoc Perry Owens wrought that Sunday afternoon in Holbrook was the result of blind luck, not expert shooting.

But the gunfight was not over with the fatal wounding of Mose Roberts. Its final chapter was written when Sam Houston Blevans, only sixteen (some say he was only fourteen), and the youngest of the Blevans clan, seized the dying Andy's gun and in a mad attempt to avenge his brothers, leaped through the main front door. He evidently saw Owens crouching behind a wagon that stood in the yard, but before he could raise the pistol, the sheriff killed him with a bullet that pierced his heart.

Suddenly it was quiet, with the boy lying dead and his blood staining the porch where he fell. The fight was over, but Owens fired several blind shots through the thin walls of the cottage. Afterwards, he was vague about the purpose of that last fusillade. If he was not aware, there were three women inside, any one of whom, or all, might have been killed. He knew that Mrs. Blevans, the mother, was in the cottage, for he had seen her trying to pull young Sam Houston back when he rushed outside. This phase of the battle is not mentioned by those commentators who laud Perry Owens to the sky as a heroic fighting man with ice-cold nerves.[2]

In the space of two or three minutes at most, the Graham faction lost three of its most dependable adherents: Andy Cooper and Mose Roberts were dead, and John, who recovered from his wound, was sent to the Territorial prison at Yuma for five years. Sam Houston Blevans cannot be regarded as a Graham warrior.[3]

Even with only Charlie Blevans left of the Blevans clan to carry on the feud, the Graham partisans still outnumbered the Tewksburys two to one. However, as events proved, the latter had the support of Justice of the Peace John Meadows and Sheriff Bill Mulvenon. Later, when Sheriff Perry Owens invaded Pleasant Valley with a posse of thirty men, ostensibly hunting rustlers, he spent his time ransacking the hills and mountains in a vain attempt to capture Tom Graham and a number of his followers. So, with the law on their side, the Tewksburys had no reason to feel discouraged.

On September 16 a Graham scout reported that a group of Tewksbury men were camped on Cherry Creek below the Tewksbury ranches. Plans were made at once to raid the camp at dawn the following morning. If Tom Graham did not lead the raid, he certainly organized it. The hope was that the Tewksbury men could be caught in their blankets and wiped out. They were taken by surprise, but they seized their guns and managed to wound two of the attackers, one critically, after which they scattered in the brush. The enemy retreated to the Graham ranch, where, two days later, one of the wounded men, Harry Middleton, a Defiance Cattle Company cowboy, died; the other, Joe Underwood, a cowboy working for Tom Graham, who had been shot in both legs, survived his wounds. Before he was able to be up and about, the feud had ended.[4]

Undoubtedly the fact that the seat of Arizona's territorial government had been returned to Prescott after having been located at Tucson for ten years had something to do with the pressure put on Sheriff Mulvenon to end the lawlessness that was running wild in the government's home county. His first invasion of the troubled valley in August had been a dismal failure, but at the urging of Governor Zulock he made a second attempt. The second expedition numbered more than twenty men when it gathered at Payson. That Mulvenon was strongly prejudiced in favor of the Tewksburys was evident almost at once.

Jim Houck, who had ambushed and killed young Billy Graham, was back in the county, still posing as a peace officer from Apache County. It passes belief that Mulvenon was taken in by Houck's pretensions or was unaware that the man was an avowed Tewksbury gunman. And yet the sheriff welcomed him as an addition to his posse. Mulvenon could have found no surer way in which to inflame the Graham faction or let them know what they could expect from him. In addition to Jim Houck, George A. Newton, the rancher and ex-jeweler from Globe who had been drawn into the conflict as a Tewksbury supporter, was present in Payson.

On the evening of September 20, Sheriff Mulvenon conferred with Justice Meadows. It is obvious from what followed that they decided to use Newton as an intermediary with the Tewksburys, for Newton left Payson during the night and was next seen at the Tewksbury ranches. An hour before dawn the following morning Mulvenon and his posse reached Perkins' store and took possession of it. They were in sight of the Graham ranch and the cabin of Al and Ed Rose, both active Graham supporters. Had the sheriff, with his overwhelming force, gone on at once and surrounded the Graham and Rose houses, the fight that occurred a few hours later might have been unnecessary.

Joe McKinney, another visiting deputy sheriff from Apache County, was in the valley with a small posse, hunting the two men who had held up a Santa Fe train at Navajo Springs. They had joined up with Mulvenon's posse at the Houdon ranch, south of Payson, apparently "just for the hell of it," to quote McKinney. He was no man's fool and for the past several months had been bobbing in and around the feud country without becoming involved in the fighting. Soon after reaching Perkins' store, however, Mulvenon gave him a role to play that made him an active participant.

The strategy to which Sheriff Mulvenon was about to resort does him no honor; but if trickery could end the Pleasant Valley War, he was ready to employ it. He ordered McKinney to take five men and make a detour of three or four miles to the south and then return to the store after daylight, passing the Graham and Rose places on their way back. He hoped that the appearance of strangers minding their own business as they passed, would decoy the Graham men into coming out. The remainder of the horses were concealed some distance away and the rest of the posse stationed in concealment behind the wall of the new building Perkins was putting up for his residence. It was an ambush and as cowardly as such confrontations always are.

Half an hour after daybreak McKinney and his men rode past the two houses as planned, and then tethered their broncs at the rack in front of the store. They remained inside only a few minutes, when they came out and rode off in the opposite direction, giving the impression that they had found no one in the Perkins store. The maneuver was successful. They were no sooner out of sight than signal shots were exchanged between the two houses. Half a dozen men emerged from the Graham place and hurried to the corral. The first ones to finish saddling up were Charlie Blevans and John Graham. They rode to the store and circled it suspiciously, apparently not sure that it was deserted. Next they turned toward the stone wall of the unfinished building. The wall had been run up only four or five feet, but death lurked behind it that morning.

Mulvenon reared up as they approached, a double-barreled shotgun loaded with buck in his hands, and commanded them to throw up their hands. Experienced as he was in such matters, he knew it was a command that would not be obeyed. Charlie Blevans and John Graham swung their broncs and reached for their guns in the same motion. Mulvenon's shotgun roared twice in quick succession and the rifles of the possemen belched a deadly requiem. Charlie Blevans and John Graham were knocked out of the saddle by the impact of the slugs that rained into them and lay sprawling in the dust, Blevans dead and Graham dying.

He was left to die by himself as best he could; Mulvenon wanted Tom Graham, and he led his men on the run to the Graham house. Two men, Louis Parker and Pat Bonner, galloped away as the posse closed in. They were permitted to escape without a shot being fired. A woman with a baby in her arms stepped out of the house a moment later. She was the wife of Joe Underwood, who had been wounded in the skirmish with the Tewksburys on September 17. She told Mulvenon that only her husband and Miguel Apocada, a Mexican who worked on the Graham ranch, were left in the house; that Tom Graham and the others had fled.

The sheriff found this to be true. He next turned his attention to the cabin occupied by the Rose brothers. Al Rose was there alone. He refused a summons to come out with his hands raised, but after thinking it over, he did. Some accounts say that Mulvenon handcuffed Al Rose and the Mexican together and left them at Perkins' store to await his return. The author has found no proof of this.

Bill Mulvenon realized that Tom Graham had bested him again. Smarting with defeat, he ordered the posse to proceed to the Tewksbury place at once.

We have it from Joe McKinney that Mulvenon told him as they rode that they would find the Tewksburys waiting for them and that there wouldn't be any trouble, which confirms what had been said previously about his having had an "understanding" with them.

When the sheriff and his posse reached their destination, they found Ed and Jim Tewksbury, George Newton, Jim Roberts,

George Wagner, Joe Boyer, and Jake Lauffer waiting for them. They surrendered without protest.

Mulvenon gathered up his nine prisoners and began the long return ride to Prescott. They were given a preliminary hearing before Justice Meadows, at Payson. He discharged Al Rose and the Mexican, there being no evidence of a criminal nature against them; the Tewksbury brothers and their cohorts were held for the grand jury for the killing of Hampton Blevans and John Paine at the Middleton ranch on August 10. When they reached Prescott, they were released under bond for their appearance before the next grand jury. Two days later they were all back in Pleasant Valley, free to come and go as they pleased. It had been quite a performance, expensive and of little consequence. The Prescott *Courier* and Coconino *Sun* attempted to put a better face on it, going so far as to say, "It seems probable that this last effort to make a peaceful abiding place of Pleasant Valley will be successful." A different opinion was expressed by the hard-hitting Globe *Arizona Silver Belt*. "We do not share the belief that the feud can be settled for all time by the courts," it editorialized. "As long as men remain in both factions, bearing wounds inflicted by their enemies, thirsting for revenge, the lives of those who have in any way been connected with the quarrel will be in imminent jeopardy."

It is true that following Mulvenon's second invasion of the feud district the conflict took on a new phase. No more raids or pitched battles occurred; it was man against man now; killing an enemy or suspected enemy from ambush. The death toll continued to grow. Many of the slain were never identified. Charlie Perkins listed six unidentified men who had made the mistake of venturing into that hate-ridden country and paid for it with their lives.

There were now five graves in the little cemetery on the Graham ranch. Of the Graham brothers, Tom alone was left. John Blevans was on his way to Yuma in shackles; the other Blevans boys had been killed, along with some of their close friends and associates. One wonders what thoughts must have marched across Tom Graham's mind as he counted up the carnage. He had played a prominent role in the war. Miraculously he had escaped receiv-

ing a scratch, although from the first he had been a prime target
for Tewksbury guns.

Since returning from Prescott, Ed and Jim Tewksbury had
been careful to give the appearance of not being connected with
the sniping and ambushing that was rubbing out two or three
men a week. They had a date to face the grand jury on December 1. That they were carrying out their end of the pact they had
made with Mulvenon and Yavapai County District Attorney John
C. Herndon seems fairly evident. They expected to be indicted in
connection with the killing of Hampton Blevans and that the indictments would then be dismissed for lack of evidence to convict.
Their enforced inactivity must have weighed heavily on the
Tewksbury brothers, for late in November, Jim Tewksbury,
Glenn Reynolds and a third Tewksbury partisan, name unknown,
killed Al Rose from ambush at the Houdon ranch on Spring
Creek. While Al's partners were cooking breakfast, he went out to
find the horses they had hobbled the previous evening. He was
within a few yards of the concealed killers when he was cut down
by a blast from a shotgun in the hands of Glenn Reynolds, later
sheriff of Gila County.[5]

Rose's body was strapped over his saddle and taken to the
Graham ranch, where he became the sixth man to be buried there.

XII

A Honeymoon and a Hanging

Tom Graham was thirty-three when he left Pleasant Valley on the first of October and set out on the long ride down the Salt River Valley to Phoenix. The fall work on the ranch was over and he was leaving behind him a force of staunch supporters who would, he was sure, look out for his interests in his absence. He was accompanied by Charley Duchet, a strange character who was known to most men only as the "Frenchman." Even such first-rate grass-roots historians as Will C. Barnes and Earle Forrest have admitted to knowing little or nothing about Duchet—who he was, where he came from or why he had attached himself to Tom Graham. Whenever possible, he never permitted the feud leader to get out of his sight. On the record, he was not a gun fighter. But he was an excellent watchdog. No doubt it was in part due to him that Tom Graham seemed to live a charmed life.

The mission on which the last of the Graham brothers was now engaged was of a very personal nature. He must have had reason to believe he could pursue it to a successful conclusion. In his enamored state of mind, however, it is unlikely that he was aware of his audacity in daring to ask any young woman to share her life with him, especially beautiful young Anne Melton, the daughter of fire-eating, hell-and-brimstone Elder W. J. Melton,

the Baptist preacher and farmer of nearby Tempe. Elder Melton
was in Phoenix conducting one of his "revivals," and she had accompanied him.

Like her father, Anne had a mind of her own. She was very
young, between seventeen and eighteen. Photographs of her at
that time show her to have been an extremely attractive girl, of
good figure, with dark, intelligent eyes.

It must be left to the scientists who have investigated the mys-
teries of the chemistry of love and sex to explain why the handsome young cattleman and feud leader from Pleasant Valley suddenly became the most important thing in her life, and why after
a whirlwind courtship she took him for her husband. They were
married on October 8, at her home in Tempe, her father conducting the ceremony.

The influence she was to exert on Tom Graham became apparent when, several days after their marriage, at her behest, he
went to the office of the sheriff of Maricopa County and requested
him to inform Sheriff Mulvenon that he would come to Prescott
and surrender himself if any charge had been lodged against him,
if Mulvenon would assure him that he would be protected. The
latter responded by coming to Phoenix and placing him under
arrest for complicity in the killing of the Navajo sheepherder at
the beginning of the Pleasant Valley War.[1] Graham gave bail in
the amount of three thousand dollars and was to appear before the
December grand jury in Prescott. This meant that he would be
there at the same time the Tewksburys and their followers would
be in town to face the charges leveled against them. That the two
factions could be brought together without violence erupting
seemed unlikely, but Mulvenon assured Graham that he would
have enough deputies on hand to keep the peace.

With Anne riding at his side, Tom Graham took his bride
back to Pleasant Valley to spend their honeymoon. No more unlikely place to spend a honeymoon could have been found than
that ravaged, blood-stained land. Its natural beauty remained unchanged, but there were scars, however, that could not be ignored,
such as the graves out in the ranch yard. Anne had been raised on
the frontier and was well acquainted with the harsh lonely life it
imposed on its womenfolk. Few women remained in the valley;

they envied the lucky ones who had got out with their families intact. She tried to conceal the fear that constantly stalked her. She never ran out into the yard to wave good-by to her husband as he rode off without wondering if she would ever see him alive again.

Tom Graham was not deceived by the brave face she put on for him. It made him realize how much he was asking of her, and it imposed a greater restraint on him than the law had been able to do. For reasons of their own the Tewksburys were also holding back. But both factions were watching each other carefully and preparing to move to Prescott in force for the December meeting of the grand jury. They got started about the same time, and that they reached Prescott without clashing was largely due to Tom Graham's promise to his wife that the Graham party would fight only if attacked.

The two factions rode into Prescott within an hour of each other and camped at the O.K. Corral and Store, which should not be confused with the more famous O.K. Corral at Tombstone, where the Earp-Clayton battle occurred. The Tewksburys were the first to reach town. When the Graham warriors arrived, they camped beside them, each side ignoring the other. Obviously it needed only some insignificant act, a drunken man's threat, to touch off a conflagration.

The feeling in town was tense. Prescott realized that it was sitting on top of a bomb that might explode at any moment. Special deputy sheriffs were everywhere to keep the peace. They were not needed, for the clan leaders wisely realized that if violence occurred, it would prejudice the court against them.

The legal action that took place the next day followed the predicted course: the charge against Tom Graham was dismissed without argument; indictments were returned against Ed and Jim Tewksbury, Jim Roberts, George Newton, Jake Lauffer, Joe Boyer and George Wagner for the killing of Hampton Blevans at the Middleton ranch on August 10, 1887. Although John Paine, the Hash Knife cowboy, was killed at the same time, his name does not appear on the indictment, which cannot be explained. The seven men were released under bond to appear for trial. Their cases were not called until the following June, when they were dismissed for lack of evidence to convict. Again the law had accomplished nothing and the feudists were free to continue slaughtering one another.

With the coming of winter there was the usual slackening of range activity, and when snow came to block the trails, the vendetta lost its sting. Spring came and with it the prediction that the uneasy peace of the past months would vanish in a blast of gunfire. Several times during the summer the old feud sputtered into flame, but not finding fresh fuel to feed on, the sparks burned out and failed to ignite another rash of violence, as in the past. However, an incident occurred on August 4, 1888, that was to have grave repercussions. As Jake Lauffer, a long-time Tewksbury partisan, stepped out of his cabin a shot from the brush crashed into his right arm. The haste with which he darted back into the house undoubtedly saved his life. That same day two other men named Cody and Coleman were fired at as they rode up to Lauffer's ranch, one of the bullets wounding Cody's horse. Who fired the shots was never learned, but to a certainty they came from Graham guns. That faction had held a long grudge against Lauffer for his part in the slaying of Hampton Blevans at the Middleton ranch.

If this narrative has one black-hearted villain without a redeeming trait, it must be the ubiquitous Jim Houck who had assassinated young Billy Graham. On the evidence, he was a liar, braggart, coward and thief as well as a wanton killer. That he was responsible for the triple lynching that occurred at the Bear Spring Ranch in the Mogollon Mountains, forty miles north of Pleasant Valley, on August 11, is the unanimous conclusion of the writers and investigators who have sat in judgment on him. He has no defenders.

Although the evidence to prove it is lacking, there seems to be little reason to doubt that the rustling that was still being carried on in Pleasant Valley was connected with the Bear Spring tragedy, which resulted in the lynching of young James Stott, owner of the ranch, and James Scott and Billy Wilson. In the many stories dealing with the event, the names of the Tewksbury brothers are often mentioned as doing business with Stott, an allegation that becomes believable when one considers the maneuvering and presence of Jim Houck, their long-time ally.

James Stott was only twenty-two, but he had spent two years cowboying in Texas before coming to Arizona and could not be considered a green tenderfoot. He was from North Billerica, Massachusetts, where for forty years his father was superintendent of the Talbot Woolen Mills and had accumulated a modest fortune. Life in that quiet backwater did not appeal to his son. After graduating from Wilmot Academy, the same hunger for adventure and excitement that sent so many young men West in those days took hold of him and eventually landed him in Holbrook, Arizona, in 1886. There, Sam Brown (the same Sam Brown whose livery barn figured in the Battle of Holbrook in 1887) took him under his wing and advised him to buy the partially improved homestead that became Bear Spring Ranch.[2]

With money he received from his father, young Stott put up new buildings, fenced pasture and began to stock his range. Two years after he established his Bear Spring Ranch, he had between two and three hundred horses on his range. Some of them wore blotched brands, indisputable evidence that they were rustled animals. Of course he knew it; he couldn't possibly have been naive enough not to have known. Beyond doubt he was dealing with rustlers, and he alone knew their identity—a dangerous bit of knowledge to have.

Young Stott may not have regarded buying rustled stock as a heinous transgression—others were doing it—but in Western eyes it was a serious offense. It gave the snooping Jim Houck the weapon he needed to make good his boast that he "would be running sheep on Bear Spring range before Stott made final proof on his claim and got U.S. title to it."

Houck must have felt very sure of himself. It was already August and Stott was to take title in September.

When in Holbrook, Stott always dropped in at Brown and Kinder's livery barn to exchange a few words with Sam Brown. On one such occasion he found a young man from the East talking with Brown. The stranger was broke and obviously in the last stages of what used to be known as "consumption." Brown suggested that Stott take the stranger out to the ranch and let him do the chores to pay for his board. Fred Clymer, the invalid, was delighted at the prospect, and when Stott returned to Bear Spring, he accompanied him.

A frequent visitor at Bear Spring was Jim Scott, a Hash Knife cowboy who was riding bog (pulling steers out of the muck) on Silver Creek between the Little Colorado River and Snowflake. He was a Texan and had arrived in Arizona about the same time as Stott. Both he and Stott were young, which must have helped them to enjoy each other's company. In that mountain wilderness visitors were scarce. You appreciated the few that happened by.

Stott was in the habit of making the long trip to Holbrook once a month. He was in town early in August when he encountered a young man, a miner who had come down from the big camp at Durango, Colorado, and was on his way by saddle and packhorse to try his luck at Globe. His name was Billy Wilson. On inquiring the best way to get through the mountains, Stott suggested that the stranger accompany him back to Bear Spring and spend the night there. He would put him on the Canyon Creek trail to Pleasant Valley next morning. Wilson accepted this proffered hospitality and he and Stott left Holbrook together the following day. Sam Brown spoke with them briefly as they were about to pull out. He was to recall the incident, and it is one of the important pegs on which hangs the true story of what occurred at Bear Spring Ranch. No one was in a better position than he to account for the presence there on the night of August 10 of James Stott, Billy Wilson, Jim Scott and the "lunger" Fred Clymer.

There are many accounts of what transpired there shortly after breakfast on the morning of August 11. In a clumsy attempt to escape the suspicion that he had arranged the multiple killings to get possession of the Bear Spring Ranch, Jim Houck told at least three conflicting stories. At first he charged that Stott, Scott and Wilson were the three men who had attempted to kill Jake Lauffer and his friends and that the Bear Creek slayings were committed in retaliation. That was not only too far-fetched for belief but it involved the Tewksburys. Houck got off of that story in a hurry and came up with an even more preposterous tale. He now claimed that he had arrived at Bear Spring Ranch with five deputies, armed with warrants for the arrest of Stott, Scott and Wilson, charging them with having rustled livestock in their possession. The alleged warrants were nonexistent, as several Arizona newspapers stated after a thorough investigation.

Houck's account of what followed, as published in the Flagstaff *Champion* of August 18, was that a few minutes after he served the warrants a party of forty masked outlaws rode up to the cabin, took possession of the prisoners and marched them some distance into the trees, where they lynched them.

Why Houck failed to realize that one of the four men who had been trapped at Stott's ranch that morning was still alive and able to tell the true story of what happened is beyond explanation. It is no greater mystery than why the attackers failed to kill Fred Clymer, the consumptive. The theory that it was because he was unacquainted with them does not make sense; Billy Wilson was equally a stranger.

According to Clymer, eight men—not forty and not masked— rode up to the house before breakfast, were fed and then told Stott, Scott and Wilson that they were "going to take a little walk." Wilson, suspecting what was about to happen, refused to go, but he was forced to comply. The lynchers led their men down the trail and disappeared with them in the trees. Clymer saw no more of them. Fearful of what had happened, he did not attempt to investigate until the morning was half gone. Making his way in among the trees, he had gone only several hundred yards when he saw the lifeless bodies of Stott, Scott and Wilson dangling from the limb of a pine, their faces distorted with the agony of death.

Historian Earle Forrest, who is not given to exaggeration, says of Clymer: "In terror he fled. Not even stopping to catch a horse, he ran and walked all the way to Holbrook, where he told his terrible story to Sam Brown." In his weakened physical condition that would have been impossible. We know that Clymer brought the first news of the lynching to Holbrook and told it to liveryman Brown; but it was August, the hottest time of the year, and under a glaring sun he could not possibly have run and walked those sixty miles. Certainly he encountered someone on the road who picked him up and drove him to town. On learning the nature of the news Clymer was carrying and not wanting to become involved, the stranger seemingly had not disclosed his identity.

On reaching Holbrook, Clymer went to Brown's barn at once

and told his story. Because of his connection with young Stott, Brown was both shocked and enraged, and somehow felt responsible for the young man's death. From what Clymer could tell him, it seemed obvious that the only reason for hanging Scott and Wilson as well was that they were strung up to silence them. It didn't explain why Clymer had not been shot or hanged with the others. Certainly he had not been spared out of pity.

Brown and the little group who had gathered in his office found it much easier to agree on the purpose behind the removal of young Stott. Somebody wanted the Bear Spring range and had taken this way of getting it. Stott's legal rights to it having expired with his death, it was now up for grabs by whoever dared to take possession.[3]

Most accounts agree that Jim Houck's name was mentioned several times during the course of that conversation in Sam Brown's office, for he had no standing with men of good repute in Holbrook. He was running a sizable band of sheep at what he called Houck's Tank, a dozen miles or more west of Bear Spring, the operation being limited by the scanty supply of water available.

With a companion, Brown left town for Bear Spring the following morning to see "for himself what had taken place," as he put it. Save for the chickens feeding in the yard, he found the ranch deserted. The horses that Stott had been running in his pasture were gone. "A short distance from the cabin we found the dangling bodies of the men who had been lynched," he reported. "We cut them down and buried them. They had been hanging there for four days." This is proof that it had taken Clymer two days to reach town with his news.

A stake was driven into the ground at the head of each grave to mark its location. Much later a dispute occurred between Sam Brown and Will Barnes, who at that time was operating the Esperanza Cattle Company with its headquarters at the Long Tom Ranch, not far from Bear Spring. Both men claimed to have buried the victims of the lynch mob. To the day of his death Sam Brown insisted that Barnes had had nothing to do with burying the three men. He also refused to accept Barnes' story that the body of Jim Stott had been returned to his home in Massachusetts and Scott's remains shipped to Texas. Both Brown and Barnes were old men by that time, and either's memory could have been faulty. But the former had an excellent reputation for his veracity, and the author accepts his word as final.

On returning to Holbrook, Brown communicated by telegraph with Stott's parents, informing them of the death of their son. They wired back that they were leaving for Arizona at once. Railroad transportation being what it was in 1888, almost two weeks passed before they arrived in Holbrook.

In the meantime Houck had showed up in Holbrook and spread his conflicting stories. Feeling against him was running high. Frank Wattrous, the druggist, Sam Brown and several others got him into the livery barn and demanded that he give them an exact account of his whereabouts on the day of the lynching. This Houck refused to do. He became so angry that he started to draw his gun, but they had him covered before he could get his pistol out of the holster. "I told him," Brown recalled in his old age, " 'You organized that lynching party. You're acquainted with every rustler and outlaw between here and Pleasant Valley. You organized a bunch of them to hang those boys and for their trouble to get Stott's horses.' He said he'd make me prove what I was saying in court. I told him he wouldn't dare to meet me in a courtroom. Of course he never did, but he was right about one thing; he said nothing would be done about the lynching; and nothing was."

When Stott's parents arrived at Holbrook, they were driven out to Bear Spring by Sam Brown. Mrs. Stott and her daughter had visited the ranch the previous summer, but Brown had not met them at that time. On reaching their destination on this sad occasion, they found Jim Houck in possession, with his sheep grazing in the old Stott pasture. He was in a surly mood and let them know at once that they were not welcome. Before leaving Holbrook several days later, Mrs. Stott related that when she told Houck that somebody would be made to pay for this crime (the lynching), "he boasted of his part in it." [4]

Sam Brown led the grieving parents to the grave of their son, and as they stood there with bowed heads, they decided to leave him where he was and not have his body sent back to Massachusetts as they had planned. So, despite tales to the contrary, Jim Stott still sleeps beneath the pines in Mogollons, and so does Jim Scott. His remains were not shipped back to Texas, as some would have it.

Jim Houck did not prosper at Bear Spring. He could not have remained there long. There is no record of his having filed on the old Stott claim. In fact it was not until fifteen years after the tragedy that a man named Bailey proved up on it and took title.

No one can say with authority what finally became of Jim Houck, although there is a story that he was killed in a saloon brawl in Bisbee. After eighty-odd years the Bear Spring lynching has become only a vague memory. A day spent in Holbrook recently failed to turn up anyone who was interested in recalling it.

XIII

To the Last Man

When news of the triple lynching at Bear Spring Ranch sifted down through the mountains to Pleasant Valley, it touched off a wave of speculation among Graham followers as to who from their neighborhood might have had a hand in it. Jim Tewksbury had been ill for several weeks; Jake Lauffer was still incapacitated with his shattered arm. That excused them. They thought of John Rhodes, another of Jim Houck's intimates.[1] Rhodes had not been accounted for in several weeks. He was a far-ranging rider who was widely acquainted with the rustlers who roamed the distant reaches of the mountains to the east. He could have organized the lynching party. He was capable of it. But although suspicion centered on him, no proof was ever uncovered.

The following weeks passed quietly. No one would believe it, but the Pleasant Valley War was over—or nearly over. News spread that Jim Tewksbury was dying. A big, strong man, still in his early thirties, he had suffered a severe attack of measles and the disease had settled in his lungs and quickly developed into what used to be called "galloping consumption." Late in November, he was taken over the mountains to Globe where, as reported in the Phoenix *Herald* of December 6, 1888, "Jim Tewksbury died of consumption at 5:30 P.M., December 4, at his sister's home in Globe."

Of the clan leaders only Ed Tewksbury and Tom Graham were left. In response to his wife's continuing plea to pull up stakes and leave Pleasant Valley, the latter promised that he would go "when I can leave without giving Ed Tewksbury any right for saying he had run me out."

At best that was an indefinite promise. But when in the summer of 1889, Anne informed him that they could expect an addition to the family, he did not hesitate any longer about leaving. He turned his cattle over to a man named Young,[2] who was to run them on shares. Packing a wagon with their personal belongings, with he and Charley Duchet acting as outriders and Anne doing the driving, they set out on the Payson Trail for Prescott. Near Tempe, he found a farm that was to his liking. He bought it and settled down to raising wheat, barley and oats.

Being farm-bred, it was not a new experience for him. He prospered and made friends. But when George Newton, the Globe jeweler, ranchman and long-time Tewksbury partisan, disappeared mysteriously on September 18, 1891, suspicion focused immediately on Tom Graham and the Pleasant Valley men who had fought on his side during the vendetta. Sheriff John Montgomery of Maricopa County called him into Phoenix for questioning. Graham must have convinced him that he was not connected with the disappearance of the missing man nor knew anything about it, for the search for the man took off in other directions.

When old Mark Blevans had vanished, a few years back, it was presumed, especially by his sons, that he had been cut down by Tewksbury guns and buried in some out-of-the-way place. Newton appeared to have dropped out of sight even more mysteriously. He had left Globe on the morning of September 18 with the announced intention of crossing the mountains to his Pleasant Valley ranch. He was as familiar with the trail ahead of him as anyone, having used it repeatedly.

Several men spoke to him as he was riding out of Globe, leading a pack horse that was heavily laden with supplies. Early in the afternoon, as he was nearing the Pinal Creek ford, which he would have to cross, he met a man named Crampton, who warned him that he better turn back; that Pinal Creek, a branch of Salt River, was running high due, he figured, to a cloudburst up in the Sierra Anchas. Newton told him that he knew where the eddies and quicksands were and that he would have no trouble crossing.

Crampton was the last person to see him alive, and from the subject of their brief conversation it must be assumed that Newton ventured to use the ford. Days passed before he was listed as missing. His wife offered a substantial reward for the recovery of his body. A search party set out from Globe and examined Pinal Creek all the way downstream to its confluence with Salt River, which was not difficult, now that the flood had passed. They found Newton's pack horse buried in the quicksands but no trace of Newton or his saddle horse. Finding the dead pack animal convinced many people that Newton had lost his life at the ford. Others maintained that while he had had trouble there, he had managed to go on and that he had been killed by a sniper between Globe and the river.

Newton was carrying a $10,000 insurance policy on his life. The insurance company demanded proof of his death before honoring the policy. Mrs. Newton instituted a lawsuit to compel them to pay. Seven years passed before she was able to collect, and by that time most of the principal had been spent on legal fees.

Some writers have not hesitated to add Newton's death to the list of men killed in the vendetta. They may be right. No one can say for sure.

In June, 1892, Tom Graham's partner S. W. Young informed him that a rough count of the herd they owned jointly showed that it had increased to over seven hundred head. It meant that their limited range was becoming overstocked. Despite his wife's entreaties not to go, Graham decided to return to the ranch, gather his share of the cattle and drive them to Prescott, where they would be readily salable.

He went unarmed, for he had given Anne his word that he would never pack a gun again, not even to save his own life. Duchet went with him. The cattle were rounded up, divided, and with the assistance of two of Young's cowboys, driven to Prescott without incident. In light of what was to follow, it remains a mystery why Ed Tewksbury—if he was determined to rub out the last of the Grahams—did not kill him before he left the valley with his cattle. He must have had many opportunities and with little likelihood of being called to account.

To Tom Graham, happy with his wife and two-and-a-half-year-old daughter, the old feud days must have seemed far behind him. But Anne was obsessed with the feeling that their home was being watched. One night she was sure she saw two men at one of the windows. She blew out the lamp at once and in the morning found fresh tracks where she insisted she had seen the pair. Graham could not deny that someone had been at the window. But he was not alarmed, his feeling being that a couple of Mexican farm hands employed in the neighborhood had been doing the snooping for a lark. Across the yard the young Mexican who had been working for him for a few weeks had just finished hitching a four-horse team to a wagonload of grain that was to be driven to town that morning. When Graham began to question him about the snooping, the man became so enraged at being suspected of having a hand in it that he threw up his job on the spot and demanded his wages. Graham paid him and told him to clear out.

The incidents of that morning—August 2, 1892—became so clearly stamped on Anne Graham's mind that she was never able to forget them. At breakfast her husband decided that he would drive the load of grain to Tempe. It was only a few minutes after eight o'clock when he drove out of the farmyard and disappeared down the road to town. Half an hour later, as he was approaching the Double Butte schoolhouse, two men fired at him from a mesquite thicket beside the road.

The team bolted and ran a quarter of a mile to the ranch house of William T. Cummings, where Tom Graham died that afternoon, but not before identifying his two assassins—Ed Tewksbury and John Rhodes.

The shooting had been witnessed by three children who were cutting across the fields and came up in back of the two men. The oldest of the children was Ed Cummings, a boy of twelve; his sister, Molly; and a younger girl named Gregg. The children spread the alarm and neighbors gathered quickly. Led by expert trackers, a posse took up the trail of the two fugitives. After a chase of ten miles, Rhodes was captured; Tewksbury, mounted on a faster horse, escaped.

Rhodes refused to talk, even when confronted with the ugly evidence that some of the horse tracks found at the scene of the shooting matched the hoofprints of the animal he was riding. The three children were questioned separately and the descriptions they gave of the two bushwhackers tallied in every detail.

Tempe never witnessed such an outpouring of public wrath as followed the killing of Tom Graham. Rhodes had been lodged in the Tempe jail and an abortive attempt was made that night to bring him out and lynch him. But the law prevailed for once.

A warrant was issued against Ed Tewksbury charging him with murder. Sheriff John Montgomery, of Maricopa County, was roundly criticized for not bringing his man in at once. As a matter of fact, he didn't know where to look for him. He asked Sheriff Findlay, of Pima County, for his assistance. Findlay was well acquainted with Tewksbury. He located the wanted man in Tonto Basin and placed him under arrest. Evidently fearful that a successful attempt might be made to lynch Tewksbury, Sheriff Montgomery dispatched a deputy to Tucson and wired Sheriff Findlay to take his prisoner there. That was done and in the early hours of morning he reached Tucson by train and was behind bars in the Maricopa County jail before the town was aware that he had arrived.

Contrary to many accounts, Ed Tewksbury and John Rhodes never faced trial together, not even a preliminary hearing. Evidence against both men appeared to be conclusive, yet neither, in the end, was to mount the gallows platform. The law got to Rhodes first, but after a bitter preliminary hearing lasting ten days, it set him free.

It seems incredible that the law could have been so blind to the facts. Certainly that was the feeling of the men and women who crowded Justice Huson's courtroom on that long-ago morning in Phoenix when he delivered his unbelievable decision.

Anne Graham was present throughout the long hearing. She had testified that before he died her husband had told her that Ed Tewksbury and John Rhodes had shot him. Seats had been reserved for her father and her in the front row of spectators, close to the reporter's table. Rhodes was seated with his back to her. The climax of the hearing came when District Attorney Cox put the three children on the stand to tell their story. Justice Huson appeared not to be impressed by their testimony. As he reached for a pen and began writing, Anne Graham suddenly pulled her husband's pistol out of her dress and held the muzzle against Rhodes' back. She pressed the trigger as people held their breath. But the gun misfired, the hammer falling with a loud, mocking click. "Let me shoot him," she screamed as her father wrenched the gun out of her hand. "Let me kill him, let me kill him; they will turn him loose," she continued to scream as she was ushered out of the courtroom.

Justice Huson had evidently decided on his ruling in advance, for as the Phoenix *Gazette* reported in its next issue: "Upon the conclusion of the District Attorney's argument there was hardly a pause before Justice Huson rendered his decision. He said in a rather indistinct voice, 'I have listened carefully to all the testimony in this case and, although I was at first inclined to believe the defendant guilty of the murder, the defense has so conclusively proved their alibi that I must release the prisoner.' "

The stunned, angry crowd poured out into the street denouncing Huson. It turned ugly and the cry was raised to hang Justice Huson in effigy. His honesty was questioned. "We cannot conceive upon what grounds the defendant was discharged," said the Tucson *Star* in its next edition. "Why go to the useless expense of an examination which is but a travesty upon law and justice?"

The wave of indignation that swept across southern Arizona did not disappear overnight. On August 27, a week after the charges against John Rhodes were dismissed, a huge mass meeting at Tempe resolved: "That the action of one, W. O. Huson, justice of the peace at the City of Phoenix, in relegating to himself the powers of judge and jury in the recent preliminary examination of John Rhodes, accused of the murder of Tom Graham, is hereby condemned . . . that it is the opinion of the meeting that the evidence presented at said examination was in the minds of all honest men sufficient to bind the accused over to await the action of the grand jury."

There were two questions that the aroused citizenry demanded to have answered (but which never were). First: what was the alibi that Judge Huson ruled had been established by Rhodes' attorneys? Second: Rhodes was penniless but had been defended by Joseph Campbell, the most expensive attorney in the Territory. Who had supplied the money to retain him?

After three quarters of a century those questions remain unanswered. Is it possible that the money spent in the defense of Rhodes—and would be spent lavishly in the defense of Ed Tewksbury—was an echo of the old sheep-cattle confrontation in Pleasant Valley? The murdered Tom Graham was a cattleman; Rhodes and Tewksbury were sheepmen. Daggs Brothers were now out of the sheep business and owned the bank of Tempe. But in those days men kept their grudges alive a long time. There can be little doubt that the name of Graham was still anathema to them.

Friends of Rhodes had spirited him out of Phoenix the day after his acquittal, and although he lived out his life in Arizona, he disappears from this narrative.

On August 18, 1892, Edwin Tewksbury began his long fight to save his life. A preliminary hearing held him for trial for killing Tom Graham on practically the same evidence that had acquitted Rhodes. On September 7, the grand jury found a true bill against him; and on December 5, he was arraigned and bound over to stand trial in the district court of Maricopa County, on May 10, 1893. Representing him was the aforementioned Joseph Campbell and A. C. Baker. Their legal maneuvering resulted in one stay after another being granted. When such means were exhausted, Campbell and Baker appealed for a change of venue, alleging that the defendant could not secure a fair trial in Maricopa County, citing the mass meeting at Tempe, local editorial comment, and the prejudiced attitude of Phoenix citizens. Undoubtedly this was true. The district attorney opposed the change of venue, but it was granted and the case transferred to Pima County (Tucson) on July 10. It was not until December 14 that Ed Tewksbury came to trial for the first time.

Never before had such an array of legal talent been gathered in an Arizona courtroom. Joe Campbell as chief defense counsel led the questioning. The evidence adduced followed closely the testimony given at Tewksbury's arraignment and John Rhodes' preliminary hearing. The defense sought to establish an alibi. It put a cowboy named Stencel on the stand who swore that Tewksbury was with him in Tonto Basin, far from Tempe, on the morning of the murder. Some of the jurors must have believed him; the majority did not.

The trial lasted only a week. On December 21, Ed Tewksbury's fate was placed in the hands of the jurors. It took them two days to reach a verdict. They filed back into the courtroom and took their seats in the jury box. The foreman handed the clerk a slip of paper.

"We, the jury," it read, "duly impaneled in the above entitled cause, upon our oaths, do find the defendant guilty of murder and recommend him to the mercy of the court."

But this was far from the end of it; the battle to save Ed Tewksbury's life had just begun.

By legal technicalities that are beyond the lay mind to understand, Campbell and his associates succeeded in winning a new trial for the defendant. It took time and money. The plea for a new trial was granted in March, 1894, but it was not until early January, 1895, that Edwin Tewksbury faced a jury for the second time. The prosecution called dozens of witnesses and the defense even a greater number. No new evidence was submitted, but this time Joe Campbell and his associates had selected a jury that would give them what they wanted.

After eight days of parading witnesses to the stand and argument and counter-argument, the fate of Ed Tewksbury was placed in the hands of the jury. Following four days of deliberations, it reported to Judge Sloan that it was hopelessly deadlocked and could not reach a verdict. This was what Campbell had expected. Judge Sloan discharged the jury and Campbell immediately petitioned the court to free the defendant on bail. Campbell's original bid for bail was denied, but on February 6 it was granted. Altogether Ed Tewksbury had been confined in prison for two and a half years. His long confinement had shattered his health. His father had died. He went to Pleasant Valley, but there was nothing there to hold him. Whatever assets the Tewksburys might have had were dispersed by now. The few cattle that remained were running wild, unbranded. He did not attempt to reclaim them. When he left Pleasant Valley, it was for the last time. He had relatives living in Globe. He joined them and spent the rest of his life there. After the prosecution dropped its charges against him in 1896, he was appointed a constable and Deputy Sheriff of Gila County. Nominating well-known gun fighters for its peace officers was standard Western town procedure.

Tewksbury died of natural causes in Globe on April 4, 1904. His passing produced a number of newspaper stories to the effect that he was the "last man" of the Pleasant Valley feud, which was not true. John Blevans had come out of prison and was living quietly in northern Arizona. As has been mentioned, his death did not occur until 1928, when he was killed in an automobile accident. The "last man" to set out on the trail from which none return was old Jim Roberts. He was seventy-five. Following the conclusion of the Pleasant Valley vendetta, he had served for forty-four years as a peace officer in several riotous copper-mining camps, including a long stint as town marshal of Jerome, the wildest of the copper towns. In his old age he moved to nearby Clarkdale and at his death was still in harness as a special officer for the United Verde Copper Company. The final summons came on the night of January 8, 1934. He was found lying on the ground in back of the Clarkdale Drug Store. The doctors said his heart had failed him.

Today, if you inquire in Arizona about the part Jim Roberts played in the Pleasant Valley War and how many men he killed, you will get only hazy and mostly inaccurate answers. But almost anyone will tell you how he foiled the robbery of the Clarkdale branch of the Bank of Arizona in 1928. The two bank robbers were fleeing in a speeding car when a bullet from his ancient single-action Colt killed one and he captured the other after the car crashed.

When the U.S. Post Office Department got around to establishing a post office in Pleasant Valley, it named it Young, for S. W. Young, Tom Graham's partner in the Graham ranch. And a lean-to built as an addition to the Graham cabin became its official location.[3]

Young is easily reached today by surfaced road from Holbrook to the north or from Prescott to the west. It is a peaceful, picturesque village with three hundred inhabitants. The visitor can find food and lodging in—of all places—the old rock-walled Perkins store of vintage memory.

THE FENCE WAR

XIV

The Sea of Grass

When the buffalo were gone and the Indians had been placed on reservations, the Texas Panhandle became a vast, unknown and empty land of seemingly interminable distances stretching away to the horizon in every direction, the silence broken only by the whining of the wind and the barking of the coyote and the wolf. That vacuum was not to last for long. In a shorter space of time than occurred anywhere else in the history of range lands, little more than a decade, the Texas Panhandle was to be cut up, seized, fought over and parceled out to the strong. In its transition from uninhabited wasteland to teeming cattle empire, no man was to play a more important part than Charles Goodnight.

We last saw him mourning the death of his partner, Oliver Loving, at Fort Sumner, New Mexico, in 1867. It may be considered the end of the first half of his long life; the second half begins in 1870, when he married his boyhood sweetheart, Mary Ann Dyer, and brought her out to Pueblo. He was becoming wealthy, with his three Colorado ranches and an irrigation project on the Arkansas River. He was also interested in a slaughtering and packing operation at Trinidad. Spreading out even further, he became one of the organizers of the Stock Growers' Bank of Pueblo.

He was vulnerable beyond escape when the panic of 1873

swept the country. He lost the mansion in Pueblo that he had built for his bride, the ranches, the meat-packing plant. The Stock Growers' Bank was the first to go. When he realized the extent of the disaster, he shipped Mary Ann off to California to live with relatives.

"There I was in '75 with a wife and a mixed herd of sixteen hundred Longhorns and not much else," one of his leading biographers reports him as saying.

He had other assets, not immediately cashable, not the least of which was his proven tenacity in overcoming adversity. As fall neared, he instructed Leigh Dyer, his brother-in-law, to gather the sixteen hundred head of cattle and begin drifting them southward to the Texas Panhandle. He joined Dyer and the herd before it crossed the Cimarron. If the Goodnight crew was an overly large one for the work in hand, it was because he refused to turn men off who had proven their worth and loyalty. With the range cattle business in the doldrums, they could not expect to catch on elsewhere.

Fifteen years and more had passed since Goodnight began his acquaintance with the Llano Estacado. Now, as he trailed southward with his small herd, he found it unchanged, "broad, level, gray, barren . . . sublime in its vastness, in its stillness." [1] He had long fancied that he knew something about the Llano, but as the drive pushed on southward day after day, he realized how limited that knowledge was and that it was confined to the eastern and southern edges of the great tableland.

In his trail-driving days in New Mexico he had crossed the upper Canadian River many times and knew it crossed the Panhandle in an east-west direction. That was one of the few facts he possessed. He didn't know where he would cut it, but the Canadian was his destination.

In the crew there was a Mexican vaquero who went by the name of Little Frank but was oftener called Panchito. He hailed from Las Vegas and claimed that as a boy he had herded sheep across the New Mexico line into the Panhandle. Goodnight suspected that the truth was that Panchito had been in the *comanchero* trade. However that might be, he had some knowledge of the country. To take advantage of it, Goodnight had him ride at his side and allowed him to have his say about pointing the herd.

Late in October they reached the Canadian about where several years later the town of Tascosa was to be established. A glance at a map will show that they could hardly have missed striking the river. They turned up it, looking for a place to establish a winter camp. They found what they were seeking at Rano Creek. Goodnight divided his herd, and leaving half of his crew and cattle there, found a second spot to his liking in the brushy breaks of an unnamed creek ten miles further west. Timber not being available for building of any kind, the men burrowed into the creek banks and made dugouts in which they could hole up for the approaching winter.

Several varieties of gramma and short, curly buffalo grass carpeted the plains in every direction. To Charlie Goodnight's practiced eye it was the finest cattle range he had ever seen. Following range tradition, he could have laid claim to a big slice of it, but he had no thought of remaining on the Canadian. He wanted to establish a home ranch where he could settle permanently, with good grass, water and plenty of timber for the buildings a home ranch should have. Panchito told him he had seen such a place—a great canyon in the Cap Rock—and could take him to it. Of course he was speaking of the canyon in which Mackenzie had defeated the Comanches and put them afoot. It had been named Palo Duro by the early *comancheros*.

Though Panchito was given to gasconade, Goodnight had found him a fairly truthful man. Being able to speak good "cow-pen Spanish," he drew the man out. "Other talks followed," he recalled. "I didn't want to go off on a wild-goose chase, but I know I'd already decided that I wanted to see the Palo Duro."

An interruption occurred. Word came down to Rano Creek from the west camp, where Dave McCormick was holding forth, that a great band of sheep, as many as a hundred thousand head, according to McCormick, was moving down the Canadian. A dozen or more *pastores,* under the direction of a *mayordomo* (overseer), were herding the animals. At this time of the year it was common practice for the sheepmen of Las Vegas to combine their bands and send them into the Panhandle to graze until spring, when they would be driven back into New Mexico for shearing.

Goodnight sent word to McCormick by Panchito, ordering

him to see the *mayordomo* and inform him there would be no trouble if he turned his sheep around and moved back up the river, but they would not be permitted to graze on Goodnight range. That message was delivered and agreed to, but two mornings later the sheep crossed the deadline. His fighting Irish blood up, McCormick and his men scattered the goats that were leading the band and drove three or four hundred sheep into the river, where they drowned or died in the quicksands.

Eventually Goodnight had to pay for the carnage, but the deadline was not crossed again. For days his crew was kept busy pulling the polluting carcasses of the drowned sheep out of the water. Shortly thereafter, accompanied by Panchito, Goodnight left the Canadian and headed south into the Panhandle to find the Palo Duro. Several weeks of seemingly aimless wandering followed.

Goodnight was not acquainted with Captain Marcy's report of his discovery of the source of Red River, published in 1853. Had he been, he would have realized that the place he was trying to find had to be in the vicinity of the sources of the Red, and that the course he was taking was leading him far to the south of it. By chance, when he decided to turn back, he struck off to the north-west.

The Mexican had seen so many canyons that he was hopelessly confused. Goodnight now led the way, and then one day as they moved along the rim of the Cap Rock, Panchito pointed below and shouted:

"*Al fin! Eso es cierto!*" (At last! It is certain!)

Charlie Goodnight was often to recall the feeling that coursed through him as he stood there seeing the Palo Duro for the first time. With its grass, live water and protecting timbered walls it was all that Panchito had promised, and more. As it spread out a thousand feet below him, he could not discover any way of entering it, but if the Comanches had been in the habit of wintering in the Palo Duro, there had to be a way—perhaps several.

He did not attempt to explore it. That would have to wait. The first order of business now was to return to his camps on the Canadian and then set out on the long trip back to Colorado to borrow money so he could buy supplies to get his outfit through the coming winter.

He was back on the Canadian by the first of the year and wintered there. With the coming of spring the cows began to drop their calves. He could not move until the youngsters were strong enough to travel. In the meantime he sent Leigh Dyer and the Mexican to the south to scout out the approaches to the Palo Duro and locate the Indian trail into the canyon.

They were gone a long time. When they returned, their news was good; Goodnight abandoned his camps on the Canadian and grazed the herd southward. It was fall before they reached the network of creeks and canyons at the headwaters of the Red. Where the Tule flows into Palo Duro Creek, they made camp. It was not until October 23, 1876, however, that Goodnight followed the old Comanche trail into Palo Duro Canyon. Where the canyon widened out for ten miles or more, he staked out a spot for his home ranch.

You will recall that Mackenzie found buffalo in the Palo Duro. They were still there. In his *Recollections* Goodnight gives several estimates of their number, saying in one place "ten to twelve thousand," and later "several thousand." Undoubtedly many of the animals had been born in the Palo Duro and never left it. With gunfire the shaggies were stampeded up the canyon and off the grass that was to be reserved for the cattle, a maneuver that could be repeated whenever the need arose. Getting the cattle and the wagon into the canyon was a more difficult matter.

Although the old Indian trail had doubtlessly been used for several centuries, the traffic that passed over it had left no trace of its passing on the flinty surface. When it became apparent that the mules could not get the wagon down, it was taken apart and lowered in pieces with ropes. In the week that followed, all hands toiled from daylight to sundown improving the road. With few tools and muscle having to take the place of blasting powder, there wasn't a great deal they could do. When they were done, Goodnight drove the wagon down and up the trail to try it out. He came back to camp shaking his head. "It's rough—damn rough," he told Dyer. "But it's passable. We can bring the stuff in."

Excluding wandering sheepmen from New Mexico and out-

laws, he didn't have a neighbor within a hundred miles. Far to the
east Fort Elliott had been established, its principal business being
to keep the Indians on their Indian Territory reservations. He
was far beyond its influence. His ranch in the Palo Duro, which he
always referred to affectionately as "the Home Ranch," was the
first and only cattle ranch in all the Texas Panhandle. He was not
to have it to himself for long.

Goodnight was in Colorado during the winter of 1876, where
he received an ultimatum from Molly. In the months they had
been apart, he had not been able to get a letter off to her more
than two or three times. She named a day when he was to meet
her in Denver, and either agree to "come out to civilization, or
take me to the Palo Duro with you."

"I didn't know which way to jump," he recalled years later.
"The Palo Duro was no place for a woman. I figured the loneliness would kill her. But I couldn't give up the ranch. I was deep
in debt. I'd just borrowed thirty thousand dollars at eighteen per
cent. I met her at the train and she was delighted when I told her
that she'd be going with me when I returned to the canyon."

Beef prices were high again and men of means were seeking
good investments in the range cattle business. That happy circumstance brought John Adair, of Rathdair, Ireland, and Goodnight
together and led to the partnership they formed which was to
mark the turning point in the latter's life.

Adair belonged to the landed gentry of Ireland and was the
owner of several large estates. Although a rich man, he had never
been honored with a title, perhaps because he was a moneylender.
He was both a gentleman and a snob, a not uncommon combination, and, with justification, regarded himself as an all-around
sportsman, shooting and riding to hounds.

On coming to New York in 1866, he established a brokerage
business. Following the practice that had made him wealthy, he
borrowed great sums of money in England and the Continent and
let it out at several times what it was costing him. Being prosperous and personally attractive, society opened its doors to him, and
in 1869 he married a remarkably beautiful young widow, Cornelia
Wadsworth Ritchie. The Wadsworths were among the first families of New York. Her father, General James S. Wadsworth, had

become famous as a military leader in the Civil War before he was fatally wounded during the Battle of the Wilderness. His father, a native of Connecticut, had founded the family fortune through his land speculations in New York State prior to the building of the Erie Canal.

Cornelia's first husband, Montgomery Ritchie, also came from an illustrious family, being the grandson of the statesman Harrison Otis, of Boston. He died in 1864 of a disease contracted in the war. After five years of widowhood, she married Adair. She was thirty-two.[2]

In her diary Cornelia Adair relates how her father's close friend, General Phil Sheridan, commanding the Department of the Missouri, arranged the elaborate, military-escorted buffalo hunt that introduced her husband and herself to the American West. She doesn't mention that newspapers opposed to the Administration labeled the expedition a wanton waste of taxpayers' money. "It was this hunting trip," she says, "which caused us to become interested in the West, and we resolved to return the following year and purchase a large tract of land."

They were back in Denver ten months later, where, having closed out his business in New York, Adair opened a brokerage office. Being determined to embark in the range cattle industry with its allegedly fabulous profits, he spent a year running up and down the country looking for a favorable opportunity. Friends advised him to contact Colonel Charles Goodnight.

The "Colonel" was a purely honorary title and applied to him in Colorado long before it became a standard practice in Texas.

John Adair was not the first foreigner to get into the booming beef cattle business; Scottish and English investors were pouring thousands of dollars into what soon was to go down in history as the "Beef Bonanza." The individual owner, marketing his own cattle, was selling out or being absorbed by the big foreign- or eastern-financed companies. Gullible investors residing far from Western range lands, often with an ocean intervening, had to have someone to conduct their business if the expected dividends were to be forthcoming.

It produced a character new to the range cattle business—the ranch manager. If he was honest and competent, he was priceless.

Not all were. That was the precarious margin on which absentee ownership operated, and why it often ended in disaster.

Adair undoubtedly realized that as a foreigner and a tenderfoot he was regarded as easy pickings. It made him doubly cautious about where and with whom he placed his money. It can be taken for granted that he had made some inquiries about Goodnight before they sat down together to talk business in March, 1877.

Goodnight had come to this meeting primed to extol the possibilities of expanding the Palo Duro ranch into a large-scale operation. For the first time he was addressing himself to a polished man of the world. It imposed no handicap on him, for he regarded Adair as an equal. The latter sensed as much and thought to take him down a peg.

"Are you a religious man?" he asked.

"No. A teetotaler but not religious."

"Then you've never read the Bible?"

"Oh, yes. I've read it a couple of times and I intend to read it again. It's a damned good book."

Adair smiled, but he got the rebuff.

Several other conversations followed, and Adair agreed to make the three-hundred-mile trip to the Palo Duro, accompanied by Mrs. Adair. He left it to Goodnight to make the arrangements. On the first of May they left Denver and made their way to Trinidad, where they outfitted for the journey to the canyon. Including the Adairs, who rode the entire way in the saddle, there were eight in the party: Charlie and Molly Goodnight (she drove one of the four wagons) and four cowboys. Intent on upgrading his cattle, Goodnight had bought a hundred head of fine Durham bulls. Two of the cowboys trailed them along in the dust behind the wagons and the light army ambulance in which the Adairs were to sleep.

They were twelve days reaching the Home Ranch. Once they were forced to go without water for two days. It was a trying experience. Adair complained; Cornelia took it in stride and won Goodnight's everlasting respect.

They encountered no one. With the exception of Mrs. Bill Olds, who had accompanied her husband to Adobe Walls in 1874, Molly Goodnight and Mrs. Adair were the first reputable white women to set foot in the Texas Panhandle. The stillness of that vast, silent land, where the wind never stopped blowing, must have weighed heavily on Molly, knowing it was to be her future home.

On May 15, Goodnight led the way down the four-mile trail to the floor of the canyon and the Home Ranch. While Mrs. Adair enjoyed herself going up the canyon under escort to shoot buffalo, Adair and Goodnight explored the country and ironed out an agreement to go into partnership. It was not until June 18 that it was effected. It was heavily loaded in Adair's favor and was to run for five years. Under its terms Adair was to finance the enterprise, with Goodnight furnishing the foundation stock and directing the ranch at a salary of twenty-five hundred dollars a year, which with operating expenses was to be paid out of the annual earnings. Additional cattle and twenty-five thousand acres of land were to be bought. Adair's investment, with ten per cent interest, was to be repaid in full. At the end of five years, all assets were to be divided, one third going to Goodnight and two thirds to Adair. The former suggested that his partner's initials—JA connected—should be the brand name.

Soon after the departure of the Adairs, the skulduggery began with the appearance in the Palo Duro of Jot Gunter, the widely known land speculator and one of the most successful in Texas.

Operating out of Sherman, Texas, the firm of Gunter, Munson and Summerfield was a formidable organization, with its lawyers, surveyors and land locators. No great amount of capital was required to get started in the business. However, you had to be smart, and no one ever questioned but what Jot Gunter was smart. The situation in which he operated was legitimate and can be quickly explained.

When Texas entered the Union, it retained ownership of its public lands, including so-called "school lands" amounting to millions of acres. Needing money desperately, the State government offered such lands for sale. There had been many buyers, but up to 1875 the Panhandle State-owned lands had not been touched. To increase business, Texas began selling land certificates. At the time of purchase the buyer did not have to designate any particular acreage, which enabled him to hold off until he saw interest developing in some special area. He would then have a blanket survey made, pay for the land with his certificates, and turn a handsome profit.

The speculators did an active business in buying and trading certificates among themselves and often were able to corner the market. When Goodnight set out to buy range, he found that Jot Gunter's firm had surveyed him in.

"Gunter tried to hold me up for one dollar and twenty-five cents an acre for what they had bought for ten cents," Goodnight recalled with a chuckle in after years. "I had to do business with him, but I was as smart as Jot. I bought twelve thousand acres as a starter, but with the privilege of spotting in what I was to take. I bought a piece here and a piece there and made a crazy quilt out of his blanket survey. I had to pay him six-bits an acre, but I got what I wanted along with an option to buy another twelve thousand acres the next year.

"I took all the good land and water I could find and when I got through I knew the canyon was so broken up that no big outfit would try to move in on me. Adair authorized me to buy more land than our contract called for. I bought land anywhere and everywhere I could get it—twenty cents per acre, some twenty-five, some thirty and thirty-five. The largest amount I ever bought at one time was one hundred and seventy thousand acres in the Tule country at twenty-cents an acre, which necessitated the formation of the Tule Ranch."

The expansion of the JA was to continue through the years, and in the middle eighties reached a maximum of 1,325,000 acres, on which ranged more than one hundred thousand cattle.

Goodnight's operations had become so extensive that when he left the Home Ranch in the spring of 1879 and headed for Dodge City, Kansas, some one hundred and fifty miles to the north, the urgent purpose of his errand was to recruit a large crew of competent men to work the JA ranges. Booming Dodge, the so-called Queen of the Cow Towns, with its daily cowboy population of a thousand men or more (coming and going) was the most likely place to find them.

For roughly two-thirds of the way Goodnight had to blaze his own trail. He had no directions to guide him. At Cimarron Crossing he picked up the old, long unused buffalo hunters' trail to Adobe Walls. In the years to come, the route he was pioneering was to be carved deep in the prairie sod by untold thousands of Texas Longhorns and to take its place in history as Goodnight's Palo Duro-Dodge City Trail.

When Texas trail drivers deserted the famous Chisholm Trail en masse for the new Western Trail that crossed Red River at Doan's Store and went curling up through the Panhandle to Dodge, they rewrote the whole book of trail driving. Although not in Texas geographically, Dodge City was a "Texas" town. Among the arriving and departing owners, trail bosses and cowhands, there were very few to whom Goodnight was not known, either personally or by reputation.

Despite his frank pronouncement that any man working for him who was caught drinking or gambling on the job would be fired on the spot, which was flying in the face of cowboy tradition, he got the men he wanted. Over the years his dictum against gambling and drinking cost him the services of several men whom he regretted losing, among them Sam Dyer, one of Molly's brothers. He was adamant, however.

"It paid off," he recollected. "I often had as many as fifty men on the payroll and never a shooting incident." [4]

The Dewees brothers, the Driskills, the Snyders and other owners who were sending one or more big herds up the Western Trail to Dodge were in the habit of arriving at Doan's Store a day or two ahead of their cattle to confer with their trail boss and inspect their herds. Needing cattle to stock his empty ranges, Goodnight reasoned that there was no better place than Doan's Store to find a bargain. He was not interested in buying steers and spayed cows; he wanted breeding stock.

He was prepared to buy as many as fifty thousand head. After a week of dickering, he settled for forty-two thousand five hundred, range delivery to be made on Sweetwater Creek below Mobeetie. After completing arrangements for receiving them, he returned to the Home Ranch. Taking five of his cowboys with him, he rode west into New Mexico to intercept the herds coming up the old Goodnight Trail.

"I bought about two thousand twos and trailed them to the

Palo Duro and turned them out on grass. Counting everything we had about fifty thousand head on the JA by then, which wasn't a patch to what the range could accommodate. But winter was coming on and I had done the best I could. Adair wrote me to go slow. That was the thanks I got. I don't know why I didn't tell him to go to hell and quit. But I knew I had a fortune made, so I kept my mouth shut."

About the time the first snow fell, Kansas and Texas newspapers published scare stories about a "great Indian uprising," stating that "thousands" of Kiowas and Comanches had jumped their reservations and had invaded the Panhandle. The figures given were a gross exaggeration; including women and children not more than five hundred were crossing the Panhandle. They were out to "make meat," not war. The majority were Quahadas led by Quanah Parker. Goodnight arranged a meeting with him and offered to give him two beeves a day if he would agree to lead his band back to the reservation when they were rested. Quanah agreed, and the Indians were voluntarily returning to the Territory when a company of cavalry arrived from Fort Elliott to hurry them along. It was the last and final appearance of the red men in the Panhandle.

Other changes were taking place. Mobeetie was growing. In Donley County, the prohibition settlement of Clarendon had become firmly established and a cluster of buildings marked the site of upcoming Tascosa. Eighty miles north of the Home Ranch, T. S. Bugbee was ranging upwards of thirty thousand Longhorns. Further down the Canadian, Bates and Beals, Henry Cresswell, Mose Hays and others were ranching. Goodnight could name a dozen. By the fall of 1878 men who had grown accustomed to the loneliness of the great plains were saying a little regretfully: "The Panhandle is sure filling up."

In a land where organized law had yet to make its appearance and anything as valuable and readily salable as cattle were roaming almost at will over thousands of square miles of unfenced range, it was as certain as taxes that the rustler and the outlaw would soon be moving in to take their toll.

Even when local law enforcement was weak or nonexistent, large-scale range depredations could be carried on successfully only when and where a great number of cattle or horses and mules were easily reached. It was no less important to have a safe and quick means of disposing of the stolen stock. And the operation had to be carefully organized. Nowhere were conditions more favorable to the rustler than along the Western Trail during the trail driving season, roughly from May to October.

John Sellman, who had been run out of Fort Griffin for various offenses, and his gang, said to number as many as forty, operated south of Mobeetie. Dutch Henry's gang, even more numerous, claimed rustling rights north of the town. Dutch Henry's honest name was Henry Born. He was shrewd, daring and well educated. His particular pleasure was to steal mules and horses belonging to the U.S. Army.

The course the Western Trail followed in the hundred miles from Sweetwater Creek to Mobeetie to the North Canadian, in what used to be called No Man's Land, was ideal for the business in which he was engaged. His men were acquainted with the various places at which trail herds camped for the night. To swoop down on a resting herd, cut out fifty to a hundred steers and make off with them was comparatively easy. After they had been hustled out of Texas and across the line into Indian Territory, they were rested for a day and the old brands vented. In leisurely fashion the stolen steers were then driven north until they cut the old and now unused Cut-Off Trail, which left the Chisholm Trail at Pond Creek and ran westward for ninety-six miles to Longhorn Crossing. After following the old trail eastward for a day, the cow thieves turned north into the hills and reached the end of their journey at the camp of men who were engaged in the business of buying rustled stock. After several months the cattle would be marketed at Caldwell, Kansas, and no questions asked.

When the trail driving season ended, Dutch Henry went to Wichita to spend the winter. The gang scattered. Some members, unable to resist the temptation of doing a little depredating on their own, focused their attention on the cattle in the Panhandle.

On the second or third of November, Tom Bugbee sent an urgent request to a score of stockmen to assemble at his Quarter Circle J ranch on Bugbee Creek, a small tributary of the Canadian, to decide on ways and means of putting down the rustling that was sweeping the Panhandle. The response was unanimous, for all who had been invited were being hurt. Bugbee had located a rustler camp ten miles down the river from him where four men were holding upwards of half a hundred head of stolen cattle.

The sentiment of the meeting was to capture the four thieves and string them up without ceremony as a warning to their kind. Cooler heads prevailed, however; the four men were taken prisoners without a shot being fired. Judge Nelson of the Shoe Bar Ranch delivered an ultimatum to the prisoners: "Get out of the Panhandle and stay out, or be killed on sight."

It was a sinister threat but only a threat, and it accomplished nothing. The four rustlers had been caught red-handed and expected no less than to be hanged on the spot.

"And they should have been," Goodnight conceded later. "You can't put down range outlawry by temporizing with it. To fight it, we needed an organization. But getting men to sink their differences and organize to help themselves was a tough job. It's not stretching the truth to say that the Panhandle Stock Association was born out of desperation."

XV

Barbed Wire Empire

When Goodnight drove his mixed herd of sixteen hundred head southward from the Arkansas into Texas, they were the only cattle in the Panhandle. Five years later it was the most heavily cattle-populated range in the West, a distinction it was to maintain for many years. Perhaps more remarkable was the upgrading of Panhandle livestock. The number of Longhorn bulls was decreasing rapidly and the new sires were blooded Durhams, Shorthorns and Herefords. The Hereford, with a strain of Durham blood, had proven best adapted for that region, and by 1885 the Panhandle could be described as "white face" country.

So great was the change that the upgraded cattle were referred to as American, to differentiate them from the old Texas or Longhorn strain.

The so-called "fever war" broke out during trail driving days from Texas to the Kansas cattle markets, and embargoes against the entry of Texas cattle, unless they had been wintered in the north, were written into law in Kansas and Colorado. Little was known about splenetic fever, variously called Spanish, Texas or tick fever, other than that cattle from south Texas were immune to the disease and that where they passed or grazed, native, or American, cattle sickened and died.

The case against the Longhorn left no room for doubt; he was the enemy. It was believed (quite erroneously) that his slobber or droppings contaminated the grass over which he passed and that domestic cattle following in his wake either contracted the fatal disease by inhaling or by eating the excrement he left behind.[1]

In Colorado, members of the Colorado Cattle Association intercepted herds coming up the old Goodnight-Loving Trail from New Mexico and at gunpoint forced them to divert to the east by way of Granada on their drive north. But in Colorado and Kansas it was a confrontation between Texans and Northerners. It was different in the Panhandle, where Texans faced Texans. When mossy-horned, tick-carrying cattle from south Texas began streaming across the Llano on their way north from San Angelo and Colorado City, they were regarded by the stockmen along the Canadian as just as dangerous to their upgraded stock as they were by the owners of the so-called "American" cattle of Colorado and Kansas. Just how determined they were to prevent the south Texas herds from crossing their ranges may be gathered from the following warning Colonel Goodnight addressed to his old frontier friend, George T. Reynolds:

Que Ti Qua Ranch, Aug. 20, 1881

Dear Sir:

I send Mr. Smith to turn your cattle so they will not pass through our range. He will show you around and guide you until your reach the head of this stream and then you will have a road. The way he will show you is nearer and there are shorter drives to water than any route you can take. Should you come by here you will have a drive of 35 miles to make.

I hope you will take this advice. Yourselves and I have always been good friends, but even friendship will not protect you in the drive through here, and should you attempt to pass through, be kind enough to tell your men what they will have to face as I do not wish to hurt men that do not understand what they will be sure to meet.

I hope you will not treat this as idle talk, for I mean every word of this, and if you have any feeling for me as a friend or acquaintance, you will not put me to any desperate actions. I will not perhaps see you myself, but take this advice from one that is and always has been your friend.

My cattle are now dying of the fever contracted from cattle driven from Fort Worth, therefore do not have any hope you can convince me that your cattle will not give mine the fever, this we will not speak of. I simply say to you that you will never pass through here in good health.[2]

While Goodnight's language was mild, there was no escaping the sober resolve behind it. If tick-bearing cattle were to be driven across the Panhandle on their way to the Kansas markets, they would be compelled to follow a designated trail or they would not be permitted to pass. Up and down the Canadian, stockmen fell into line and out of their united stand the efficient (and extra-legal) Winchester Quarantine was established. For three years it protected the Panhandle cattle against the fever-bearing herds.

The procedure was simple enough. Armed horsemen rode the imaginary quarantine line between ranches for the width of the Panhandle, a rider from the west meeting a rider from the east, and after conferring briefly, turned his bronc and returned in the direction from which he had come. There were threats of violence that were on the verge of spilling over into bloodshed. There was some shooting. But the offending herds from the south did not cross the deadline.

It was plain to all that the campaign had been waged success-fully because it had been a cooperative effort. Men who previously had shown no interest in forming a permanent stock association were suddenly won over to the idea. Early in March, 1881, half a hundred owners met at Mobeetie and after three days of threshing about, formally organized the Panhandle Stock Association. A constitution and by-laws were approved, not the least important feature of which was a standing reward of two hundred and fifty dollars for the arrest and conviction of anyone rustling Association cattle.

An executive committee of five was elected and given the authority to hire inspectors, range detectives, legal counsel and to spend such sums of money for the protection and promotion of the rights of Association members as it found necessary. It was such a sweeping grant of power as might have been promulgated by an entrenched political machine in a settled community; in the Panhandle, where law and order was making its first faltering appearance, it was incredible. That the executive committee could not enforce its dictums without ripping the Association to pieces was freely predicted. But the skeptics were mistaken; the Panhandle Stock Association was to survive and prosper.

However, it was powerless to do anything about the weather. When a blue norther came howling down across the High Plains, bringing zero temperatures and freezing, stinging snow, nothing could keep cattle from drifting with the storm. The drifts came from as far away as the Arkansas and the Platte, hundreds of miles to the north. Wherever they found a sheltered canyon they piled up, and the Canadian and Red River ranges were eaten clean. No native stock disputed their right to such grass as they could find, for the Panhandle herds had long since broken through the line of riders who were trying to hold them and were heading south for the Brazos and the Colorado.

With the coming of spring there was chaos on the High Plains. Cow outfits from distant ranges appeared in the Panhandle to round up what they could of their drifted cattle and drive them back to their home pastures. Meanwhile, cowboys from Panhandle ranches were combing the headwaters of the Brazos and Colorado for the same purpose.

Barbed wire had not yet made its appearance in the Panhandle, but after the bad storms and heavy losses of the winter of 1882-1883, the big outfits and many of the smaller ones accepted the fact that fencing, expensive though it might be, was the only solution to the recurring problem. The first step taken by cooperating ranchmen was the erection of a three-strand drift fence north of the Canadian which "spanned the Panhandle from east to west for approximately two hundred miles." [3]

In Texas, Wyoming, or anywhere else, wherever a drift fence was built, it was for the dual purpose inherent in its name. First, to prevent your neighbor's cattle from encroaching on your range, and secondly to keep your cattle from straying. The great Panhandle drift fence, the longest ever built, saved the grass of the Canadian in the severe winter of 1884, but cattle from the north, antelope and deer, drifting in the blizzards that beset the country, unable to proceed further when they struck it, starved and froze to death by the thousands. Their rotting carcasses lined the entire length of the fence.

It was reported, perhaps with some exaggeration, that settlers at Clarendon had found herds of antelope trapped in a pocket of the fence and "killed fifteen hundred and lived on antelope steak all winter."

When riders from the north came looking for their drifts, they had no difficulty finding them. But the tales they carried home of the disaster that had overtaken their cattle were quickly followed by a rash of fence-building in Kansas and Nebraska. This sudden concern of cattlemen for the safety of their animals was purely selfish, of course. Likewise was the feeling, now expressed for the first time, that if you were engaged in the range cattle business, it behooved you to give some thought to caring for your animals.

Goodnight was a fencing enthusiast. He built wire enclosures in the Palo Duro that enabled him to separate his pure-bred sires and graded cattle from his native stock. From the culls and range stock, he gathered his beef herds for the fall drive to the Kansas market. It was only the beginning of his dependence on barbed wire. When 170,000 acres of range in the Quitaque country, adjacent to the south, were added to the JA holdings, he erected a sixty-mile drift fence running along the divide between the Salt Fork of the Red and Mulberry Creek from the western Armstrong County line to connect with the Shoe Bar fence. Together, they formed a drift barrier a hundred miles long.

The range cattle business was booming and every outfit of any size was buying or leasing great chunks of land from various sources. Texas railroads, some of which had yet to lay a foot of track, had received huge land grants from the Legislature and they were devoting more of their energies to disposing of what they had got for free than to building highways for the Iron Horse. Texas speculators such as Jot Gunter had been their principal customers, but the picture changed drastically when Eastern syndicates entered the market.

Texas owned millions of acres of what were designated as "school lands," the sale or leasing of which were to provide funds for the advancement and perpetuation of the educational system of the State. When the syndicates began buying huge tracts of so-called "school lands" at ridiculously low prices, newspapers in different parts of the State blasted them as "unscrupulous Yankee land-grabbers making off with the children's land," and damning the politicians who were conniving with them.

The best and biggest of the out-of-state speculators was the New York and Texas Land Company. It was solidly financed and ably directed by a Vermont Yankee named Ira H. Evans. His first major transaction was the deeding to his company of 3,049,430 acres of Texas land by the financially distressed International and Great Northern Railroad. This acreage was only part of the tremendous grant given the railroad under the provisions of an act passed by the Texas Legislature as far back as 1854, entitled: "An Act to Encourage the Construction of Railroads in Texas by Donations of Land."

There were millions of acres of ten cent land in Texas when Ira Evans made his deal with the International and Great Northern. But it was located in west Texas; what he got was choice land and town sites between San Antonio and Waco, for which he paid $1.35 an acre. His next venture was the purchase of 800,000 acres in the Panhandle. The New York and Texas Land Company continued to increase its holdings. The size of its operations can be judged by its sale of the White Deer Lands, 631,000 acres in Gray, Carson, Hutchinson, and Roberts counties, to the Francklyn Land and Cattle Company, of St. Louis.

When land company surveyors began running property lines, these gigantic sales and purchases of what on State Land Office profiles appeared to be vacant range land often were found to be under fence. A cattleman building a fence did not stop when he reached intervening sections that he neither owned nor had under lease, but kept on stringing more wire until he reached range that, with some justification, he could call his own. What he was doing was illegal. That didn't bother him, for he knew his neighbors were doing the same. So the rash of fencing continued, and within three years after it began, the days of the old, open range were gone. Goodnight alone had put up six hundred miles of barbed wire.[4]

He was among the first to realize that a showdown with the

land companies was inevitable. The quasi-judicial proceedings of the Panhandle Stock Association to establish law and order in the Panhandle (always in its own favor) were now in conflict with the law and order agencies of the State of Texas. The Thirty-fifth Judicial District, embracing the entire Panhandle, had been established, and there was a court sitting at Mobeetie, with a sheriff to carry out its orders. Of even greater assistance was the company of Texas Rangers from the famous Frontier Battalion that had been assigned to the Panhandle.

Under the provisions of the Land Act of 1883, land to be used exclusively for grazing purposes could be leased from the State for as little as four cents an acre. Cattlemen leased many square miles of state-owned land, but they enclosed great sections on which they paid nothing, and they fenced it, which prevented settlers and the small outfits from reaching land they had either bought or leased.

The inequities of the law could not be denied. The New York and Texas Land Company took up the cause of the settlers and small ranchers. The campaign it launched caused such adverse criticism throughout the State that a special session of the Legislature was called to write a new law.

Had the Legislature been called into session at once, the violence that broke out in May and continued until November might have been averted. But that is to be doubted, for the nesters (the farmers, newcomers and men with a few cows) had suffered too many provocations to be held back. Almost with the first clash, the Fence Cutting War was in full cry.

From the very beginning it was a shooting war, and although the number of men killed was small—some authorities say as few as seven—more powder was burned than in the several years of the Lincoln County War. Property damage was great. Miles of barbed wire were cut, twisted and rendered useless. One of the items Panhandle merchants had difficulty keeping in stock that summer was a handy little tool known as "a patented wire cutter."

A trickle of dark-bearded men came down the trail from Dodge. After spending a day in Mobeetie, Clarendon or Tascosa, they disappeared without advertising their destination. They were alleged to be hired gunmen, brought in by the big outfits. Maybe they were, for with popular opinion solidly against them, the so-called "range hogs" and "cattle barons" were having a difficult time holding their own. Night after night they sent their crews out to protect their fences, but there were too few cowboys and too much fence to stop the depredations. In a month there wasn't a bunkhouse across the width of the Panhandle that didn't have an injured man or two lying helpless in his bunk.

With the coming of cold weather, the feud petered out. The big outfits, including the JA, Spade, Matador and XIT, had suffered heavily. They knew a new Land Act would be voted at the special session of the Legislature and they turned their attention to Austin and the politicians. On February 7, 1884, a bill known as the Enclosure Act was voted into law. It wasn't what cattlemen wanted, but they decided they could live with it, for buried in the verbiage was a clause to the effect that if one side of the enclosure was a natural barrier, it need not be fenced. It meant that a three-sided enclosure was legally not an enclosure.

The new Act proved to be no improvement on the old. Cattlemen continued to ignore it or to take advantage of its loopholes. The small fry, unable to make any headway by themselves, turned to the land companies for help. They got it. Ira Evans, president of the New York and Texas syndicate and the South Western Immigration Company, joined forces and got the Enclosure Act amended to compel the big cattle outfits to build gates that would allow men owning land within the enclosures free access to their property. It was an important victory. Whether it was his honest conviction that what he called the "little fellers" should be admitted to membership in the Panhandle Stock Association or just an act of appeasement, Goodnight jammed a resolution through the Executive Committee giving any man, even though he owned only half a dozen cows, the right to membership. It was an empty gesture, for it was well known that only the big owners had a voice in shaping Association policy.

Powerful as Goodnight was, he was taken aback when he realized that Ira Evans, by his buying and selling great tracts of land, had maneuvered himself into position to embark on what had always been his real purpose, namely, to colonize the Panhandle. New York and Texas Land Company advertisements began to appear in Midwestern newspapers offering section and half-section land for sale, no money down and years to pay. Arable lands were offered, with water no more than thirty feet below the surface, which could be made available to the farmer by a windmill.

The Association countered with a propaganda campaign picturing west Texas and the Panhandle as suitable only for stock raising. The country was described as unfit for farming of any kind and warned prospective settlers not to be duped by the "false misrepresentations of unscrupulous land agents, immigration schemers and glib railroad promoters."

A letter appeared in the Kansas City *Star* over the name of Charles Goodnight stating that there were no arable lands in the Panhandle; that the water in the few streams was impregnated with salts of gypsum, and unpalatable.

The Panhandle Stockmen's Association, in convention assembled, passed a resolution to the effect that it was a well-known fact that the Staked Plains (west Texas and the Panhandle) was semi-desert country, suitable only for stock raising; that it would not produce a crop; that it was the humane duty of the Association to warn all prospective settlers that failure and disappointment awaited those who attempted to till the unfavorable soil.[5]

Cattlemen were annoyed and angered by the campaign being waged against them. They struck back by planting articles disputing the claims of the land companies in farm journals and such newspapers as they could reach. But they were waging a losing battle. They were the entrenched interests and the settlers were the underdogs. Public opinion favored the latter, and such influential newspapers as the Wichita *Eagle,* the Fort Worth *Gazette,* the little but belligerent Tascosa *Pioneer,* the Kansas City *Star* and others supported them.

Said the *Pioneer* "The man who declares that he can draw a line in the West which marks the terminus of arable lands, misrepresents its conditions, and is an enemy of its interests." The Fort Worth *Gazette* blazed forth with, "The prevailing notion in regard to this great table-land [west Texas] must be abandoned. It has been held a desert, and was long so marked on the maps; but it deserves no such designation, being naturally for the most part very fertile soil, covered with rich grasses. The sandy belts which cross it are the only exception to the rule. . . . The time will come, we doubt not, when the Staked Plains will be famous for its crops of wheat and other small grain." [6]

The passing years have proven this to have been an overly optimistic stretching of the facts. Modern agronomists have found that only thirty-one per cent of the Panhandle can be classed as suited for agriculture.

A reporter for the St. Louis *Globe-Democrat* caught Colonel Goodnight in Clarendon and asked:

"Can a farmer make a living as far west as this?"

"Yes," was the honest answer. "But he can't make money. He may, by hard work, do a little better some seasons than a living, but he can't get rich. The only way a farmer can do well here is to combine stock raising with farming." [7]

The panic of 1873 had swept away his modest fortune and left him impoverished. But he was back on top again and could regard himself as a wealthy man. When the first five-year contract with Adair expired, there was left after all interest and indebtedness had been deducted a clear profit of slightly more than half a million dollars to be divided between them, a third to Goodnight and two-thirds to Adair. The partnership had been continued under a second five-year agreement and was still in effect when Adair visted the JA Ranch in 1885. At the new headquarters on the Tule a comfortable house of native stone had been built for his and Mrs. Adair's exclusive use. On this occasion, however, she had remained in London and he was accompanied only by his valet. He was amazed by the improvements that had been made.

"But he shuddered when he looked at the books and saw what the fencing had cost," Goodnight wrote his friend Garettson in 1918, thirty-five years later. "I don't believe he realized that without the exclusive use it gave us of our grass and the water in the earthen tanks I had dug that we could have weathered the extended droughts without being crippled." [8]

It was Adair's last visit to the JA. On his way back East, he was taken ill and died in St. Louis on May 14, 1885, leaving his entire estate to his wife. She informed Goodnight that she wanted the partnership continued without any dislocation; thanked him for all he had done and promised that, her health permitting, she would visit the ranch at least once a year.

It was a happy arrangement. It left him free to lead the uphill fight against the State Land Board's crippling interpretation of the Range Lease Act.

XVI

Fenced Off

In the fall of 1885 the Land Board sent out so-called "grass commissioners" to investigate violations of the Leasing Act. They were headed by General Henry E. McCulloch, not a name to be tossed around carelessly in Texas. In November, he reported that eighteen million acres were being grazed free. His fellow commissioner, W. T. Gass, reported that he had found five million acres of school lands illegally fenced in the Panhandle, adding that "the law cannot be enforced by civil process." [1]

The report aroused a furor of excitement. State Comptroller Swain stated publicly that the Government should send the Rangers to tear down the illegal fences. Treasurer Lubbock agreed and said they should begin by making an example of the 750,000 acres of pasture land that Goodnight was using in defiance of the law. Governor Ireland was not adverse to taking such action, but he announced that he would not call up the Rangers until the county governments and courts had demonstrated that they could not cope with the situation.

It was all the encouragement the Land Board needed to set about revising the provisions of the Legislative Act they had been appointed to administer. Arbitrarily it proclaimed that it would lease no more land for less than eight cents an acre (double the price stipulated in the Act); that for what it considered good and sufficient reasons it might refuse to lease any watered lands; that sales should be made only to actual settlers; and that no watered lands belonging to the State would be sold.

Knowing they were in trouble, Panhandle stockmen, Goodnight among them, swung into action. Lease fees had to be paid in cash and in advance. Goodnight led a party of his neighbors to Austin and tendered the State what they claimed was the amount due, figured at the cost stipulated in the Land Act. Treasurer Lubbock refused to accept the proffered fees on such terms. He called in Attorney General Templeton, who agreed with him on the stand he was taking. Before the stormy session was over, Governor Ireland sat in.

Goodnight, as spokesman for the Panhandle cattlemen, led the fight. As reported in the Texas press, it was "hot, acrimonious and violent."

"You cannot legislate for me," he thundered. "I will pay the lease fee as written into law, but before I pay what you're demanding [the Land Board], I'll see you all in hell."

There was no way of avoiding a legal battle now. The Attorney General ordered the District Attorney of Wheeler County to secure indictments against the violators of the Enclosure Act, and the Stock Association countered by engaging the services of the best legal talent in the State to defend its members.

When the grand jury of Wheeler County was summoned into session in January, 1886, composed to a man of cattlemen of one level or another, with Goodnight as foreman, its action could only be described as farcical. The Attorney General stated in his official report, "the farcical judicial proceedings were shamelessly carried on under the pretext of punishing the illegal enclosure of these lands, but it would appear in fact for the real purpose of securing immunity against punishment by preordained verdicts of not guilty."

Goodnight was foreman of the grand jury, the members of which were, like himself, cattlemen. When they gathered in Old Clarendon in January for their deliberations, they were in the preposterous position of voting true bills against themselves. But they did, being confident that convictions could not be obtained.

The first bill returned was again Goodnight for "Unlawfully fenc ing and herding on Public School Lands." Two days later, six more indictments for the same offense were found against him.

Before it had finished, the grand jury voted a total of seventy-six true bills. It took the court clerk several days to inscribe them. When they were ready, the Colonel put them in a market basket and delivered them to Judge Willis. Willis impaneled a jury in due course, the members of which, with one or two exceptions, were cowboys in the employ of the accused. Judge Willis was not ignorant of that circumstance. His excuse was that the scarcity of population made it impossible to impanel a jury of twelve men in Wheeler County who were not connected with the cattle business.

The legal travesty began with an agreed statement of fact, the defendants admitting enclosure of certain land, while the State acknowledged a tender of leasing fees had been made. The trial got under way with defense attorneys contending that their clients had bid four cents an acre for certain lands and that leases had been awarded by the county surveyors with tenure for a period of ten years; that the required leasing fees had been tendered the Land Board. Judge Willis then charged the jury that if this defense was found to be true, it should render a verdict of not guilty. Which it did forthwith.

Attorney General Templeton had come up from Austin and sat through the farce. On returning to the capital, he instituted impeachment proceedings against Willis. It precipitated a bitter fight, and being an election year, it aligned heavily populated (comparatively, that is) east Texas against west Texas. Angry men stalked the streets and the legislative halls at Austin. It was freely predicted that the threats and vituperation that filled the air would result in bloodshed. More of the animosity was directed at Goodnight than at Judge Willis, who was held to be only the cowman's dupe and tool. Scurrilously, he (Goodnight) was held up as the "Panhandle Bullionaire," the "Usurper of the Children's Land," and "Range Hog." His hands were far from being lily-white, but such abuse only stiffened his determination to win by whatever means were available. In this instance, that entailed the expenditure of money.

Willis wanted to resign his commission. Goodnight refused to permit him to do so. Finally the impeachment proceedings were dropped and Willis returned to Clarendon in triumph. Goodnight hung on in Austin, fighting for an equitable lease law. He got it passed. He had paid for it. "The Willis impeachment and the lease fight cost me twenty thousand dollars," he informed Mrs. Adair, "but we upheld the honor of the Panhandle."

How honor had been served is difficult to understand, unless the bribing of public officials was justified when employed in a good cause. However that may be, under the Land Act of 1887, cattlemen were now secure in their rights and at the same time the way was open to the colonization of the Panhandle. Cattle prices had been tumbling and the Panhandle was suffering from another long drought. These were problems that, hopefully, could be taken in stride. But there was another factor now on the horizon which was to revolutionize life on the High Plains and end its isolation for all time. To the northeast, the Kansas Southern Railroad had crossed the line into Texas; to the southeast, the stuttering, stumbling Fort Worth and Denver City Railroad had passed Quanah, in Hardeman County, and was pressing forward with sudden vigor for the Panhandle.

The Kansas Southern had recently changed its corporate name to Panhandle and Santa Fe for the logical reason that the Atchison, Topeka and Santa Fe had taken it over and merged it into the Santa Fe System. It was pointing for El Paso, on the Mexican border, hundreds of miles to the south. Locators and surveyors were already deep into Potter County. In September they reached the hitherto unimportant village of Amarillo. That the road was in a hurry became evident when it announced that its grading crews would continue working throughout the winter. Early the following year the Panhandle and Santa Fe rails reached Amarillo. It gave the sleepy town a mild boost.

To the southeast, the Fort Worth and Denver, after several financial crises, was booming along, too. Its end of track had reached Memphis, in Hall County, and it was grading into Donley County with the expectation of being in Clarendon by Christmas. With one railroad bound for El Paso and the other for Denver, of necessity their tracks must cross somewhere in Potter County.

Goodnight speculated that the junction—the first railroad junction
in west Texas—would be made at Amarillo. "When that occurs,"
he wrote Mrs. Adair, "every section of land within a hundred
miles of the spot will be snapped up in a hurry. New towns are
certain to spring up along the railroads. Clarendon is filling up
already with squatters waiting to decide which way to jump. We
cannot expect the range cattle business to continue on the old
scale. I believe our interests would be best served if we divided
the property."

The partnership with Mrs. Adair, that had begun so pleas-
antly, had become a series of annoying vexations, partly his fault,
for the only woman he ever understood—and who understood him
—was Molly.

His letters to Mrs. Adair about division became more insistent.
Only after months of negotiations was it accomplished. To make
it possible, he agreed to take the short end of the stick, for he was
tired and worn out. He gave her the JA—which he often regretted
—and the ranch on the Tule, keeping for himself the Quitaque
Ranch, with its one hundred and forty thousand acres of land and
twenty thousand cattle. On December 27, 1887, he left the ranch
in the Palo Duro and moved over to the station on the Fort Worth
and Denver, which the railroad named Goodnight in his honor.

The buffalo was becoming a museum piece, but in the Palo
Duro Goodnight had ranged a small herd over the years and had
succeeded in crossing the buffalo with the cow, producing an animal that he named the cattalo. Because it was an excellent forager
and immune to extremes of cold weather, he seriously believed
for years that it might supersede the cow as a commercially profitable range animal. When he moved to Goodnight, which was to
be his home for the following forty years, he took them with him.

Amarillo, having garnered two railroads, was booming. Any
doubt that it was to become the commercial capital and metropo-
lis of the Panhandle was dispelled when the Chicago, Rock Island
and Pacific shot across the Plains and made Amarillo a division
point. It has been said many times that the railroads opened the
West; that where the rails went, civilization followed. Certainly
they opened up the country and put thousands of men and women
on the land, the majority of whom would not have left their

homes and farms in the East and ventured westward if the covered wagon of the pioneers had been the only means of transportation.

The newcomers who were streaming into the Panhandle were typical of the great majority of immigrants who had been lured westward by the prospect of making a fresh start in life and bettering their lot. Most of them were poor and ill equipped for the struggle on which they were embarking. This raw land held no welcome for them. As farmers, homesteaders, nesters, they were not wanted by the range lords. Not only were they reviled, branded as rustlers, shot at by nightriders if they came to their cabin door, but the land itself, with its ever-encroaching sagebrush and mesquite, was against them.

We do not know what percentage of the Americans who spread out over the plains and prairies of the West in the decade of the eighties had their place of origin in the North, as opposed to the South (using those designations in their Civil War connotations). Regional, political and social differences were still alive, and they were not left behind. If they disappeared sooner in the Texas Panhandle than elsewhere, it undoubtedly was because all encountered the same harassment. A range war usually refers to a confrontation between cattlemen and sheepmen. But not always. Sheep did not enter into the conflict in the Panhandle. And yet it was war. In it were all of the elements that culminated in the bloody eruption in Wyoming, which has taken its place in history as the Johnson County War. If it stopped short of that, it was largely because of the wisdom, courage and generosity of one man —Timothy Dwight Hobart. If Charles Goodnight was the "first man of the Panhandle," then humble, kindly, forthright Dwight Hobart was number two.

At the time when events ushered him into prominence in the Texas Panhandle, it seemed that the conflict between the cattle outfits and settlers had reached a point where their differences could not be settled amicably. "I don't take that view," Hobart told a meeting in Mobeetie. "If both sides will sit down together and will give a little, I'm sure we will find a way out of our troubles. I say that because I believe most men want to do the right thing." [2]

It was a position from which he never departed his faith in his fellow men, his willingness to compromise, to listen to the other man's side of the argument without condoning injustice. Some men mistook his gentleness for weakness. They soon learned their error. It didn't make them like him any better, but he won their respect. Because he befriended the little man, the farmer and the settler with a few head of cattle, the big outfits regarded him as their common enemy until it dawned on them that the policy of live and let live, which he advocated, had as its end result peace and increased profits for themselves.

Hobart was a Vermonter, a cousin of Ira Evans, the president of the New York and Texas Land Company. Evans brought him down from his home in the village of Berlin, where he had been teaching school, and started him at the bottom of the company's ladder, sending him out as chain man with a party of surveyors running lines west of San Angelo in Tom Green County. He was young, twenty-seven, largely self-educated and totally inexperienced. Next he was made assistant town-lot agent in the company-owned town of Troup, in Smith County. Being a salesman didn't appeal to him, and at his request he went back to surveying, this time joining the crew that was running lines from the headwaters of the Middle Concho to the Pecos. Applying himself diligently to making himself a competent civil engineer, he succeeded so well that two years later he was placed in charge of the work being done in west Texas in today's Mitchell and Scurry counties, until recently Comanche country.

"In his first three years in Texas, 1882 to 1885, he acquired a knowledge of Texas soils, climatic conditions and natural phenomena," says L. F. Sheffy, his biographer, "that prepared him for a career he was to follow for the next fifty years." [3]

His letters home and numerous entries in his journal reveal how deep was his love for that high, lonesome land, with its big sky, great distances and buffeting winds with their invigorating soprano scream.

Hobart was sent up to Mobeetie from Austin in 1886 as land agent and surveyor, with a small party of civil engineers. His first job was to check the accuracy of the original surveys made by William Nelson in 1873. He established his headquarters in the office of Lawyer Temple Houston, the youngest son of General Sam Houston. Settling down to work, he discovered almost at once that what he had regarded as a routine assignment was in fact a bewildering, seemingly insurmountable undertaking. Wherever he checked a Nelson survey, he found it to be in error—errors so glaring that he wrote President Evans that "Nelson must have done most of his work seated at his desk."

Fort Elliott stood on land that the Government had leased from the New York and Texas Land Company. Hobart's surveys showed that the company did not own the land. Equally disturbing was his discovery that the town of Mobeetie stood on company land. Many settlers were found to be occupying lands which they believed they owned, but for which the deeds proved to be invalid. Hobart wrote the company that in such disputes it would be his policy to favor the settlers. The adjustments he made were so satisfactory to all concerned that the animosity he had encountered at first completely disappeared, and his reputation for honesty and fair play became widespread. It took him three years to settle all claims for and against the company. It was accomplished without a single lawsuit.[4]

The success he was having was rewarded by President Evans, and in 1887 he was placed in complete control of all New York and Texas Land Company holdings in the Panhandle.

He took office fully aware that it wasn't only the members of the Stock Association who opposed his land policy; there was a third party to the conflict, the "free-grassers," who were militantly opposed to all fencing, whether by the big brands or the farmer-stockman. They centered their fire on Goodnight, charging that he and his associates had wangled the Land Act of 1887 through the Legislature by widespread bribery and corruption. They demanded that leasing be made illegal and the Panhandle declared open range.

They had no hope of having their demands met. But they were numerous enough, and loud enough, to unite the two factions opposing them. Evidence of it came a few weeks later, when Goodnight, who had not budged an inch, suggested to Judge Plemons, recently elected to the Legislature from the Panhandle, that a "four section" law, which would give settlers sufficient land for stock-farming, might have to be considered. Plemons was shocked, thinking of the horde of settlers it would bring in and the new towns that would arise.[5]

"That's exactly what Hobart has been advocating, Mr. Goodnight. It would ruin you."

The old warrior shook his head.

"Nothing will ruin us, Judge, that settles the country."

Hobart expressed his satisfaction when the conversation was repeated to him. "I'm glad to hear that the Colonel is coming around to my way of thinking," he observed.

SOME SHACKLEFORD
COUNTY HISTORY

XVII

Conflict on the Clear Fork

Its violence, lawlessness and general depravity long ago assured old Fort Griffin, on the Clear Fork of the Brazos, in Shackleford County, Texas, a permanent niche in history. The civilian town of Fort Griffin, however, gave the fort its hell-roaring reputation. Known in its day as the Flat, the town was at the foot of Government Hill, on which the military post was perched.

When Texas appealed to Washington to build a fort on the Clear Fork to protect its citizens from being scalped and butchered by the Comanches, the War Department took the matter under "advisement," being in no mood to give succor to its recent rebel enemy at-arms. But in 1867, following several Indian outrages, it ordered the establishment of Fort Griffin, and with bureaucratic malice garrisoned the post with Negro troops.

Aside from patrolling the country to the north and west and turning back raiding Comanches, both real and imaginary, Fort Griffin achieved no military importance in the dozen or so years of its existence. But just being where it was, with its threat of retaliation, had a persuasive effect on the Indians. They continued to run off the white man's horses and take a scalp, when opportunity offered, but not almost at will, as they had done in the past. They were losing their grip on the country; being pushed

back. For years Weatherford had been accounted the farthest town
west that was "safe." That line was not a hundred miles west of
Weatherford. Fort Griffin, atop its mesa on the Clear Fork, played
a part in that advancement.

As the soldiers converted their wages into fun and pleasure at
the earliest possible moment, Fort Griffin's monthly payroll of
about ten thousand dollars was an irresistible bait that drew forth
from their distant environs a small assortment of crooks, gamblers,
thimbleriggers, whores and whisky peddlers. They reached Fort
Griffin by one means or another and set up in business on The
Flat.

After entertaining some of the most notorious characters in
Western folklore, Fort Griffin and The Flat might have passed out
of existence after a few years and been forgotten had it not been
for Frank E. Conrad, the young and enterprising post sutler. The
great slaughtering of the buffalo was going full blast and Dodge
City (not yet a cow town) was booming with the trade of the hide
hunters. Beside the Santa Fe tracks flint hides were piled twenty
feet high for half a mile, awaiting shipment. Some hunters were
working as far down in the Panhandle as Red River to be in position to intercept the great southern herd when it began its annual
migration northward.

Fort Griffin was much closer to the buffalo range than Dodge.
It was handicapped by not having a railroad. However, the Texas
and Pacific had reached Fort Worth, only a hundred and twenty-
five miles to the east, and was inching westward. In the meantime
there was a good wagon road over which heavy loads of hides could
be moved from Fort Griffin to the railhead.

Having considered the possibilities, Conrad plunged into the
lucrative hide business by outfitting a large party of hunters with
wagons, horses, guns, ammunition and supplies on credit and
agreeing to pay Dodge City prices in cash for the hides they
brought in.

The venture was so successful that by the fall of 1875, Fort
Griffin was being labeled the Hide Hunter Capital. Eight- and
ten-yoke ox teams were pulling four, even six, hitches of wagons
over the road to Fort Worth, grinding the soil in the deep ruts to
powder.

The population of The Flat had tripled. It was lawless, violent, lewd. Of its hundred women, less than half a dozen could lay any claim to decency. The Bee Hive, its gaudiest saloon, opened for business. Over the main entrance hung a picture of the traditional beehive, adorned with the following doggerel:

> Within this hive we are alive,
> Good whisky makes us funny.
> So if you're dry, come in and try
> The flavor of our honey.

Frank Conrad was growing richer by the minute. At one time in the fall of 1876, he had two hundred thousand flint (unsalted) hides spread out on three acres of ground on the east bank of the Clear Fork. He took all winter to transport them to Fort Worth. He seems to have realized (which few others did) that the buffalo would soon be killed out and that the hide business was only a fleeting bonanza. He came down from the hill and opened a general store on The Flat. His stock of goods, probably the best in Texas, was valued at $40,000.

About the time that the buffalo killing was beginning to peter out, Fort Griffin got a lift from an unexpected source. For years the Texas Longhorn trail to the northern markets had been up the Chisholm Trail. In May, 1877, bound for Ogallala, Nebraska, Maxwell and Morris, with a mixed herd of fifteen hundred head, turned off the old trail at Belton (below Waco) and headed northwest, hoping to clip off a hundred miles or more from their long journey.[1] They had no trail to follow. Because it was convenient, they went up the Leon River. Reaching the end of it, they struck north, their only compass the north star. After forty miles of wandering, they came by chance to Fort Griffin. Armed with the information gathered there, they struck out across as yet unorganized Baylor and Wilbarger counties and reached Red River, which they crossed at the place where Doan was to have his trading post. Following the North Fork of Red River, they went up through the Panhandle and eventually reached the Arkansas River crossing, four miles west of Dodge City. The Jones and Plummer Trail brought them to their destination. By their calculations they had clipped two hundred miles off the old route between Belton and Ogallala.

Though unaware of it, they had pioneered what was soon to become the Western Trail, destined to be the second most heavily traveled cattle trail in the United States. Over it an estimated million Longhorns and no fewer than a hundred thousand mustangs were to pass, transforming Dodge from a buffalo hunters' town to the Cowboy Capital of the West. The Chisholm Trail was forgotten, with Fort Griffin becoming an important trail town as the big herds passed its doors and pointed north.

Having survived the collapse of its hide-hunting prosperity, which followed the practical elimination of the buffalo from the Plains, The Flat welcomed the cowboy. But its economy and importance received a blow from which it never recovered, when the Government abandoned Fort Griffin in 1881. The exodus began, and it continued. To the discerning eye it was evident that the advancing railroads would soon be criss-crossing Texas and make trail-driving unnecessary. When that came to pass, The Flat no longer would have any reason for its existence.

A few hardy businessmen hung on until the Texas Central put its rails into Albany, the county seat, some twenty miles to the south. Packing up their wares, they moved to Albany. The buildings they left behind them were torn down, and for years The Flat was just a plowed field.

Fort Griffin was not the first military post on the looping Clear Fork of the Brazos. On the north bank, a few miles up the river from Fort Griffin, Camp Cooper was established in 1856. Situated on a gently sloping plain that ran down to the river, and surrounded by low hills that made it indefensible if attacked (which fortunately never occurred), it was garrisoned by four companies of the Second U.S. Cavalry.

The primary duty of Camp Cooper was to control the Indians who had been placed on the nearby Comanche reservation, a state, not a Federal, establishment. Ironically the military soon found itself equally as busy protecting the Comanches against the Texans, who wanted them moved north of Red River into Indian Territory. It presented a vexing problem for Camp Cooper's first commander, Lieutenant Colonel Robert E. Lee, the Virginia aristocrat, hero of the Mexican War and late superintendent at West Point.

The Second U.S. Cavalry was a new regiment, recently organized at Jefferson Barracks, St. Louis, from which it had marched to Texas, in December, 1855. Its ten companies numbered 750 enlisted men, forming with its 800 horses, 600 mules and 25 wagons, a military caravan several miles in length. In its officer corps were the men who, a decade later, were to form the very flower of the Confederacy's armed might.[2] On reaching Texas, the regiment had been spread out among the new posts. Why Robert E. Lee was assigned to miserable, unimportant, unhealthy Camp Cooper is a secret buried in the files of the War Department.

When he saw the rows of tents pitched out on the open plain opposite officers' row, with its crude log cabins, and beheld the still unfinished headquarters building that was to be his home, he became so embittered that he thought of resigning his commission. As days passed and the camp sweltered in the humid heat that hung over the river, the temperature often standing at 120 degrees, he realized that in his official position he was more of a policeman than a military officer. His letters home to his wife, Mary Custis Lee,[3] back at Arlington, spoke eloquently of his discouragement. He told her he was going to request a transfer from his Department Commander. Later, his request evidently having been refused, he wrote: "My military career is at a dead end."

Of course, as the world knows, it was only beginning. Obviously the harsh rawness of west Texas could not have failed to have an abrasive effect on a man of his gentleness, refinement and humanity qualities that were to win him the respect and affection of both sides in the great conflict ahead. His tour of duty at Camp Cooper lasted for fourteen months, ending on July 28, 1857. It has been said that the majestic loneliness of west Texas did something for Robert E. Lee—it taught him humility, patience and human understanding. Undoubtedly his months at Camp Cooper made a lasting impression on him, but in his collected letters he does not refer to west Texas with affection.

Camp Cooper continued to function long after Lieutenant Colonel Lee left. Its monotonous existence was enlivened in December, 1860, when Captain Sul Ross and his Texas Rangers rode in and requested the assistance of a company of troopers for a showdown with Peta Nocona's Comanches at Pease River (as related in a previous chapter). Captain Stephen Carpenter, Lee's successor, supplied the men Sul Ross requested. After the victory at Pease River, the reservation on the Clear Fork was closed and the Indians removed to Indian Territory. Camp Cooper continued to function as a U.S. Army post. But not for long; the War Between the States was soon to rip the nation asunder. Throughout Texas sentiment was four-to-one in favor of seceding from the Union. In February, 1861, a secession convention was called and it voted to put the question to the people. The result was never in doubt; Governor Sam Houston, Texas hero that he was, was deposed and Texas cast its lot with the Confederacy.

Scattered throughout the State from the Rio Grande to Red River were a score of U.S. Army posts, well supplied with guns, ammunition and military stores. Their capture was the first order of business. It was accomplished without a shot being fired when General David E. Twiggs, commanding the Department of Texas, with a scratch of the pen turned over all U.S. facilities to the rebel government. The ease with which the turnover was accomplished might have been expected, for seventy-five to eight per cent of the U.S. officers serving in Texas were Southerners. What had become the routine takeover of the different forts ran into difficulties when Texas Colonel W. C. Dalrymple and a large party of Rebels reached Camp Cooper. Young Captain Carpenter, the commandment, was in no mood to haul down the Stars and Stripes and turn the camp over to the insurgents. Dalrymple and his followers withdrew to the crest of the surrounding hills and sent out word for reinforcements. When they arrived, they took up a position on the hills with Dalrymple and his men. Realizing that he was not only badly outnumbered but that the camp, from its unfavorable position, could not be defended, Carpenter changed his mind and struck his colors. Had he not done so, the course of history would have been changed and the first shots of the Civil War would have been fired at Camp Cooper instead of Fort Sumter, as they were six weeks later.

During the war Camp Cooper was occupied by a detail of the Frontier Battalion. Their principal duty was to oversee the Union prisoners who were shunted there where they could be maintained at minimum expense to the Confederacy. Although the members of the Frontier Battalion stationed in Camp Cooper were an accredited part of the Texas militia, they did not wear Confederate gray. In fact, Confederate gray was not seen in that part of Texas until 1869-70, when among the trail crews bound north with the big herds, veterans could be spotted still wearing some part of their old service uniforms— patched pants, a shabby jacket or battered campaign hat. "Hearts overflowed at the sight," says Glen O. Wilson, in the *Southwestern Historical Quarterly*.[4]

By then Camp Cooper was forgotten and had all but disappeared; doors, windows, and anything of value had been carted off to do service elsewhere. A thorny mesquite thicket had begun marching across the old parade ground. But as recently as ten years ago it was still possible to find out on the flat, the ruins of a cottage, built of stone and lumber purloined from Camp Cooper. It overlooked the river, and when the tall pecan trees lost their leaves, the ranch house that all Shackleford County knows as "the Larn place" could be seen some distance to the south on high ground above the far bank of the Clear Fork.

In west Texas the term "ranch house" covers almost anything enclosed by four walls. Therefore you should know that the Larn place could be properly described as a mansion. It was a two-storied house of twelve rooms, with double chimneys at the ends of its peaked roof, which was topped by a square cupola, with a "widow's walk" and encircling benches, convenient for meditation and for spying (a use to which rumor said it was often put). Although showing signs of age—John Larn built it in 1877—the marks of time are softened by the patina of romance and tragedy that cling to it. According to local legend, the etched glass in the fantail above the doors of the main entrance came from the commandant's headquarters at Camp Cooper. Certainly much of the stone and lumber used in building the great house came from there.

By the mid-1870's Shackleford and the surrounding counties had become one of the foremost beef-producing districts in Texas. Its economy was solidly linked to the ups and downs of the range cattle business, which was, in fact, the only major industry. Law enforcement was negligible, which was an invitation for the cow thief and range outlaw to move in. Their depredations became so successful that the rustlers organized and allotted to one another the territory in which each group was to work. When not gainfully employed, they had Fort Griffin and The Flat to resort to for relaxation. There were times when the known and suspected rustler population of The Flat exceeded anything ever known elsewhere.

That was the situation when young John Larn came down from Kansas and went to work punching cows for Joe Matthews, the most powerful and respected cattleman in Shackleford County. Larn was a handsome, laughing young man with a fast gun. Matthews was impressed with him and his ability to lead men. In him old Joe realized he had found the strong right arm he needed to wage war on the rustling ring that was making his life miserable.

There is nothing in the evidence to warrant the accusation that Joe Matthews organized the vigilante action of the cattlemen that spread terror in Shackleford County and parts of Throckmorton and Haskell counties. But it can be taken for granted that he subscribed to the movement to eliminate the rustler gangs, nor can it be doubted that John Larn rode with the masked nightriders who strung up an estimated sixteen men in less than three months. It may have been true, as it was alleged, that among those lynched were at least two innocent men. The raids accomplished their purpose, however, and the wholesale rustling ended. When the range quieted down, it was noticed that a number of familiar faces had disappeared from The Flat.

Mary Jane Matthews, old Joe's pretty daughter, was as impressed with Larn as her father was. Local romanticists say it was a case of love at first sight. Certainly she was deeply in love with Larn, an affection that never wavered. They were married when he was twenty-one, and they moved into the "honeymoon cottage" he had built on the old parade ground at Camp Cooper.

When the sheriff of Shackleford County resigned a few months later, Larn's name was put up as his best possible successor. He was easily elected. As his chief deputy, he appointed John Selman, with whom he had struck up an acquaintance at The Flat. If the name John Selman rings a bell in your memory, it should, for he was the same John Selman who on the night of August 19, 1895, was to kill John Wesley Hardin, the man with forty notches on his gun, in the Acme Saloon in El Paso. Selman was an old man by then. In his younger days he had run afoul of Charlie Goodnight, who had categorized him as a "worthless punk" (one of the earliest-recorded uses of that expression as a term of contempt).

Beyond doubt Selman was a cattle thief at various times, noted for his quick and deadly trigger finger, but never any match for Wes Hardin. Hardin was standing at the Acme bar when Selman entered the saloon and shot him in the back, the first bullet—three were fired—passing through Hardin's hat and entering his head. To escape the stigma of having shot an enemy in the back, Selman came up with the unique defense that Hardin and he were seemingly staring at each other, eye to eye, when he fired, but that what he was seeing was only Hardin's reflection in the back-bar mirror. Ex-Senator A. B. Fall assisted in his defense and won an easy acquittal.

Soon after he became sheriff, Larn put together a force of hard-riding deputies, captained by Selman, who became the scourge of the county. A number of known criminals were arrested and convicted of various crimes. Cattlemen and the general public, who had been clamoring for law and order, applauded. Presently, however, a number of robberies occurred in different parts of the county. Ranchers returing home after the sale of their beef cattle, with large sums of money on their persons, were held up and robbed by masked bandits in broad daylight. In two instances they were killed while resisting the thieves.

Although Sheriff Larn and his deputies scoured the country in an effort to apprehend the guilty parties, the crimes went unsolved. Reports began to circulate of large numbers of cattle being run off and disappearing mysteriously. Larn and his men cut the trail of the rustlers and followed it into adjoining Jones County, where they lost it. Old rangemen, excellent trailers themselves in their time, shook their heads; they couldn't understand how the trail left by several hundred steers could be lost in the open country along the upper Clear Fork. Maybe it was their grousing that gave rise to the whisper that it was Larn himself, and his deputies, who were plundering Shackleford County.

Larn appeared to have plenty of money. He built the mansion across the Clear Fork from the honeymoon cottage, and early in 1877 it became their new home. The Larn place was soon a house of mystery to the surrounding neighborhood. The big yard and pasture were enclosed by a rock wall, topped off by a barbed wire fence. It was an effective way of warding off intruders; to approach the house, the visitor had to use the front entrance, which exposed him to view from within.

Of the many legends connected with the Larn place, perhaps the one oftenest heard concerns the handsome rock wall, still standing a few years ago. According to the tale, Larn engaged two dry-wall masons (a lost art today) to build it for five hundred dollars, paying them a hundred dollars down. When they were finished, instead of completing payment, he killed them and buried their bodies in the sands of the Clear Fork. Some years later there was a great deal of digging on the river bank. Two human skeletons were found. Although no identification was possible, it was believed that they were the two masons, which ignores the fact that one of Larn's supposed victims turned up at Fort Smith, Arkansas, and identified himself.

Any place where crime and tragedy occur is easily invested with legend. The Larn place was no exception. Numerous tales exist about how Larn climbed to the cupola of his home at dusk and seated himself on the bench, his rifle across his knees, supposedly scanning the surrounding country for enemies or to await the coming of his henchmen, who, however late they arrived, were gone before dawn.

Strangely, Mary Larn was never aware of the mysterious comings and goings. Throughout her life, whenever she heard such tales, she branded them as false and without foundation. She had two children by John Larn, both boys. The first died very young. Will, the second boy, grew to manhood and after an absence from Texas of many years, returned to make his home with his mother's family. As handsome as his father, he was a restless man, a loner, apparently unable to escape from the shadows of the past.

A year after taking office, Larn resigned his position. Selman and the other deputies followed suit. Bill Cruger, a native of Albany, was named to take Larn's place. From the first, Cruger appears to have been obsessed with the feeling that Larn was responsible for most of the crimes occurring in Shackleford County. He appealed to the Texas Rangers to aid him in gathering evidence against his predecessor.

Larn knew he was suspected of various crimes. He conferred with his gang, who had moved back to The Flat, where they felt perfectly at home, and told them they were to lay low for the time being. To give the impression that he was busy at something legitimate, he put in a low bid for the Government contract to supply Fort Griffin with beef. It called for the delivery of three slaughtered steers a day.

Butchering the cattle and delivering the meat kept the gang occupied. Neighbors noticed, however, that despite this drain on Larn's herd, it continued to increase. It spurred Sheriff Cruger into action. He got a search warrant from a justice of the peace in Albany and accompanied by a detachment of Rangers rode to the Larn ranch. They found Larn at home. He came out of the house and confronted them, armed, as usual. Cruger informed him that he was there to search the place for evidence to connect him (Larn) with the disappearance of several head of cattle from a neighboring farmer's small herd. Selman and several other members of Larn's so-called "gang" came up and took their places beside him. Larn waved them back and told Cruger to begin his searching.

As for what followed, you have your choice of which conflicting tale to believe. One widely circulated story (and generally believed in those long-ago days) had it that Cruger found upwards of two hundred hides of mutilated brands buried in a deep hole on the river bank, the believers ignoring the fact that it would have taken an excavation thirty feet deep to hold them. Other tales trimmed the number down to two or three, while the sanest said the sheriff had found nothing at all. Surely if he found anything it was very little, for when he returned to Albany, he did not file any charge against Larn or seek a warrant for his arrest.

But by now Bill Cruger was determined to bring John Larn to trial, something which many prominent cattlemen and big landowners were equally determined must never happen. They

knew if Larn was put on the stand and chose to talk, he could blast
their reputations by revealing their past affiliation with him.

Several weeks later Cruger obtained a warrant on Larn, charging him with being a cattle thief. He swore in eight possemen
and with great secrecy left Albany and headed for the Larn stronghold. They arrived during the night and concealed themselves.
In the morning, when Larn stepped out of the house and headed
for the cow barn, a milking pail over his arm, they jumped him.
He was unarmed. Fantastic tales are told of how he offered to pay
Cruger five hundred dollars if the sheriff would let him get his
gun. Cruger wasn't that sporting. He read the warrant to Larn
and, manacling his hands, placed him in a wagon and started for
Albany with him.

You may read that Cruger responded to Larn's plea to allow
Mary and the boy to accompany Larn to town. You need not believe it. By the time Mary finished dressing herself and her son,
her husband was long gone. Hitching a team to a buckboard, she
set out on the road to the county seat.

It was not yet noon when she reached Albany. Accepting hospitality of friends living on Court House Square, she set out to
find a lawyer who might get Larn released on bail. His plea was
promptly rejected. The town was buzzing with excitement. Little
knots of the morbid and curious gathered about the log cabin on
Hubbard Creek that was the Shackleford County jail, in which
Larn was lodged, with several other prisoners, to await his appearance in court the following morning. As you may have surmised, it was an appearance he was never to make. Sometime after
midnight a dozen masked men clad in the long, impersonable yellow slickers common in range country, overcame the jailer and,
raising their rifles, blasted the life out of John Larn.

Mary was given his body and took it back to their home on the
Clear Fork and buried him beside their first-born. In time, she
erected a monument over his grave and surrounded the plot with
a stone wall. She tried to continue living in the big house, but it
was too silent, held too many memories. Old Joe Matthews' door
was open to her and she finally moved in with him and the rest
of the family.

Years passed before she remarried. Her second husband was a

frontier Baptist preacher. He joined with her in a valiant effort to remove the tarnish that clouded John Larn's name. They had very little success, for it was a matter about which very few people were willing to talk. The old-timers just shook their heads and turned away. A number of damaging secrets had been buried with John Larn, and they were not interested in digging them up.

MONTANA BONANZA

XVIII

From Gold to Cattle

On the evening of May 26, 1863, Bill Fairweather and his three companions, returning from Bannack City empty-handed after weeks of prospecting, struck bonanza in an unknown gulch on Alder Creek which, because it was choked with alders, they promptly named Alder Gulch. The white population of what was to become Montana Territory less than a year later could not then have numbered more than two thousand. It was Indian country, the home of a score of buffalo-hunting tribes, including the Western Sioux, Blackfeet, Crow, Flathead and Piegans.

Up the gulch, on Daylight Creek, the new camp of Virginia City mushroomed almost overnight into a bustling city of fifteen thousand gold-crazed men and women who had put their lives on the line just to get there. The hardiest had come over the mountains from the west; the great majority up the hundreds of miles of dangerous trail from Utah, or by steamboat to Fort Benton, which left them two hundred miles from their destination. Considering its remoteness, the stampede to the Montana diggings was second only to the great rush to California. Nor was it a will-o'-the-wisp, bright today and gone tomorrow. When Alder Gulch and the other placers in the Virginia City district began to fade,

Helena (Last Chance Gulch) and other districts spread their treasures before the astonished eyes of the muckers.

The Mormon-owned narrow-gauge Utah Nothern came up through Monida Pass into Beaverhead Valley and gave Montana its first railroad. With it came telegraphic connection with the outside world, and Ben Holladay's stagecoaches and relay stations took the danger out of going back and forth between Virginia City, Eagle Rock and Salt Lake City. Although the changes came rapidly, one of the Territory's great natural resources, the undulating, seemingly illimitable miles of rich grasslands, was ignored in the mad pursuit of gold. As in the days when the fur companies exercised a feeble control of the country, roving bands of Indians, buffalo, elk, deer and antelope roamed the plains.

Aside from a cow or two with which some of the early settlers arrived in Montana, there were no—or at best very few—cattle in the Territory. In 1858, James and Granville Stuart embarked in the livestock business on a very modest scale. From their camp on the Emigrant Road (the California and Oregon trail) at Green River crossing, east of Fort Bridger, Wyoming, they began buying and trading for poor and worn-out horses and oxen in the emigrant and army trains. The brothers found that after resting the animals and keeping them on good grass, they were as fit as ever and could be resold at a fancy price.

The Stuarts were so successful that with the approach of winter in 1869, they drove their mixed herd of cattle and horses north into the Beaverhead Valley. The Stuarts' herd of sixty head of cattle were followed a few weeks later by a herd of seventy-five head, also acquired on the Emigrant Road, belonging to Robert Hereford. They were among the earliest herds to reach Montana, but not the first. In his journal, Granville Stuart, Montana's foremost range cattleman, awards the honor of being first to Robert Demsey, John M. Jacobs, Robert Hereford and Jacob Meek. "In 1856 they drove six hundred head of cattle and horses up into Montana and wintered on the Stinkingwater. These cattle fattened on the native grasses, without shelter other than that afforded by the willows, alders and tall rye grass along the streams." [1]

He continues: "These herds all increased rapidly and when

gold was struck at Alder Gulch every emigrant train brought in a few cattle; ranches were established and by 1863 cattle growing had become an industry of considerable importance."

He records that Nelson Storey, of Bozeman, drove the first herd of Texas cattle into Montana in the spring of 1866. Storey had purchased six hundred head of Longhorns in Dallas, Texas, and had driven them north without having a trail to guide him as this was prior to the opening of the Kansas cattle market. He arrived safely in the Gallatin Valley in early December and located where Fort Ellis was established later. In 1878, a thousand head of stock cattle from Oregon were placed on the Sun River range. The first small beef herd trailed out of Sun River was sold in Salt Lake City.

There is little in this record to justify Granville Stuart in saying in 1863 that "cattle growing had become an industry of considerable importance." Montana was without a law covering marks and brands until 1864. But cattle were not Stuart's chief interest at the time nor for some years later. He and his elder brother James had opened a store at Deer Lodge and were doing well and spending whatever time they could take from the business to prospect.

In 1852, a French Red River half-breed named François Finlay, better known as Benetsee, had discovered colors in the sands of the creek that came to be known as "Benetsee's Creek." It was light, float gold and he could not find it in quantity to make working it worthwhile. Rumors about his alleged discovery were strong enough to draw the Stuarts to Benetsee's Creek. The best luck they had was to find gold that ran no better than ten cents to the pan. The Stuarts failed to find any evidence that Benetsee had done any digging, so quite rightly they claimed to have been the discoverers of gold in Montana. Whether that distinction belonged to them or to Benetsee became the subject of a lively debate that continued for years. It is generally agreed today that Benetsee was the discoverer and that James and Granville Stuart confirmed and publicized the fact that there was gold in the gravel of Montana's creeks.

The Stuarts were honest, able, thrifty men, better educated than their fellows and (for the time and place) cultured men. When the first rich strike was made on Grasshopper Creek and the camp at Bannack became a brawling, bustling town of five hundred inhabitants, the brothers moved a stock of general merchandise there and opened a second store. Along with their other activities they were roasting charcoal and doing blacksmithing. In their stores a shelf was set aside for basic drugs and medicines. Although Granville Stuart's knowledge of materia medica must have been extremely limited, no doctor being available, he prescribed for their customers, apparently with satisfactory results.[2]

Soon after the big strike in Alder Gulch and Virginia City began to boom, they went into partnership with Judge W. B. Dance and opened a store there, trading under the name of Dance and Stuart. The extent of the business the leading stores in Virginia City were doing can be gathered from this note in Granville Stuart's diary. "November 29, [1863] Gilette's wagon train arrived from Fort Benton, bringing six hundred pairs of heavy leather boots for Dance and Stuart. The freight from St. Louis here has cost thirty-five cents a pound. The boots are not what are liked here by the miners and I see that we will not make any money on these goods."

When the great Alder Gulch discovery occurred (and actually for some years thereafter), there were no courts in Montana Territory other than so-called "Miners' Courts," which functioned without the sanctity of statutes or system of organized law. To say the Territory was lawless would be to imply that it had laws that were being flouted; actually, there was no law. Prior to the opening of the world's greatest placer diggings, it hadn't mattered too much, but now with men and women flocking in by the thousand and everyone seemingly getting rich, it created a vacuum in which criminals of every stripe quickly surfaced.

All gold camps, past and present, giddy in their days of prosperity, have been the scene of violence, but nowhere else has the number of robberies, shootings and killings that occurred in the Montana diggings come close to being equaled. The miners, determined to do something about the situation, elected a sheriff. Ironically, the man they chose was dark, dapper Henry Plummer, a refugee road agent from Nevada and California—about whom they knew nothing.

Plummer had some executive ability. Appreciating the opportunity that was now his, it didn't take him long to organize a gang of road agents and gunmen who soon were terrorizing the different mining districts. He planted an agent in each camp who kept him informed as to which miner had made his fortune and was preparing to leave the diggings, and the route he was taking. The agents developed a system of marking departing stagecoaches that were carrying treasure so that confederates would know which ones to stop. In his scheme of espionage, Plummer's greatest achievement was in placing Clubfoot George Lane, a cobbler by trade, in Dance and Stuart's Virginia City store, where he occupied a corner near the door with his bench. The cripple was a popular man around town and the information he ferreted out and passed on to the indicated outlaw rendezvous resulted in the killing of at least seven men.

When Plummer's gang was fully recruited, it was estimated to number at least fifty men. They had regular meetings at several hideouts. Rattlesnake Ranch, on the road between Bannack and Virginia City, where big George Ives, a merciless thug, was in command, was a favorite hangout. Dempsey's Ranch on the Stinkingwater, twenty miles below Virginia City, was another—or Daly's Ranch on Ramshorn Creek. These various "ranches" were not ranches at all, being no more than a log cabin and brush corral.

In less than eighteen months they accounted for two score of killings in which robbery was the motive. In addition they killed three friendly Bannock Indians just for the hell of it, and in a duel among themselves one of the gang, George Carrhart, was mortally wounded. When a man named Dillingham, Plummer's chief deputy in Virginia City, was discovered to have warned a prospective victim who was about to start for Fort Benton, three members of the gang, Haze Lyon, Buck Stinson and Charlie Forbes, were named to "take care of him." On June 30, 1863, they caught him in the outskirts of a crowd attending a miner's civil trial and blasted the life out of him.

To quote Larry Barsness, the Virginia City historian, "These men were not the gunslicks of Western fiction. They were ordinary saloon goons, who, by their numbers and tactics, were able to wage a successful gang warfare." [3]

It soon became an almost daily sight to see such Plummer worthies as George Ives, Ned Ray, Whisky Bill Graves, Bill Hunter, Haze Lyon, Bill Moore, Charlie Reeves and Buck Stinson, drunk with prosperity and rotgut whisky, swaggering up and down Wallace Street, Virginia City's main thoroughfare. Plummer himself began spending more time in town and letting it be known that he was about to launch a vigorous campaign to eliminate the road agents who were terrorizing the district. Some people were taken in by his smooth talk and believed him; others wondered why it was that whenever a holdup or killing occurred, he was invariably fifty miles away. Presently the unvoiced suspicion spread that he was not only protecting the thugs, but that he was the actual leader of the gang. Plummer, cocksure of himself, failed to realize that he was treading on quicksand.

It seems unnecessary to dwell at length on the day-to-day life of Virginia City, for it was tailored to the pattern established in other gold camps that preceded it. In the beginning the six miles of gulch above town wound through hillsides of pine and Douglas fir, with little groves of quaking aspen in the sage. Fires and man soon denuded the hills and left the beautiful natural setting ugly. Daylight Creek, a sparkling, fast-running stream as it came down the gulch and cut through town, quickly became polluted and befouled. Every stick of dressed lumber used in slapping buildings together had to be hauled the seventy-five miles from Bannack, which made it expensive.

Many of the business buildings were so poorly and hastily put up that in a year they were sagging. The narrow streets were a sea of mud after every heavy rain. High-wheeled, heavily laden wagons often sank to the hubs in the mire, requiring as many as sixteen yoke of oxen to extricate them. The principal intersection at the corner of Wallace and Jackson Street collected so much water that a wag put up a hastily scrawled sign reading:

Wallace Street has been chartered a canal.
A ferry boat will be put at the Jackson
Street crossing.

The *Montana Post* thought this good enough to warrant printing it on its front page.

Along with the gamblers and thugs had come the whores—painted, coarse-grained castoffs of the St. Louis underworld. A little later came the pigtailed, heathen Chinese. They huddled together at the foot of Wallace Street, and with their well-known facility for establishing themselves on foreign soil, they soon had their own shops, gambling dens, joss house and theater. They were thrifty, industrious and hard-working but, preceded by the threat, first raised in California, that it was their evil intention to put the white man out of his job, no claim-owner would employ them. That prejudice did not extend to their women, dainty little things who were much more desirable in a miner's eyes than the overage prostitutes on Cover Street. It became the highlight of the evening to crowd into the Chinese "theater" and watch them cavorting in their silk pantaloons and screeching songs that were discordant and not understandable to white men's ears. Their favors were purchasable, the negotiations being conducted by the girl's owner.

Virginia City had a fighting mayor with the improbable name of Paris F. Pfouts. His firm, Pfouts and Behm, was one of the leading wholesale and retail establishments in town, along with Dance and Stuart, Tootle and Leach, and Rockfellow and Dennee. All were agreed that the almost daily murders and robberies were injuring their business and imperiling the future of the town, and that something had to be done, even if it meant imposing vigilante law. The events of the following two days convinced them that the time for action had come.

It was mid-December. Out hunting near Ives' hangout in the Ramshorn Mountains, Bill Palmer killed a grouse. Going to recover the bird, he found it had come to earth beside the frozen, bullet-riddled body of Nicholas Thalt, a young German miner who had been missing for a week. Palmer went to Ives' place and, finding Long John Franck and George Hilderman there, asked them to help him carry the body to his wagon. They refused. Palmer got the dead man to Nevada City, a mile up the gulch from Virginia City, where it lay for the rest of the day. Several hundred miners, idled by the freeze-up, came to gawk at it and swear vengeance on the young German's killers. They were convinced that the guilty parties were George Ives and his pals.

At dawn a large party set out for Ives' place. They found Ives,

Long John and a man known only as Tex there. They put them under arrest and started for Nevada City with them. On the way back they picked up a fourth man, George Hilderman. Ives took it lightly, being convinced that Plummer would put in an appearance, take charge of the "prisoners" and that would be the end of it. Clubfoot George Lane had been dispatched to Bannack with word that Ives had been arrested.

The trial, an open-air affair, began the following morning, a wagon box being used as the judge's bench and another wagon serving as the jury box. As the morning wore on, the crowd grew until it numbered a thousand or more. It included several hundred armed men, among them a number of Plummer's followers. Jim Williams, the sheriff of the district, was on hand with a score of deputies.

A great log fire was kept burning to warm the judge, prosecutor and jury as the trial proceeded. Between the fire and frequent visits to the adjacent saloons, no one suffered from the cold. Ives was found guilty and sentenced to be hanged. Thirty minutes after the verdict was rendered, he was placed on top of a packing box and a noose dropped over his head. When the box was kicked out from under him, he made his drop and strangled to death.

The following day the trial resumed. Hilderman was banished from the Territory under penalty of being shot if seen after the passing of ten days; Long John was freed, having purchased immunity with his testimony; Tex was freed for lack of evidence against him.

On December 23, a proclamation was published over the names of Paris Pfouts and twenty-one other leading citizens that a Vigilance Committee had been formed, for the "laudable purposes of arresting thieves and murderers and recovering stolen property."

Within the next twenty-four hours no fewer than twenty-five additional men, all prominent in the camp's affairs, joined up. It was tantamount to a declaration of war on the criminal element. Sheriff Jim Williams was named captain. Accompanied by half a dozen Vigilantes, he set out for Deer Lodge at once to capture and hang Whisky Bill and Alex Carter. Red Yeager, a gang messenger, got there ahead of them and the two men fled. But the

Vigilantes saw Yeager pass them and surmised why he rode so swiftly. Returning cold and empty-handed, they stopped at Rattlesnake Ranch and captured Yeager. They took him on to Dempsey's ranch on the Stinkingwater and dragged the information out of him that he was a member of the outlaw gang. In an effort to buy himself out of trouble, Yeager named other members and charged Bill Brown, the barkeep at Dempsey's, with having written the warning he had carried to Deer Lodge. That was enough for Captain Williams and his men. They condemned the pair to death. They were found dangling from the branch of a cottonwood on New Year's Day.[4]

Before January was over, a number of bodies were discovered swaying in the breeze beneath a convenient tree. The Vigilantes were doing their job thoroughly, riding hundreds of miles through cold and snow to string up road agents who had been tried *in absentia* and found guilty. On January 9, they went after the boss man himself, Henry Plummer, and two of his lieutenants, Ned Ray and Buck Stinson. Carrying warrants for their execution, a posse under the leadership of Captain Williams set out for Bannack. They knew the saloon crowd was friendly to Plummer and would not support them, but they went about their business and took the three wanted men into custody. Placing them on horseback, their hands tied, they led them to the livery barn and cast their ropes over a projecting beam used for raising hay to the loft. When the nooses were adjusted, they whacked the horses on the flank. The animals bolted and left the three men dangling in the air.

Ned Ray and Stinson went out cursing Williams and his posse; Plummer died screaming and begging for his life. The following morning Dutch John Wagner, a well-known member of Plummer's gang, rode into Bannack not knowing what had happened. The Vigilantes strung him up without ceremony.

Four days later in Virginia City the Vigilance Committee hanged five men, with several thousand miners looking on from windows and rooftops. Early in the morning the town had awakened to find the camp surrounded by several hundred armed men who permitted anyone to enter but no one to leave. Caught in the net were an unknown number of men the Vigilantes had marked for death. Their agents began ferreting them out, and by early afternoon they had rounded up half a dozen. Clubfoot George Lane was one of them, also Jack Gallagher, Frank Parrish, Boone Helm, Haze Lyon and Bill Hunter. During the excitement Hunter escaped by crawling through a drainage ditch.

One by one the captured men were brought before the Vigilante's Executive Committee and sentenced to death. In a body they were marched up Wallace Street to an unfinished building at the corner of Van Buren, where they were placed on packing boxes and ropes adjusted over a convenient beam. They were ushered into eternity, one after the other, amid the jeers of a gawking crowd. Bill Hunter, the escapee, was captured on January 2 and promptly shared the fate of the others.

In a matter of days the Vigilantes had hanged twelve men. It left eight more on the list Red Yeager had given Captain Williams. Learning that the eight had taken refuge at Hell Gate (Missoula), two hundred miles to the north, they set out in below zero weather, took the culprits by surprise and strung up all eight.

Twenty-one men hanged in less than a month! It was a sort of record. But before the Vigilantes coiled and put aside their ropes, they strung up a man for a killing he had perpetrated on February 14. Two weeks later the notorious Jack Slade was lynched on the overhead crossbeam of the Elephant Corral gate with the Committee's approval.

Slade was not a member of Plummer's gang. Aside from being obstreperous when he was in his liquor and shooting up a saloon, he had done no wrong in Virginia City. But he was a recognized "bad man" and his past reputation did him in.

As the weather moderated and miners began to return to the diggings, they found, for the first time, that the roads and trails were safe. There were no more hangings, but the Committee continued to round up and punish petty criminals, flogging those who were found guilty. Honest men did not object to the highhanded methods of the Vigilantes. For two years they were in absolute control. Then their ranks were infiltrated by newcomers to Montana of dubious character. Fortunately for the public good, elections were held and civil officials elected as the Vigilante movement crumbled and went out of existence.

In 1864 the great strike in Last Chance Gulch at Helena, second only to Alder Gulch, was made. Half of the Virginia City crowd stampeded over Boulder Hill to the new diggings, merchants and shopkeepers joining in the exodus. In a matter of a few weeks every other building in the surrounding camps, such as Nevada City and Junction, had a For Rent sign on its doors. It was a lasting blow from which Virginia City never recovered. But the big firms, doing a wholesale as well as a retail business, like Dance and Stuart and Pfouts and Behm, felt it less than the others, Helena having to draw its supplies from Virginia City. The old camp had an open road to Fort Benton, head of Missouri River navigation, to the east, and the railhead of the Utah Northern a few miles to the west. (It should be interjected that no railroad ever laid its tracks into Virginia City.)

But that strangle hold did not last long. The Legislature handed out toll road and toll bridge charters with reckless abandon. Presently several thousand men were engaged in one way or another in the freighting business between Fort Benton and Helena. With goods and food moving in freely, no matter what the weather, there was no repetition of the flour riots that had bedeviled Virginia City in 1865, in which the price of flour was forced up to a dollar a pound.

In 1874, as the result of much politicking and skulduggery, Montanans were given the opportunity to vote on moving the capital from Virginia City to Helena. Helena won. "Old Virginia," as it soon came to be called, began to fade rapidly. There wasn't much reason for it to continue; the placers that had made it rich and famous were exhausted, and business had gone elsewhere.

Very few people noticed, but Mormon ranchers had put several thousand sheep on Montana ranges, and two young Germans, Nick Bielenburg (sometimes referred to as "Butcher Boy" Bielenburg because his first connection with cattle was as a retail butcher) and his friend Konrad Kohrs, had trailed in between twenty-five hundred and three thousand ungraded Oregon cattle of crossed Shorthorn and Durham strains and were ranging them on the headwaters of the Madison River. The herd had been driven across the rocky, sun-parched Idaho plains from the western crossings of the Snake River and brought into Montana by way of Raynold's Pass. Of course no one saw in these feeble beginnings the birth of a great livestock industry that was to populate Montana's vast, empty ranges until they were second to none in America.

In the decade following the rush to the Alder Gulch diggings, changes had been wrought in western Montana that must have seemed incredible even to the men who were responsible for them. Eastern Montana—the cattleland of the future—remained largely as it had been in the days of the fur traders and trappers, with a remote military post or two supposedly maintained to guarantee the safety of the white man against Indian attack. Actually eastern Montana was still Indian country. The nomadic Blackfeet, Crows and Sioux came in to collect their Government annuities but otherwise roamed wherever fancy dictated, their war parties stealing horses and taking scalps. Steamboats on the Missouri were fired on or burned if they grounded.

By 1873 the fur trade had lost its importance. Of far greater concern to the Indians was the wanton slaughtering of the buffalo. No longer were the plains black with shaggies. Growing Indian wrath boiled over three years later in the Battle of the Little Big Horn in which Custer and his immediate command were annihilated. It was at once both the Indians' greatest victory and most crushing defeat, for never again were they to confront the troops in battle. (Wounded Knee, in 1890, was a massacre, not a battle.)

The hostiles were put back on their reservations and military posts established to keep them there. The Northern Plains became safe for the white man, if not for his property. Bielenburg and Kohrs (Con Kohrs to all who knew him) and other pioneer cattlemen began moving their herds out on Montana's virgin ranges. Being unsurveyed land, title to it could not be taken, but simply by being in possession a settler could lay claim to it. The rush to get in on a good thing attracted capital, and by 1879 cow outfits were digging in as far east as Arrow River and Judith Basin.

There was not a more interested observer of what was occurring than Granville Stuart. He had disposed of his several business interests and was a wealthy man at forty-five. Although already widely known and respected as one of the Territory's foremost pioneers, in the summer of 1879 he took the step that was to bring him everlasting fame as the victorious leader of the great Horse Thief War and father of the range-cattle trade of Montana.

XIX

Raw Land

The first big and adequately financed outfit to put cattle on Montana grass was organized by Granville Stuart under the firm name of Davis, Hauser and Company.

"During the summer of 1879," to quote Stuart's journal, "a co-partnership was entered into between A. J. Davis of Butte, Erwin Davis of New York City, Samuel A. Hauser [later governor], and Granville Stuart of Helena, Montana, for the purpose of engaging in the business of cattle raising. The capital stock of the firm was one hundred fifty thousand dollars. The brand was 'H.' The firm name Davis, Hauser and Co. The interests were divided into thirds; the Davis brothers one-third, Hauser one-third, and Stuart one-third. I was elected superintendent and general manager and instructed to begin at once to look about for stock cattle that could be purchased at a satisfactory price."

He is in error in saying the original brand was H; it was D-H. But that was changed almost at once when it was found it could not be burned without blotching. It then became the D-S, with the firm name altered to Davis, Hauser and Stuart.

"By the first of January," Stuart continues, "I had contracts for about two thousand head that could be purchased in Montana and Oregon. The price paid ranged from $14 to $17 per head according to the number of steers in the bunch. The young calves were thrown in with the mothers. By the first of March I had contracted an additional two thousand head of Oregon cattle."

Throughout his long career on the range Stuart's early preference for Oregon cattle (and Oregon horses) never lessened. Over the years he bought them by the thousands, sending trail crews across Idaho to Burns and Baker City, Oregon, and often going himself. Between 1882 and 1886, when more than half a million Texas Longhorns were put on Wyoming and Montana ranges, he stocked the D-S almost exclusively with Oregon-bred cattle, in which, as has been previously noted, the Durham strain predominated.

Their color and configuration were not uniform, traits that breeders of purebreds came to prize. But they were chunky, put on more weight than the Longhorn, were excellent foragers, were easier to work than Texas cattle, and had the stamina to survive the bitter Montana winters. Oregon horses held many of the same advantages over the smaller Texas mustang. They were strong-legged and sure-footed, were equally intelligent and easier to handle.

A word or two should be said about the great reservoir of livestock that had been accumulating for years in eastern Oregon, and for which, prior to 1877, there was no market. In the four decades when thousands of emigrants had made their way over the Oregon Trail, the majority had reached their destination with a cow or two (barnyard cattle), as well as oxen, bulls and horses. Turned out to graze on virgin grass, they had multiplied beyond belief. The root stock of Oregon's horse herd came from several sources, the animals the pioneers brought in being implemented by the fine animals the Hudson's Bay Company had brought in during the years when Great Britain was in possession of the country, and by excellent strains of Indian ponies bred by the Nez Percé.

It is a matter of record that before any market developed, Oregon was so glutted with cattle and horses beyond any conceivable internal need that they were sold for as little as three dollars a head. When Montana and Wyoming stockmen put in an appearance, the price skyrocketed to fifteen dollars. John K. Rollinson, in his estimable *Wyoming Cattle Trails*, says: "They were a bargain at fifteen dollars. A horse that could be bought for that price in Baker City was worth forty dollars when it reached Wyoming." [1]

The range cattle business in Montana and Wyoming followed a somewhat parallel course up to and including the years of the so-called "Beef Bonanza," the one great difference being that the Longhorn never achieved the dominance on Montana ranges that it did in Wyoming. Geography had something to do with it. Wyoming was easily reached by the great herds of Texas cattle being driven up the Texas Trail and the Goodnight Trail. They were turned out on Wyoming grass without any thought being given to what the range would sustain. It was not until overcrowding became apparent that the trail herds were sent on north into Montana. Ultimately overgrazing was to compound the disaster that struck the High Plains from the Canadian border to Texas in the great die-up of 1887.

Long before stock growers everywhere became convinced that the white-faced Hereford was the best of all beef range animals, the Longhorn's preeminence was being eclipsed by cross-breeding it with Oregon Durhams. In fact by the time the swing to the Hereford became widespread, the full-blooded Longhorn had all but disappeared from the High Plains. The bulls were sold for what became known as "bologna beef." The Texas mustang was also disappearing and being replaced by the Oregon horse. All that remained of the great Texas invasion of the north were the cowboys and their drawl. "These men were bred and born on the range," wrote Stuart. "Their understanding of cattle was almost supernatural, their patience, ingenuity, faithfulness, and loyalty to their outfit can not be described." [2]

In the early spring of 1880, Stuart set out from Helena to find range on which to locate the D-S home ranch. The weather was at its worst, with snow, freezing rains and icy winds. For much of the time—twelve weeks in all—he traveled alone. It was not until after he had crossed the Yellowstone, far to the south, explored the valleys of the Big and Little Horn rivers, Rosebud Creek and the forks of Tongue River that, in Miles City, he engaged two men to accompany him. Following a wide sweep to the northeast without finding what he wanted, he turned west and crossed the

Musselshell. He was looking not only for good grass range but for hay land from which as much as a hundred tons of hay could be cut for winter feeding. Permanent flowing water and timber were also essential.

On June 29, on Ford Creek, a sparkling stream that came tumbling down out of the Little Snowies, to the south, and within several miles of the foot of the Judith Mountains, he found what he was seeking. It was all there—water, grass, hay land and a magnificent stand of yellow pine. As Brigham Young is alleged to have exclaimed on gazing at Salt Lake Valley for the first time, Stuart could have said, "This is it!"

D-S cattle that were being held on the Beaverhead were started for the home ranch at once, while an advance crew arrived on the scene to construct the needed buildings. Neighbors were non-existent. But that situation changed drastically a few weeks later, when Captain Dangerfield Park and two companies of the Third U.S. Infantry marched in and began building Fort Maginnis (named for Martin Maginnis, Montana's Congressional Delegate). The land Captain Park marked off for the military reservation included more than half of the hay meadow Stuart had laid claim to. He protested to no avail. It was the beginning of his long feud with the army.[2] In one of his blasts he wrote: "The officers constantly drink to excess. The men are young, mostly foreigners (German and Irish) and so incompetent that they couldn't find their way to the privvy after dark without a lantern. Instead of protecting the white rancher against marauding Indians, their real concern is to safeguard the Indian's fancied right to depredate and steal at will."

Throughout his active years on the range, Stuart's favorite target was the whole Indian Reservation system, which he held to be responsible for the degradation of the Indian: "The annual appropriation of the government for several years has been ample to board every one of the agency Indians, big and little, at a first-class hotel, yet somehow all of this money does not seem to fill a long felt want (for the Indians either) for he remains the same dirty poverty-stricken thief that he became when first placed on a reservation. It is a well-known fact everything brought from the East shrinks most awfully in this high, dry altitude, yet this scientific fact would hardly account for the portly and robust appropriations becoming so thin and emaciated, that when they finally reach the Indians they are like the darkie's fish, 'all swump up.' The Indian knows he is being robbed and in turn becomes a thief, stealing our horses and eating our beef [the result of] the united efforts of the government and the reservation agent to 'civilize' and enlighten the Indian by so far as possible isolating and cutting him off from civilization."

By the first of October the D-S home ranch buildings were almost finished. Out on the range line, cabins had been built. Stuart had designed the main house, a U-shaped building consisting of two large cabins, with loopholes, standing some forty feet apart and connected at the rear by a paling of logs set into the earth in an upright position. The space between the buildings, closed at the front by gates, was to be used as a corral in which a dozen horses could be penned. It gave the place the appearance of a fort. As additional buildings were required, it was Stuart's intention to build them around two sides of a square to form a compound, leaving the southern end open for entering and leaving. When the furnishings and his books arrived from Helena, followed a few days later by his Indian wife and their three daughters, the place began to take on a homey air.[3]

In the seven months prior to September, 1881, there had been an amazing increase in the number of beef cattle turned out on the grass of eastern Montana, the total approaching the one hundred thousand mark. The D-S had brought in a second five thousand head and an additional one hundred horses; Bielenburg and Kohrs had three thousand head on Flat Willow; James Fergus an equal number on Armell's Creek; Power Brothers and Charles Belden had brought two herds into Judith Basin; Robert Coburn and Henry Sieben between them had another five thousand head on Flat Willow. In Custer County an English company brought in five thousand Texas cattle and located their home ranch at the mouth of Otter Creek. Many smaller outfits had located on Elk Creek and elsewhere, while two hundred and eighty miles to the east, the Northern Pacific Railroad, recovering from its financial disaster, had finally crossed the Missouri River at Fort Union and was driving its rails up the Yellowstone.

It had been an unusually dry summer and the expected autumn rains had not fallen. On September 16 a prairie fire was reported burning out of control on the Grass Creek range. A hurried call for help was sent to the various ranches.

"We sent a crew of men," says Stuart, "when reports of a fire on Crooked Creek near Haystack Butte were sent in and men hurried to that locality, then a disastrous fire near Black Butte that threatened to destroy a horse ranch. Fires sprang up in all directions almost simultaneously and spread with alarming rapidity. The flames swept up McDonald Creek at the rate of a mile a minute. Great columns of black smoke rolled up in every direction, filling the air with ashes and cinders. At night, lines of flame crept along the ridges, flinging a lurid glare against the sky line. For ten days every available man in the country, with wet gunny bags, fought the flames with desperation, some of them sinking in their tracks from exhaustion. In spite of almost superhuman efforts more than five hundred square miles of the finest grass land in eastern Montana lay a blackened waste. We lost no fences or hay but the loss of so much grass was a [severe] hardship." [4]

As a rule a prairie fire resulted from man's carelessness or lightning. In this instance with the skies holding clear and a number of fires burning in different directions, it was obvious that they were of incendiary origin. There was a meeting of stockmen at Fort Benton to discuss the situation and form a protective association. The consensus was that the bands of Canadian Indians that had crossed the border and invaded Montana ranges were responsible for the losses many had suffered. In the past these Indians, Northern Piegans, Assiniboines, Bloods and Crees, had crossed the international boundary at will to hunt buffalo. They were now finding it as agreeable and more profitable to slaughter the white man's beef and steal his horses.

The losses to stockmen resulting from the incursions of the Canadian Indians totaled an estimated $60,000. As a result a campaign was launched that drove the intruders back across the line. With them went the whisky peddlers who had triggered most of their depredations. Bull-Who-Goes-'Round and other chiefs were warned that if they and their bands reappeared on American soil, they would be met with gunfire.

The Eastern Montana Stock Growers' Protective Association requested the Government to place more troops on the boundary. The matter was referred to General Terry, commanding the Department of the Missouri, who declined to act, having no troops available for patrolling the border. The newspapers found nothing alarming in the situation until it was learned that the Montanans had dispatched a sharply worded communication to Major James Crozier, commanding the Canadian Mounted Police at Fort McLeod, demanding that he take steps to prevent British Indians from violating the boundary. Without justification many newspapers came out with scare headlines warning that an international incident was in the making. Actually the British were as anxious to keep their Treaty Indians on their reservations as the Americans were.

The authorities at Fort McLeod and Fort Walsh recovered eighteen stolen horses and turned them over to the sheriff of Chouteau County. Other animals were recovered. These summary measures had a good effect on the Indians. After a small party of Bloods were caught with a number of fresh hides in their possession and three were killed on the spot, an equal number escaping, there was very little depredating from the north. But shortly thereafter Montana stockmen were to be confronted with a plague of range thievery from another direction that made their past difficulties with the Canadian Indians seem trivial.

Despite Stuart's low opinion of the military, he acknowledged that the nearness of Fort Maginnis had some advantages: it gave the D-S telegraphic communication with the outside world, a post office and a place where most supplies could be purchased, which relieved its isolation.

The long, severe winter of 1881-1882 was at hand. On December 11, twenty-four inches of snow fell. There was very little sage on the D-S range to hold it, but there wasn't wind enough to blow the snow away. The temperature moderated for several days, then plunged to sixteen degrees below zero. The snow crusted and the cattle could not get to the grass which, though sear, was as nutritious as ever, the grama not dropping its seeds until spring. Stuart and his crew were on the range every day, spreading hay and keeping waterholes open. Other outfits were doing the same. Large gray timber wolves, running in packs, were everywhere. When a rider set out in the morning, he carried strychnine with him to poison the carcass of any cow or steer that had been pulled down during the night. Every brand was suffering losses, the extent of which could not be estimated with any accuracy until the spring roundup.

Stuart placed the D-S losses at thirteen per cent: five per cent to native Indians; five per cent to predators; three per cent to weather. Other outfits suffered more severely. The English company on Otter Creek, in Custer County, was almost completely wiped out. "Their cattle [all Texans] did not reach Montana until late in the fall and they were thin and worn from the long drive," wrote Stuart. "Practically the entire herd perished. The sheriff of Custer County could find but one hundred and thirty-five head in the spring to satisfy a judgment held by Charles Savage of Miles City for supplies. The cowboys with the outfit were never paid their wages." [5]

An excellent calf crop tended to offset the heavy losses. Losses were a part of the business. Following the publication of Brisbin's *The Beef Bonanza*, which pictured in glowing colors the wonderful possibilities of the range cattle business in Montana, magazines and Eastern newspapers printed all sorts of tales about the ease and rapidity with which vast fortunes were being accumulated by the "cattle kings." In such accounts profits were figured at one hundred per cent and no mention made of severe winters, storms, parched summer ranges, predatory animals, hostile Indians and rustlers, or of the danger of overstocking the ranges. What followed was what might have been expected. Herd after herd of Texas cattle were put on Montana ranges by outfits that knew little or nothing about the cattle business. Anxious to learn, they joined the Montana Stock Growers' Association with which the Eastern Montana Stockmen's Protective Association had affiliated. At the summer meeting in Helena, in 1883, two hundred and seventy-five "members" were present.

"Things were changing so fast you had to be there to believe it," Granville Stuart recalled. "By the 1st. of October there were six hundred thousand head of range cattle in the Territory, together with several hundred thousand sheep and a great number of horses. It was as much stock as the ranges could safely carry. In the fall of 1883 there was not one buffalo remaining on the range and the antelope, elk and deer were indeed scarce." [6]

X X

The Horse Thief War

In view of what occurred elsewhere, it was freely predicted that the increasing number of sheep being put on Montana ranges would lead inevitably to a sheep-cattle war. Contrary to such expectations, no serious confrontation occurred. That was due in large measure to the fact that many cattlemen were setting aside part of their range for sheep. But there was a sanguinary conflict just ahead on another front.

A conservative estimate of the value of Montana livestock (excluding sheep), spread out over seventy-five thousand square miles of practically uninhabited country, amounted to $35,000,-000. But great as the investment was and although stockmen were paying a major share of the tax money the Territory was collecting, the very nature of their business left them without any Government agency to which they might look for assistance in protecting their property against the range thieves who were rapidly becoming a scourge.

During the summer of 1883 there were few, if any, stockmen who escaped being hit by the widespread plundering. However, it was not until after the pooled beef roundups that fall, when tallies could be compared, that the losses of the past six months due to rustling were realized. The most startling figure arrived at pertained to the number of horses that had been stolen. Rustlers could quickly get horses out of the country and run into Canada or Dakota. Once in their hands there was little chance of recovering them.

Without horses the range cattle business could not function. That sobering fact set off some wild talk. Con Kohrs, a heavy loser, declared that the situation called for the application of vigilante law; that a regiment of cowboys be formed and sent out to string up every horse thief they located. Others were of the same opinion. But for the moment the fiery talk and threats of reprisals did not get beyond the talking stage.

Stuart was among those present at Custer station, eighty-five miles west of Miles City on the advancing Northern Pacific, from which the D-S had shipped its beef after a drive of only one hundred and twenty-five miles.[1] He agreed with his friend Kohrs that something would have to be done to put down the rustling, but he insisted that whatever action was taken should not be in the name of the Stock Growers' Association, which later could be held accountable in the courts. He took that same stand at the second annual meeting of the Association in Miles City in April, 1884, at which four hundred and twenty-nine members were present, including the Marquis deMores and Theodore Roosevelt from Dakota and representatives of the Wyoming Stock Growers' Association.

"My talk did not have the conciliatory effect that I expected and seemed only to add fuel to the fire," says Stuart. "The Marquis was strongly in favor of a 'rustlers' war' and openly accused me of 'backing water.' The Marquis was strongly supported by Roosevelt. In the end cooler heads prevailed and it was voted that the Association take no action."

It is obvious from what followed that his position was misunderstood by his associates; he was as ready to take action as anyone, but that whatever had to be done should be done by individuals who were ready to accept responsibility for whatever they did.

There was a meeting of stockmen at the D-S soon after the spring roundup. Stuart never identified who was present. It cannot be doubted, however, that they were the men who planned and successfully waged the great Horse Thief War that broke the back of organized outlawry on Montana ranges, and that Con Kohrs was one of them.[2]

When the Northern Pacific crossed the Missouri River, it marked the virtual end of the Missouri's steamboat trade. Fort Benton, which at one time had dreams of becoming the country's leading inland port, began to dry up at once. As the steamboats disappeared, the woodyards along the river were abandoned. They furnished a splendid rendezvous for horse thieves and rustlers. Bates Point and Rocky Point and the mouth of the Musselshell were their favorite hangouts. Pouchette Creek and other old yards farther down the river were also gathering places for them.

If they can be said to have had a leader, it was John Stringer, a former buffalo hunter and wolfer, better known by his sobriquet of Stringer Jack. He was a tall, handsome man, with piercing gray eyes, and fairly well educated. Unlike the men with whom he associated, he never drank to excess. Why he chose such a life cannot be explained unless it was the power he wielded over ignorant men and the danger to which such a calling exposed him.

The ranchers who met at the D-S in May, 1884, surely at Stuart's request, regarded themselves as a vigilante committee, pledged to bringing law and order to the range by eradicating the thieves who were preying upon it. They were all brand owners and not hired hands. They had a fairly good idea of who the men were that they were going after, and where to find them. But wanting to be sure, they decided to hold off for a month. Two of their number were appointed to gather additional information in the interim.

On June 25, Narcisse Lavadure and Joe Vardner, suspected horse thieves, came up the Judith River and, unnoticed, pulled up above the pasture where J. A. Wells had a small herd of cattle, guarded by a single cowboy. Lavadure and Vardner saw that the cowboy had a string of eight horses, which interested them. After watching the place for the better part of the morning, they saw the cowboy saddle up and cross the river. As soon as he was out of sight, they rounded up the seven remaining horses and hurriedly drove them up the river. They had not got far when they encountered Bill Thompson, a neighboring rancher, who recognized the animals and ordered the two men to stop. Lavadure answered by whipping up his gun and firing at Thompson. But his horse plunged as he fired, and the shot missed its mark. Thompson, who was well armed and mounted, gave chase. He shot and fatally wounded Vardner. After a run of six miles he captured Lavadure and brought him and the horses back to the Wells ranch, where he found Wells, his cowpuncher and a third man. It was decided to lock up the prisoner for the night and take him to Lewistown in the morning and turn him over to the sheriff. Thompson went home. During the night a party of armed men broke into the cabin in which Lavadure was being held and took him outside and hanged him.

On July 3, Sam McKenzie, a Scottish half-breed, was caught in a canyon a few miles west of Fort Maginnis with two stolen horses in his possession. After the horses had been positively identified as having been stolen from the Rezin Anderson ranch, McKenzie was hanged from the limb of a cottonwood.

The committee was beginning to take toll.

On July 4, another incident occurred at Lewistown, which was still no more than a small village, during a Fourth of July celebration, that confirmed the committee in their determination to rid the range of undesirable characters. In mid-June two suspicious-looking men, who answered to the range sobriquets of Rattle Snake Jake Fallon and Ed (Red) Owen, had ridden into Judith Basin with a small band of horses with a variety of brands, not proof positive but a likely indication that the animals had been stolen elsewhere.

Fallon and Owen rode into Lewistown early in the afternoon and after drinking in Crowley's saloon for an hour, they joined the crowd that had gathered at the race track at the edge of town where the festivities were to occur. Young Bob Jackson, wearing the Uncle Sam costume in which he had led the parade that morning, passed close to Owen. For some unaccountable reason the sight of the youngster in his grotesque garb infuriated Owen and he knocked him to the ground with the butt of his revolver, then made him crawl around in the dust like a snake.

A number of men, sensing trouble, hurried back into town and in Powers' store armed themselves with Winchesters. They had taken up positions on either side of the main street when the two desperadoes appeared. Stepping down from the saddle, they drew their guns and challenged the suddenly deserted street.

Owen spied Joe Doney, a cowboy by occupation, peering at him from around the corner of Powers' store. He walked toward him at once, gun leveled, and was within a few feet of the plank sidewalk when Doney shot him in the stomach. A second shot struck Owen's gun hand, causing him to drop his revolver. He quickly recovered it and snapped a shot at Doney which missed as the latter darted into the store.

There was shooting up and down the street. A bullet from Crowley's saloon struck Fallon in the side. Looking back, he saw that Owen was down on his knees but searching the hostile street for a target. Dropping down beside his partner, he caught young Benjamin Smith and Joseph Jackson (Bob Jackson's brother) as they dashed across an open space beyond the tent of an itinerant photographer, in town for the holiday. Fallon's first shot grazed Jackson's cheek and the second one pierced his hat. The third one lodged in Smith's brain, killing him instantly.

Up the street, Owen and Fallon continued to load and reload their guns until the last vestige of life was blasted out of them. Their demise was only the beginning of a Fourth of July that Montana was to remember.

Billy Downs, the ex-wolfer, was well known along the Missouri. He had a dubious reputation. At the close of steamboating on the river he had established himself and his wife at an abandoned woodyard at the mouth of the Musselshell, selling whisky to the Indians and living on other men's beef. In addition, he was suspected of being a member of Stringer Jack's horse thief ring. Although warned to mend his ways or find himself in trouble, he had continued to surround himself with the worst characters on the river. The time for talking had passed, and on the night of July 4, a committee of vigilantes arrived at his place and called on him to come out. This he refused to do, but after a short parley he stepped out, accompanied by a notorious character known as California Ed. They admitted stealing ponies from the Indians, but denied that they had any horses belonging to white men. They could not account, however, for the twenty-six horses in their corral, all bearing well-known brands. They claimed that the quantity of dried meat found in the house was buffalo meat, notwithstanding the fact that there had not been a buffalo on the range for two years. In the stable there was a pile of fresh cowhides, salted and folded for shipment, bearing the brand of the Fergus Stock Company.

That was enough for the vigilantes. Downs and California Ed were led to a grove of cottonwoods and hanged.

At the same time that one group of vigilantes left for the mouth of the Musselshell, another party left for Rocky Point, where two notorious horse thieves known as Red Mike and Brocky Gallagher were making their headquarters. They had stolen about thirty head of horses from the Smith River range and had also been operating on the Moccasin Range, and holding the stolen animals somewhere in the Badlands. The thieves crossed the river with a band of horses just before the vigilantes arrived. They were pursued and captured ten miles north of the Missouri and the horses recovered. When a tree was found, the two men were strung up without ceremony.

At Bates Point, fifteen miles below the mouth of the Musselshell, at an abandoned woodyard, lived old man James, his two sons and a nephew. It was the favorite haunt of Stringer Jack, the boss horse thief. In addition to the log cabin there was a stable and a large corral built of logs connecting the two buildings. In a wooded bottom a hundred yards from the main cabin was a tent built of poles and covered with wagon sheets. In the cabin lived old man James, his sons, his nephew Frank Hanson, and Bill Williams. Stringer Jack, Paddy Rose, Swift Bill, Dixie Burr, Orvil Edwards and Silas Nickerson made their home in the tent. Eleven men in all. When the vigilantes arrived during the night of July 8, they divided into three parties, three of their number guarding the tent, five surrounding the cabin, and one man remaining behind with the saddle horses. When they were all set, they waited for daylight.

Old man James was the first to appear. He was ordered to open the corral and drive out the horses, which he did and then darted back into the cabin. Through a porthole beside the door he opened fire on the visitors. The cabin's four walls were pierced with portholes. Almost instantly gunfire was spitting from all sides. A vigilante set fire to the hay stack. The spreading flames soon engulfed the cabin. The five men trapped inside tried to break free but were shot down as they came out with their guns blazing.

Stringer Jack and the others who had been caught in the tent managed to escape temporarily. Only Paddy Rose made it all the way to freedom, being last seen at Fort Benton on his way to Canada. Montana had become too warm for him. Stringer Jack made his last stand in a clump of willows. He was soon surrounded and chose to die fighting rather than surrender. Dixie Burr had an arm shattered by a bullet as he fled, but managed to join Bill Edwards, Swift Bill and Orvil Edwards, who had reached the river and concealed themselves in the brush under the bank.

In the afternoon the four men pushed some logs into the water, constructed a makeshift raft and at dark started downstream on the current. On the morning of the tenth as they were passing the Popular Creek Agency they were stopped by soldiers stationed there and ordered ashore and placed under arrest. Word was telegraphed to Fort Maginnis and Deputy U.S. Marshal Samuel Fischel left at once to take charge of the men and escort them to White Sulphur Springs. At the mouth of the Musselshell the vigilantes met Fischel and relieved him of his prisoners. A log was lifted into position between the roofs of two nearby cabins, ropes looped over it and the four men promptly hanged.

The committee disbanded following the battle at Bates Point. It had accounted for the death of sixteen horse thieves. Some accounts placed the number at nineteen. One hundred and sixty-five stolen horses were recovered at Bates Point and one hundred and nineteen at other places.

In the weeks that followed, a great hue and cry was raised in certain newspapers about the "brutality and arrogance of the Cattle Kings." Granville Stuart answered the critics. "There were but fourteen members of the vigilance committee," he said, "and they were all men who had stock on the range and who had suffered at the hands of the thieves. There was not one man taken on suspicion and not one was hanged for a first offense." [3]

Looking back years later, he could say, "This clean-up of horse thieves put a stop to horse and cattle stealing in Montana for many years."

TROUBLED

WYOMING

XXI

Outlines of Conflict

In the period beginning in 1840 and extending into the 1870's, no fewer than four hundred thousand men, women and children crossed what is today the State of Wyoming. They traversed that wide stretch of plains and mountains from east to west, and save for the several thousand for whom it was their final resting place, there was no thought of stopping. Their destination was the Oregon country, the Salt Lake Valley or more distant California. First came the emigrants in their covered wagon trains, bound for the great basin of the Columbia River and its tributaries, that reputed land of milk and honey about which they knew little or nothing. They didn't waste a thought on Wyoming; to them it was just the accepted way of getting to where they were going.

Pressing close behind them came the Mormons on their great pilgrimage to Zion in the Salt Lake Valley. In 1847 the first of the Latter-day Saints came up the valley of the North Platte, and they continued to come, by wagon and handcart, until sixty-five thousand had passed Fort Laramie, the trading post of the Rocky Mountain Fur Company. In their religious fervor they kept to the north bank of the Platte as they came up the river, in order to escape the contamination of the pioneers (Gentiles) bound for Oregon, who followed the south bank.

The great migration to Oregon was largely over, but the carefully organized trains of the Saints seemed to flow on endlessly. And then in 1849 the cry of gold in California generated a stampede of overnight Argonauts and gold seekers and criminal scum that turned the old Oregon Trail into a crowded, brawling highway, with every man determined by fair means or foul to get to California before the gold was all gone.

The almost constant threat of Indian attack was only one of the many dangers to be faced in crossing the Plains. Among the Forty-niners it was cholera, the germs of which they had brought with them from the Missouri River towns, that took the lives of several hundred. With the Mormons it was exhaustion and starvation in the mountains of Wyoming that thinned their ranks. Few if any died as the result of losing their way. That was almost impossible, for from the valley of the North Platte to South Pass, Wyoming, and the crossing of the Continental Divide, the three trails, the Oregon, the Mormon Road and the Overland to California, were one or, to be more exact, nearly one.

In 1849 the Government bought Fort Laramie, and for the next twenty years it was to be the most important military post in Wyoming. There, in 1851, the first Treaty of Laramie was signed with the Brulé and Oglala Sioux. The agreement called for an initial gift of $50,000, in addition to which there were to be handsome annuities consisting of sugar, coffee, salt, tobacco, clothing and powder. In return, Red Cloud, Spotted Tail, Man-Afraid-of-His-Horses and the other chiefs affixed their marks to the treaty, pledging to stop depredating along the Emigrant Trail, a pledge they had no intention of keeping. They went home well satisfied with their presents and the bargain they had made. A week later a wagon train was attacked as it neared Scott's Bluff. Three men were killed, the wagons burned and the livestock run off. It was the first of many such incidents. In 1855, General William Harney led an expedition up the Platte as far as Fort Laramie, punishing the Indians for the Grattan Massacre in which Lieutenant Grattan and twenty-nine enlisted men were killed on entering an Indian camp a few miles east of Fort Laramie. The depredations stopped for a time, but soon after Harney and his column left the country they were resumed, and they continued throughout 1865, the so-called Bloody Year on the Plains.

It is safe to say that no fewer than three hundred men, women and children were killed by Indians as they followed the great Emigrant Trail. Of that number practically none were Mormons. Their wagons were often stopped and plundered, their cattle and horses stolen, but for some inexplicable reason those singular people were not gunned down and butchered as so many others were. Many theories have been advanced to explain this remarkable fact. The one oftenest encountered is that the Indian's own religion was so steeped in mysticism that he recognized some sort of bond between himself and the spiritually indoctrinated Latter-day Saints.

With the fur trade now only a memory and the buffalo hunters gone to Montana, the permanent white population of Wyoming, excluding the military personnel stationed there, had dwindled. There were no towns; just a score of scattered trading posts. The greatest activity was the freighting business going up the short-cut Bozeman Road to the booming gold camps of Alder Gulch and Virginia City, Montana. The Bozeman Road ran north to the east of the Big Horn Mountains and was open to Indian attack for most of the way. The atrocities committed on the Bozeman Road finally led the Government to take steps to protect it. The Powder River Expedition led by General Pat Connor started north from Fort Laramie to punish Red Cloud's Sioux. Connor had twelve hundred men in his command. He marched them as far north as Tongue River, hoping to bring on a general engagement with the hostiles. But the enemy proved difficult to find. Red Cloud and the other war chiefs must have enjoyed themselves as they maneuvered back and forth, trying to lure the troops into a situation from which they would not be able to extricate themselves. In the fall, Connor returned to Fort Laramie, his only accomplishment having been the burning of an Arapahoe village on Goose Creek.

A few months later, in the spring of 1866, the War Department authorized the construction of a line of forts up Powder River. Forts Reno, Phil Kearney and C. F. Smith were built and garrisoned, only to be left woefully undermanned and inadequately supplied. It quickly became apparent that they were too far apart to support one another when attacked, which occurred almost at once.

The forts were an affront to the Indians, and warriors from different tribes flocked to Red Cloud's banner in a united campaign to destroy them. The bloody, long-drawn-out Red Cloud War was at hand. It was to be costly in the number of lives lost, both sides suffering heavily. Never before had the Plains Indians confronted the white man in such numbers. Most estimates agreed that at the peak of his power Red Cloud had no fewer than seven thousand well-armed and determined fighters to throw into battle.

There must be a few readers who are not familiar with two of the highlights of that campaign—the Fetterman Massacre in which eighty-one soldiers were killed, and the Wagon Box fight at Fort Phil Kearney on August 2, 1866, in which 1,137 Indians were slain. Red Cloud's losses were so severe that he was forced to retire and regroup his warriors before attacking elsewhere.

To the south, and despite being under the constant threat of Indian attack, the building of the Union Pacific Railroad went on at a frenetic pace. The work crews, protected by military escort, and the workmen themselves, trained to throw down their shovels and pick up their rifles at a moment's notice, were laying as much as four miles of track in a single day. Before the season of 1867 closed, the rails reached what almost overnight became the canvas and tarpaper town of Cheyenne. To it flocked several thousand assorted thugs, outlaws, gamblers, pimps and their women.

The prediction that once the railroad came through, Wyoming would begin to boom, that thousands of ranchers and homesteaders would rush in and take up land, was not realized. The lag was attributed to the Government's failure to stamp out the Indian revolt. In the Eastern press so much had been published about the wily chief of the warring Sioux that Red Cloud's name had become a household word. In the face of a growing demand for peace at any price the harassed Government dispatched a board of commissioners to Fort Laramie to treat with the hostiles.

Red Cloud, knowing he held the winning hand, refused to meet with them until the forts on the Bozeman Road were abandoned. The Government capitulated. But Red Cloud was in no hurry to talk peace. In fact, six months passed before a treaty was signed, and he was the last of the assembled chiefs to affix his signature. His demands were extravagant. They included the deeding of all lands north of the Nebraska line and between the Big Horn Mountains to the west and the Missouri River to the east, including the western portion of present South Dakota and all of present Wyoming north of the North Platte River, to the Sioux and affiliated tribes. As finally signed, it expressly stipulated that "no white person or persons shall be permitted to settle upon or occupy any portion of the same; or without the consent of the Indians . . . to pass through the same." [1] In the shaky peace that followed the signing of the second Fort Laramie treaty in 1868, the War Department built and garrisoned new forts to the west of the proscribed line. Gold had been discovered at South Pass on the Continental Divide in 1867 by a Mormon prospector. Several finds were made and they were substantial enough to start a rush in the spring of 1868. Perhaps as many as twelve thousand men were soon working the Atlantic, Strawberry Gulch and other nearby diggings, a considerable percentage of them Mormons from Salt Lake City, the principal source of supplies. They were harassed by the Indians of that region—Utes, Shoshones, Bannocks and Snakes, all expert horse thieves.

With the South Pass mines attracting nationwide attention, a group of what their emissary, Dr. Hiram Latham, described as "public-spirited citizens" sent him to Washington to petition the Congress to cut the umbilical cord that bound the district known as Wyoming to the mother Territory of Dakota, and to establish it in its own right as the independent Territory of Wyoming.

Dr. Latham must have been a very persuasive talker as well as an excellent lobbyist. He had been in Washington only a few days when the subject of Wyoming began to attract some attention. He caused to be printed a circular letter calling attention to its as yet unexploited mineral resources, its equitable climate, fertile soil and thousands of square miles of virgin grasslands in Big Horn Basin alone, on which untold numbers of sheep and cattle would soon be grazing. The good doctor distributed his letter personally to the members of both Houses of Congress.

There were, he stated, 35,000 American citizens living in the district that by popular usage was known as Wyoming. He cited the rapid growth of Cheyenne, claiming for it a population that already exceeded five thousand. He spoke in glowing terms of little Laramie City (not to be confused with Fort Laramie, a hundred and some miles to the northeast), which had become a thriving community of fifteen hundred prosperous people.

His figures were more than a modest exaggeration of the facts. But there was no one to say him nay. A bill organizing the territory was introduced in the Senate in June and approved. A month later the Committee on Territories of the House confirmed it. On July 25, President Andrew Johnson affixed his signature to the legislation and the Territory of Wyoming was an accomplished fact.[2]

One of those myths that refuse to die has it that the first Texas cattle appeared in Wyoming following the historic "Meeting of the Rails" at Promontory Point, Utah, on May 10, 1869, which marked the completion of the first transcontinental. Actually, the thousands of laborers building the Union Pacific Railroad had been eating Texas beef for almost three years, coincident with, or shortly after, the opening of the Kansas cattle market at Abilene. Beef cattle had been bought in great numbers at Abilene and driven north across Nebraska to Ogallala and sold to the commissary department of the railroad contracting firm. One of the most successful of such buyers was John Wesley Iliff. He had come to Colorado in 1859 as a young man. After trying his hand at running a store for two years, he turned to the range cattle business and established himself at Fremont's Orchard, a cottonwood grove on Crow Creek about fifty miles east of Denver on the South Platte.

Iliff was soon on his way to becoming rich and famous as one of the great cattle kings of his day, often ranging as many as eighteen thousand head of cattle at his Fremont's Orchard headquarters. Over the years Goodnight delivered to him between twenty-five to thirty thousand Longhorns. He bracketed Iliff with John Chisum as the "greatest cowman I ever knew." Speaking of his first meeting with Iliff, he says: "He came to the Apishapa where I was holding a trail herd. After looking the cattle over, he said he would buy them if I would deliver them at Cheyenne, which I agreed to do."

Goodnight's old partner, Oliver Loving, had trailed cattle to Denver but not north of there. What Goodnight agreed to do meant lengthening the Goodnight-Loving Trail to Wyoming. Keeping Denver to his west, he headed due north after crossing the Arkansas and reached the mouth of Crow Creek about where Greeley now stands. Going up Crow Creek, he arrived at Cheyenne with the first herd of Texas cattle to reach Wyoming. He delivered another herd to Chugwater the following season. After that he did not trail north of Iliff's headquarters at Fremont's Orchard, but the trail he had blazed soon became the highway for Texas herds going north.

Some beef cattle were being driven north out of Utah to the South Pass mines. Sheep from Colorado were also being put on the southern ranges of Wyoming. No cattle were entering the vast area from which white men were barred by the second treaty of Laramie. A few cattle were being driven into the Big Horn Basin from Montana. But as late as the early 1870's, Wyoming's interminable miles of undulating grasslands remained unpopulated.

The Territory had been divided into five immense counties, each larger than the State of Kentucky, running from the Colorado boundary northward to the Montana line. Laramie County, in which Cheyenne, the designated capital of the Territory, was located, was the first of the five counties to organize and provide a shadowy semblance of law and order.

It has been said, and with much justification, that the white man never signed a treaty with the Indians that he did not violate when it was in his interest to do so. In rebuttal, it can be stated that the Indians failed to live up to their part of the bargain. That was particularly true of the Plains Indians. In the eight years following the second treaty of Laramie, signed in 1868, in which they pledged themselves to peace, they continued to raid and kill whenever and wherever they deemed it safe to do so. Sometimes they miscalculated and were shot down. But despite the minor victories they achieved. it must have been discouraging to the Indians to realize that for every white man they killed two seemed to appear to take his place, while their tribal strength was being continually weakened by epidemics of cholera and smallpox that were sweeping them away by the hundreds.

Undoubtedly Red Cloud's greatest achievement, and which

was responsible for the victories he had won, had been his ability to weld the different Sioux tribes into a unified whole, their intertribal differences forgotten. That cohesiveness had begun to disappear soon after the signing of the Treaty of Sixty-eight. Even over his own Oglalas his authority began to be questioned. Spotted Tail, the principal chief of the Brulé Sioux, had broken with him, only to be murdered by one of his ambitious tribesmen, very likely at Red Cloud's urging. In the north the Hunkpapa and Minniconjou Sioux were divided between so-called "friendlies" (those who had voluntarily allowed themselves to be placed on reservations, to be fed and given allotments in money and clothing by the Government) and the "hostiles," who were determined to win or perish in an all-out "holy" war with the whites. The grievances of the latter were great. In violation of existing treaty rights, a military expedition under then Lieutenant Colonel Custer, masquerading as a "scientific party of exploration," had invaded the Black Hills, the sacred *Paha Sapa* of the Sioux. Gold had been discovered. Despite the half-hearted and futile efforts of the Army, the rush of prospectors into the forbidden country had begun. Other flagrant violations made the great Sioux War of 1876 inevitable.

Under such provocation the ranks of the hostiles swelled until they spoke for the entire Sioux Nation and the Northern Cheyennes as well. Whipped up by Sitting Bull, the able Hunkpapa medicine man, politician and—to give him his due—patriot, thousands of Sioux had left the Agencies and taken to the hills to join chiefs Gall, Black Kettle, American Horse and Crazy Horse, the last acknowledged to have been the greatest of all Sioux war chiefs.

The Government regarded the worsening situation so serious that before the end of the year (1875) one third of the United States Army was poised for action on the borders of the great Sioux Reservation. Runners were sent to the camps of the hostiles ordering them to return to their various agencies by January 31, 1876. If they failed to do so, the Army would be sent in to return them forcibly. If they came in peacefully, a Government Commission would meet with them at Red Cloud's Pine Ridge Agency to discuss their grievances. An estimated three thousand hostiles gathered at Pine Ridge, ate the food the Government provided, and

listened to the Government's offer to buy a million acres of Sioux
lands at a price to be agreed on.

This talk of dismembering their homeland for a price had no
effect on Sitting Bull or Crazy Horse, other than to confirm them
in their determination to fight the white man. As soon as the grass
came on strong and their ponies grew fat, they struck. We know
what followed: General Crook's defeat on the Rosebud and the
Custer disaster on the Little Big Horn.

Why the victorious Sioux suddenly decided to lay down their
arms and sue for peace was not because they were abashed by the
audacity of what they had accomplished. The reason was to be
found in the provision that the Congress attached to the Indian
appropriation bill that summer. It stated that unless the Sioux
agreed to give up the Black Hills and the western hunting
grounds, they would no longer be issued supplies at their agencies.
For eight years they had been receiving Government handouts
and they had become dependent on them. To have them cut off,
confronted them with a situation that left them no choice but to
submit.

When they signed the Black Hills Treaty in 1877, they signed
away their pride in themselves as well as the land they cherished.
As they lost their dominance, peace on the plains became possible.
No region was as quick to profit by it as Wyoming. As though a
log jam had suddenly been broken, thousands of Longhorns began to come up the Texas Trail and spread out over its lush
ranges.

Ninety per cent of the cattle that entered Wyoming from the
south were driven up the Texas Trail from Ogallala, Nebraska.
Coming up from the south, that is between Dodge City or Hays
City and Ogallala, the trail was known in the beginning as the
Jones and Plummer Trail. That name fell into disuse soon after
the Union Pacific built through and Ogallala took on some im-
portance as a receiving and shipping point. Located on the South
Platte, it was only a few miles across the bottoms to the North
Platte. Herds going north usually crossed the bottoms. In times of
high water they crossed at Julesburg, thirty miles to the west.

Once the Texas Trail had left the North Platte, it followed
what in time was to become the Sidney and Black Hills stage-road,

until Cottonwood Creek was reached. It then swung across to Hat Creek and on to the Belle Fourche, then over to the Little Powder and down that stream to its mouth. It pointed for Tongue River then and followed the Tongue to the Yellowstone, which it crossed at Fort Keogh. From there it ran up Sunday Creek, across to the Little Dry and after reaching the Big Dry climbed over the divide and on to Lodge Pole Creek and the Musselshell, where it ended.

Over its unwinding miles passed a vast number of Texas Longhorns, perhaps as many as half a million, as well as thousands of Texas mustangs and hundreds of Texas cowboys. In fact, the Texas invasion reached such proportions that it was suggested facetiously that Wyoming change its name to North Texas. To say that the sudden growth of Wyoming's range cattle population was even more miraculous than had occurred in Montana, cannot be dismissed as a senseless exaggeration, when the number of cattle reported for tax purposes in 1878 totaled 375,000 head. With the exception of a few thousand "pilgrim cattle" that had been shipped by rail to Ogallala from Midwestern feed lots and driven north into Wyoming, and a trickle of Oregon cattle, all were Texas Longhorns.[3]

Even at that early day seeds of the troubles that were to beset the Territory had been planted. It was taken for granted that sheepmen and cattlemen would clash and that the outlaw and the range thief would have to be dealt with. No one appears to have given much thought to the settlers (referred to derogatively as nesters) and the homesteaders who were taking up Government claims, turning under a few acres of prairie sod and producing enough hay to feed their few animals. Many of them, it was alleged (which undoubtedly was true), were improving their financial condition by slapping their unregistered brands on any maverick they encountered, as well as by butchering an occasional steer.

The newcomers, the "farmers," few of whom had had any previous acquaintance with the mold board of a plow, continued to come in in increasing numbers. Whether to be near relatives, friends, or for some unknown reason, the majority gravitated to the country east of the Big Horns on the lower Powder, Clear Creek and Crazy Woman Creek. If they had searched Wyoming over, they could not have chosen better. They built towns, sur-

vived, even prospered, and it was not long before they succeeded
in getting the northern third of Carbon County chopped off from
the mother county. Needing a name for their new county, they
drews slips out of a hat and the winner was Johnson County. From
Buffalo, the county seat, a horseman could ride for two days in
any direction without crossing the county line—unless he was in
a great hurry, as was sometimes the case.

As yet these were only peripheral problems that would be
handled in a satisfactory manner—satisfactory to cattlemen—as
soon as they found time off from getting rich to organize. Get-
rich-quick tales of the fortunes to be made in Wyoming had not
only traveled the Eastern seaboard of the United States but across
the water to England and Scotland. Being easy to reach by train,
wealthy Americans and titled foreigners began stepping down
from Mr. George Pullman's Palace Sleeping Cars at Cheyenne.
Some of them fell into the hands of sharpsters. But even that
gentry did not find it necessary to improve on the facts. ("Free
grass, by courtesy of Uncle Sam! No costs beyond the paltry wages
of a handful of cowboys. No capital investment worth mentioning
—a few rude log buildings thrown up on the public domain. No
risks—simply buy a herd and nature would do the rest.") [4]

Of course annual losses to predators, rustlers and disease could
be expected, but they were lumped together at a modest two per
cent. Weren't the winters severe? Yes, but the rugged Texas Longhorn could take care of itself. As for the prolific Texas cows,
they would double an investment of $200,000 in three years, in
addition to returning an annual dividend of seven to eight per
cent

The men who dealt in such figures were not all knaves; some
were just fools who believed they were dealing with the truth. As
for the avaricious simpletons who plunged into the range cattle
business, about which they knew nothing, they ended up broke
and disillusioned. It wasn't only the small investor who lost; half
a dozen of the big British-owned companies failed. The great
Prairie Cattle Company, launched in Edinburgh with a capital of
half a million pounds, failed with tremendous losses to its stockholders. The Swan Land and Cattle Company, another Scottish
speculation, failed due to chicanery and mismanagement. In the

aftermath, several British-owned outfits hurriedly liquidated their holdings, suffering great losses but saving something. It seemed after all that there was something more to the range cattle business than sitting in the Cheyenne Club sipping champagne and relying on the doctored book count of a ranch manager.

Obviously, some powerful, stabilizing force had to be found to combat the chaos and stagnation that threatened the future of the range cattle business. Into the breach stepped the little, and almost unheard-of Laramie County Stock Association, which suddenly blossomed forth as the Wyoming Stock Growers' Association. It was destined to become the most powerful, ruthless and tyrannical of all stockmen's associations anywhere.

It soon not only controlled the law, it *was* the law, recognizing no authority higher than its own. It either bought or subsidized leading newspapers, imported paid gunmen to carry out its edicts and marked for extinction a number of men and at least one woman.

Association policy was formulated, directed and enforced by its secretary, Thomas Sturgis, an effete, competent and arrogant young New Yorker, and his brother William Sturgis, the assistant secretary, who had reached Wyoming by way of Missouri. For more than ten years, 1876-1887, Tom Sturgis was the most powerful man in the Territory. He was a founder of the Wyoming Stock Growers' Association, president of the big, Boston-financed Union Cattle Company and the first president of the Stock Growers' National Bank. But he overreached himself, and when he left Wyoming in 1893, he had little to show for his twenty years on the Plains.

XXII

Years of Greed and Disaster

Skip a few years and consider Wyoming as it was in 1885. What Granville Stuart had predicted had happened: more cattle had been brought in than the ranges could support. And still they came. Herds of Longhorns reaching Ogallala found a ready sale. Under new ownership they were sent on north, oftener than not by the same trail outfit that had driven them up from Texas, the "Texians," as they liked to call themselves, being seduced into "giving Wyoming a whirl" by better wages than they were accustomed to earning.

For the past ten years Oregon cattle had been arriving in Wyoming by the thousand. Many had been driven into the Big Horn Basin; the rest had been trailed on east to the Pine Ridge Agency or turned out in the overcrowded Powder River country. That fall at the various pool roundups so many outfits ran a wagon (which meant a crew of six to eight men), that to old-timers it was unmistakable evidence of how the range was being overstocked. That it had happened in three or four years seemed incredible. They turned away, shaking their heads, wondering where it would end.

The fall beef roundups raised another and even more distressing problem: why had so few mavericks been gathered? Of all the reports reaching Secretary Sturgis in Cheyenne, the most dismal came from Johnson County, where the settler-homesteader-nester faction were most numerous. It was evidence enough for him that they were the guilty parties, running off every unbranded critter they could put a rope on and later marking and branding them at their convenience.

What was a maverick? By definition, any calf or yearling that had escaped the branding iron. Could an owner identify such critters? Of course he couldn't. But the range on which such an animal was found was, by established range law, taken as prima-facie evidence of its ownership. On finding a maverick, didn't it occur to a cowboy working for a big outfit, who was starting a little herd of his own on the side, that it would be immensely more profitable to burn his own brand rather than his employer's on the calf or yearling? Of course. And many of them did. If it bothered his conscience, he had only to remind himself that it was common knowledge that many of the so-called cattle kings had got their start in that fashion.

Secretary Sturgis had been waging war on mavericking for several years without much success. There were members of the Association, all in good standing, who showed little interest in his war on range thievery. He knew, or at least must have surmised, that their lack of enthusiasm sprang from the fact that they were doing some rustling themselves, or at least buying what they knew was rustled stock.

Frustrated by the failure of his campaign up to now, Sturgis trained his guns on the settlers, the so-called "farmers." He derided the idea that they were bona fide farmers. They were not tilling the soil beyond spading up a garden patch and producing a few vegetables for home consumption. But they were acquiring an increasing number of cattle. "Since they have no money with which to buy cattle," proclaimed the Secretary, "they must of necessity be stealing them."

Undoubtedly some of the homesteaders were blotching a brand now and then and picking up a maverick when the circumstances were favorable. Secretary Sturgis knew little about their financial condition. If he had inquired, he would have learned that country banks in such places as Buffalo considered them good risks and were loaning them money. But he had a good argument, and at the spring meeting of the Association he jammed through his infamous "maverick law."

Only once before in the history of the range cattle business had a powerful stockmen's association imposed such a rule on its members. It was cruel, inhuman and destined to fail. Over Granville Stuart's strenuous objections the Montana Stock Growers' Association had voted in favor of such a measure, and then rescinded it before it took effect. In Wyoming, with Tom Sturgis cracking the whip, it was a different story. Under threat of expulsion from the Association if they failed to comply, which meant among other things that they would not be permitted to take part in the roundups, the members were ordered to discharge any foreman or cowboy who owned a brand or cattle. It was further ordered that no owner could give employment to such blacklisted men.

This was a reversal of what had been standard practice since the beginning of the range cattle business. Goodnight, Chisum, Iliff, Head, Granville Stuart and other stockmen whose names are famous, had subscribed to that. Goodnight summed it up when he said: "Helping an ambitious man to get ahead by permitting him to run a few cows with your own is the best way of rewarding him for his loyalty."

There were owners in Wyoming who felt that way. They dragged their feet about firing trusted men, but a second warning from Sturgis whipped them into line. Many good men left the Territory for other ranges. A few turned to rustling for a livelihood and found it both financially and emotionally rewarding. There was added zest to stealing from a man who had done you wrong.

On the evidence, it appears that Tom Sturgis relished his position as the embattled leader of the powerful faction that regarded Wyoming as a rich and juicy dukedom belonging exclusively to themselves and having no higher purpose than their own enrichment. The group represented practically all of the Eastern and foreign money that was invested in the so-called Beef or Cattle Bonanza.[1] In addition, Sturgis had the solid support of half a dozen or more ranchers who had arrived in the Territory in 1879 and amassed fortunes in a few short years. They included Judge

Joseph M. Carey, President of the Wyoming Stock Growers' Association.

Carey was enjoying a spectacular career, and it was far from over. He had arrived in Wyoming shortly after the close of the Sioux War and set himself up as a lawyer. In 1879 he was appointed U.S. Attorney for Wyoming Territory. On borrowed money he had launched into the cattle business and put together what was now the great CY outfit, the most profitable operation on Powder River.[2]

For a sounding-board Sturgis had the Cheyenne *Leader,* the most important newspaper in the Territory, safely in his pocket; it published nothing concerning the livestock industry until it had cleared it with him. Still obsessed with the maverick situation, he rewrote the laws governing Association roundups. Henceforth, mavericks gathered in the roundups were to become the property of the Association. They would be sold at auction and the money so derived would go to defray roundup expenses, including the wages of range detectives and stock inspectors. Any surplus would be put into the Association's general fund.

Word got about that an average price of ten dollars a head would be satisfactory. Blacklisted cowboys thought that was fair. Jack Flagg had a little money. He attended the first auction and was permitted to bid, which was better than he had expected. But an Association representative ran the price up and up. Jack Flagg was no man's fool. He realized what the game was, but he played along with it until he exposed it for the fraud it was: no blacklisted cowboy or nester was to be permitted to purchase an Association maverick.

The course Sturgis was pursuing was eminently successful in intensifying hatred of the Wyoming Stock Growers' Association. Even in the Cheyenne Club, with its white-jacketed bartenders, French chef and imported waiters from Chicago, there was grumbling, the more outspoken members saying he was going too far. The fighting Buffalo *Bulletin* dubbed him "an architect of disaster."

Brushing off the bars and criticism directed at him, Secretary Sturgis continued his campaign to entice Eastern money to Wyoming. Beginning with Strahorn's *Handbook of Wyoming and*

Guide to the Black Hills and Big Horn Regions and Brisbin's *The Beef Bonanza, or How to Get Rich on the Plains,* the stream of promotional books, pamphlets and brochures had continued to flow from the presses. Without exception they were composed of exaggeration and financial fables. Even so, they produced results when placed in the hands of gullible Easterners. Western railroads and stock associations bought quantities of them and gave them wide distribution. Secretary Sturgis bought a thousand copies of a little item by his friend Colonel A. T. Babbit, manager of the successful Standard Cattle Company, entitled *The Grazing Industry and the Beef Supply.* He shipped five hundred to John Clay and Company, the leading Chicago livestock commission firm, and five hundred to the Wall Street firm of Clark, Dodge and Company, asking them: "Please give these to your clients." [3]

For six years Wyoming had enjoyed a succession of what for the Plains was considered wet summers. Grass had never burned out, but in 1886, as early as late June, reports began reaching Cheyenne to the effect that wide stretches of range on the Cheyenne River, Black Lightning Creek and the South Fork of the Powder were so bare that a strong northwest wind was enough to set the dust devils to dancing. Conditions worsened as the summer wore on. The small creeks stopped flowing. Even such a sizable stream as the Rosebud was reduced to pools of stagnant water, so impregnated with alkali that cattle would not drink it. For the same reason cowboys refused coffee made with it.

A dry summer was a new experience for Wyoming. Cattle suffered and failed to put on weight. Overcrowding made it impossible to move a herd to unused range. As a consequence, stock that was shipped east that fall was of a poor quality. They reached Omaha, Kansas City and Chicago on a dropping market. Packers and feed-lot operators combined to drive prices still lower. Back in Wyoming, Sturgis and the subservient press denied that the cattle industry had suffered a serious setback; the market was down, but they predicted it would quickly recover. Ed Towse, political hatchetman of the Cheyenne *Leader,* poured forth glad tidings of what the coming year would bring.

Little he knew of what it would bring. Wyoming was about to come face to face with disaster. It was not to be contained within any manmade boundary lines. Not only were Montana and Dakota to be scourged, as well as Wyoming, the icy bite of death was to grip the High Plains from Canada to the Texas Panhandle.

Cattlemen could have done nothing about the weather, but they were responsible for the greedy, willful overstocking that, when calamity struck, made the wholesale destruction of their herds inevitable. Had they heeded the warnings of the past summer, it would not have saved them, for it was already too late.

Although the story of the tragic winter of 1886-1887, which cowboys were to refer to as "The Great Die-up" and one of our leading Western historians has christened "The Winter of Death," [4] has had many tellings and retellings, it seems never to grow threadbare. Of the several first-hand accounts by men who lived through it, the most poignant is Granville Stuart's. The "big storm," as he calls it, which impoverished so many cattlemen ruined him financially. But of his own losses he has little to say, other than when a final tally was made they amounted to sixty-six per cent of the D-S herd. If sturdy, northern-bred, "favored" cattle could not survive the Arctic blasts, what chance did the late arrivals from Texas have that had been turned out in the fall on ranges already grazed to the roots? The answer is none. Ninety per cent of them perished.

Being a humane man, Stuart's concern was for the suffering of the cattle that died by the thousand. A steer made its way into the ranch yard and stood staring at the house as though dumbly imploring help as it froze to death. It happened in many places. The ghostly visitors were even dying on the main streets of Lewistown and other towns.

When Stuart established the D-S in 1881, thick brush and tall rye grass along the streams afforded cattle excellent shelter. That was all changed, fenced in now; the bewildered brutes piled up against the fences and died there. For weeks no trains ran. When the rails had been cleared, passengers shuddered at the sight of mile after mile of rotting carcasses beside the tracks.

Back in October, when the so-called "fall work" was over, the big Eastern-owned outfits reduced their crews. It followed that when the severe storms of January and February turned the world into a freezing wilderness, they had few men on the range. That few, for forty dollars a month, did more than any owner had the right to expect of them. Many bore the scars of that terrible winter for the rest of their lives.

Hardheaded John Clay, the former Chicago commission man and a giant in his own right, who always managed to keep a tight rein on his emotions, had been brought out from Chicago to untangle the affairs of the great Swan Land and Cattle Company. Years later he penned his explanation of the disaster that brought the range cattle boom to a painful finale. "Three great streams of ill-luck, mismanagement and greed now culminated in the most appalling slaughter of animals the West had ever seen or would see again, second only to the slaughter of the buffalo."

He might have gone further and mentioned its effect on men. Granville Stuart did, and his often-quoted words have become a fitting epitaph for an era that was gone. "A business that had been fascinating to me suddenly became distasteful. I never again wanted to own an animal that I could not feed and shelter."

Just how severe was the weather that wrought such havoc? On January 9, the first storm of the year struck. Gale-driven snow fell for sixteen hours and the thermometer plunged to twenty below zero. On January 11, a second storm howled down out of the north, depositing sixteen inches of snow on the level and piled up in drifts twelve to fifteen feet deep. For three days it snowed continuously, the thermometer never rising above twenty below.

Bad as these early storms were, they were only the prelude to what followed. On January 15, the temperature dropped to forty-six below, and it remained there for ten days, during which time blizzard-driven snow whipped across the landscape without an hour's respite. On January 29 the air was suddenly free of snow. The sun shone and a mild thaw set in. It lasted for two days, long enough to melt the top snow and form pools of water. The temperature dropped during the night of January 31. By morning Wyoming and most of Montana were sheathed with ice. The cattle left alive were so weak that few could break through the crust for grass. Jagged ice stripped the hide from the legs of those that succeeded. Blood stained the snow as they floundered about.

Storm succeeded storm throughout February, and it was well into March before they began to lose their ferocity. On March 20, a timid sun greeted the coming of spring. The ordeal was over. The creeks freed from their long confinement were soon running over their banks; grim-faced owners appeared on the range to tally what little they had left.

Throughout the terrible winter no word of disaster appeared in the newspapers controlled by Secretary Sturgis. Instead, they published fantastic tales about how cozy things were in Wyoming. Such tales were for the moneyed East, not for home consumption. Sturgis made sure that this deceptive pap was what it received. Obviously he was hoping to put off the day of reckoning until after the spring roundup, when the losses would prove to be not as great as he had good reason to believe they were.

Only a handful of members attended the spring meeting of the Association. Horace Plunkett, the ablest of all the English-Scottish imports, including the flamboyant Moreton Frewen, whose dreams of empire had collapsed and sent him scooting back to England, came down from the EK, the home ranch of the Frontier Land and Cattle Company on the North Fork of Powder River. He had made himself the most hated (by cowboys) cattleman in Wyoming. They had three counts against him. He was responsible for the attempt of the Association in 1886 to cut their wages from forty dollars to thirty dollars a month—a move that had been aborted when the men refused to work the roundup. They hated him no less for putting through the rule of no more free meals for cowboys riding the grubline. Plunkett had also sponsored the roundup boycott rule (clearly illegal) which prohibited nonmembers from participating. It meant freezing out the little feller with a hundred head of cattle. They hated him for that, too.

Plunkett was an aristocrat, not a snob, but the difference was sometimes difficult to discern. Cowboys never understood him, and although he spent nine years on the range, it must be said that he never understood them. With few exceptions he had little respect for his fellow owners. "They regard stock-raising as a gamble, not as a business," he noted. "They keep their figures in their head; never on paper."

He had suffered heavy losses in the winter just past, but he was still solvent. With only one or two exceptions could the others attending the spring meeting say the same. He knew Tom Sturgis was bankrupt, and he was not surprised when Sturgis submitted his resignation as secretary and announced he was returning to New York. Wyoming's cowboy population was glad to see him go. They raised their glasses in mocking farewell toast. Thomas B. Adams took his place. They were to find him no improvement on his predecessor.

It was obvious to all that the "good old days" of the free-grass range cattle business had ended; that henceforth the scourging of 1887 would be recognized as dividing the old from the new. Many lessons should have been learned. But few were. Perhaps that was because men—many no longer young—who had lost a fortune and had the grit to make a fresh start had no room in their single-track minds for anything else.

The Fremont, Elkhorn and Missouri Valley Railroad, later absorbed by the Chicago and Northwestern, had been building up the Platte for several years. It crossed the Wyoming line in 1887 and reached the town of Douglas. The railroad brought in a stream of settlers, almost a hundred per cent of whom took up claims on the numerous creeks in what are today Converse, Campbell and Johnson counties. It gave the eastern section of the Territory a population per square mile that was exceeded only by Laramie County (Cheyenne). The newcomers arrived with the built-in conviction that the cattleman was their enemy, and they did not lose it.

The scales were tipped more in their favor a year later when the Fremont, Elkhorn and Missouri Valley built on westward to the up-and-coming town of Casper, the county seat of newly organized Natrona County, which had been sliced off the original Carbon County, a sizable bit of real estate. Larger than all but two of our Eastern states, it included the valley of the Sweetwater and embraced the Rattlesnake Range in its western limits.

Thousands of sheep were being ranged in Natrona County. Since sheepmen and settlers regarded each other as natural allies against their common enemy, the cattleman, they felt reasonably secure. And they might have been if the sheepmen had exercised reasonable restraint, but ignoring the warnings they received, they brought in more and more bands until several hundred thousand sheep were grazing on Natrona County grass.

Innumerable conflicts occurred between cattlemen and sheep-men—such as the one in which Charles Goodnight was involved on the North Fork of the Canadian in the Texas Panhandle. Almost without exception they have been called "sheep-cattle wars." In truth, fewer than half a dozen deserve to be called "wars." What occurred in Natrona County was a "war," and it well may have been the most costly of all. It began in the summer of 1888 when Joel Hurt trailed three thousand sheep into Natrona County and did not sputter out until 1909. It cost the lives of an unknown number of men and thousands of sheep.

The cowman's bill of particulars against sheep went beyond grudging the animal the grass it ate. It included the grass it destroyed. Being gregarious and close-herded, a band of sheep cut a swath across the range with its upper and lower teeth (which the cow did not possess), grazing grass to the roots and digging up the roots with its sharp hoofs and then tamping down the soil so that it had no porosity left and could not renew itself. Furthermore, cattle would not feed where sheep had passed, their droppings leaving an odor that cattle would not tolerate. Nor would they drink water sheep had polluted.

This was utter nonsense, all of which was forgotten when stockmen discovered that there was as much money in sheep as in cattle, perhaps more, and put their own flocks on the range.

"Cowboys were known to stand off from a band of sheep and with their rifles pick off sheep after sheep until they had exhausted all their ammunition," says Alfred James Mokler in his *History of Natrona County, Wyoming.*[5] "If a herder should attempt to fight back, he, too, was generally shot at. A favorite source of amusement of some of the cowpunchers was to gather a hundred or so head of steers and drive them pell-mell through a flock of sheep, killing many and scattering the rest in all directions. Others have driven hundreds of sheep over a steep precipice. All that was necessary to get a band of sheep started over a bank was to start a few of the leaders off and then the whole band would go over with a rush and cause a 'pile-up' of the poor dumb brutes, and they were either killed from the fall or smothered by being piled one on top of the other from ten to twenty deep.

"This practice of brutality, destruction and death was kept up for about twenty years In the Sweetwater country numerous sheep camps were burned, the sheep killed and the herders shot at . . . but the men who committed these depredations were never brought into court for the reason that those who had suffered the losses were reasonably sure that a trial in the courts would result in a farce and only cause more trouble."

In the days of the open range and for some years after it had been fenced off, the cowboy and the herder had nothing in common. They were as different as the occupations they pursued, and it was said, with no little truth, that you couldn't make one out of the other. The cowboy led a vastly more exciting life. Although he worked for wages—miserable wages—it was his quixotic belief that he was nobody's "hired man." Even in a winter line-camp he was seldom alone. On the other hand, the sheepherder was a loner, his dog his only companion. Once a month or thereabouts he could expect the camp-tender to arrive with a sackful of grub. His only other visitor was likely to be the boss, come to order the flock moved to a new range.

The statements of Mokler and others that upwards of a hundred thousand sheep were destroyed in the twenty-year conflict in Wyoming cannot be dismissed as ridiculous exaggeration, nor is there any reason to doubt that as many as a dozen unexplainable murders in Natrona, Johnson and Big Horn counties resulted from that struggle.

"On the night of the 24th of August, 1905," says Mokler, "ten masked men visited the Louis A. Gantz sheep camp, which was located about forty miles from the town of Basin, and they clubbed and shot to death about 4,000 head of sheep, burned the camp wagons and shot a team of horses valued at $400. About $700 worth of grain and provisions were also destroyed. The Gantz sheep, about 7,000 in number, were being taken to the Big Horn forest reserve and the settlers along the foothills of the mountains complained that the stock was being moved unnecessarily slow and that they were destroying the home range of the settlers."

That this was a tale invented by the cattle interests to throw the responsibility for the raid away from themselves and on the so-called "settlers" seems patent. No court record reveals that any complaint against Gantz was ever filed.

"The men who committed this crime," Mokler continues, "were so bent on destruction that even the sheep dogs were tied to the wagons and burned. The men who were in charge of the sheep were given some provisions and told to leave the mountains and never return, and they lost no time in complying with the demand."

Gantz suffered his loss as many sheepmen had before him. "Nothing was ever done to bring the guilty men to justice," comments Mokler, "although it was well known who perpetrated the heinous crime."

Presumably he could have named them. Perhaps his failure to do so can be attributed to the fact that he was at the time the publisher of the *Natrona County Tribune* and in no position to risk losing the advertising patronage of the secret government that controlled the State. He had spoken out against the lynching of "Cattle Kate," in 1889, and the "Invasion," in 1892. When three sheepmen were brutally killed on No Water Creek, in the Ten Sleep country, between Thermopolis and Worland, the *Natrona County Tribune* came out fighting and blowing up such a storm that the Wyoming Wool Growers' Association offered a large reward for the apprehension of the murderers. Of the crime and the arrest of the killers, he says:

"On April 3, 1909, Joe Allemand, a sheepman from Natrona County, with his camp mover, Joseph Emge, and sheepherder, Jules Lazier, were shot to death in the night time and their bodies burned. The wagons were destroyed by fire and many sheep were slain. The crime was so revolting and aroused such wide protest that the Wyoming Wool Growers' Association took the unprecedented step of offering a large reward for the apprehension of the murderers. At the session of the grand jury held in Basin the first part of May, true bills were returned against George Sabin, Herbert Brink, Milton Alexander, Ed Eaton, Tom Dixon, Charles Faris, and William Keyes.

"At the November term of the district court, Faris and Keyes turned state's evidence, with the understanding that they should not be prosecuted. Brink was the first to be tried and he was found guilty of murder in the first degree, and was sentenced to be hanged, but a compromise was made with the court and it was

understood that the sentence would be commuted to life imprison-
ment, provided two of the others would plead guilty to murder in
the second degree and the other two would plead guilty to arson."

None of the six was in any danger of being hanged or spending the rest of his life in the penitentiary. They were men of no
consequence, just saloon roughs with records of many arrests for
petty crimes. But expensive Cheyenne lawyers had arrived in
Basin to conduct their defense. Their involvement in the case
wasn't any more difficult to explain than the prosecutor's willingness to make deals with men against whom he had evidence
enough to send every one to the gallows.

Faris and Keyes went free. The other five received sentences
ranging from life to as little as three years. Their sentences were
reduced a year or two later. Governor Joseph M. Carey parolled
George Sabin and Herbert Brink and they soon shook the dust of
Wyoming off their heels.

In killing the three sheepmen, Brink, Sabin and the others had
obviously been carrying out what the *mafioso* call a "contract."
They had done their job but had been caught. To protect itself,
the party of the second part had to protect them. And they did.
What force in Wyoming was powerful enough to engage expensive
attorneys, suborn prosecutors, judges and penitentiary officials?
Was it the Wyoming Stock Growers' Association? Was there any
other?

You decide. You be the jury.

XXIII

Tragedy on the Sweetwater

By 1889, two years after the great disaster of 1887, the range cattle industry of Wyoming was back on its feet. It was no longer the wildly speculative business it had been. With very few exceptions the British-Scottish-Irish element had withdrawn; hard-nosed Americans now owned or controlled practically all of the big outfits, and, as the Territory's heaviest taxpayers, they were determined to run Wyoming as they wanted it run. But even the protective folds of the symbolic black flag of the Wyoming Stock Growers' Association could not conceal the fact that there was trouble on the horizon. Wyoming was being criss-crossed by railroads; week after week they were bringing in more and more settlers. Mostly, these new arrivals were citizens of the United States and endowed with the Constitutional privilege of the ballot box. Joining with the others of their kind who had preceded them, they could vote and vote—and elect judges, prosecutors, sheriffs and other county officials.

What from the beginning had been a class war between the haves and the have-nots, took on new dimensions; the little fellers were not running scared any more. In Johnson County, seven men working for the Hat outfit on the Red Fork of the Powder were tried on six different charges of cattle stealing. They were ac-

quitted on every count, although the evidence left no doubt that
they were as guilty as all hell.

This was not the first time it had happened. What makes the
incident worth recording is that the Hat was unashamedly the
most notorious rustling outfit in Wyoming. It was put together in
1888 by Jack Flagg—previously mentioned—who had been a burr
under the saddle of the Wyoming Stock Growers' Association ever
since it had blacklisted him for owning a registered brand and a
hundred or so head of cattle. Soon after buying the Hat brand,
Flagg took in four partners, selling each a fifth interest in the outfit. Like himself, his partners were all able range men and had
been blacklisted by the Association. Being sworn enemies of the
big owners, they proceeded to make them all the trouble they
could.

Flagg's partners included Al Allison (his honest name was Martin Allison Tisdale and he was the son of John Tisdale who was
to play an important role in the Johnson County trouble). The
other partners were Billy Hill, Lou Webb and Thomas Gardner.
All were young men. Hill was suspected of having committed several minor robberies; the others bore good reputations, harassing
the cattle barons and running off their cattle not being considered
a heinous offense. In fact, no offense at all.

After the charges brought against them in Judge Micah Sau-
fley's court in Buffalo had been dismissed, the Judge walked out
of the courtroom and, pausing on the courthouse steps, said to Joe
DeBarthe, the editor-owner of the Buffalo *Bulletin* and no friend
of the cattle kings: "They were as guilty as any men I have ever
tried. I don't know how the stock interests are to protect themselves."

His words were music to DeBarthe's ears and he gave them the
widest possible circulation. Down in Cheyenne, H. B. Iams, sec-
retary-elect of the Wyoming Stock Growers' Association, surveyed
the assembled executive committee in dismay after reading aloud
the account of the trial in the Buffalo *Bulletin*. "Gentlemen, you
know what this means. We can't get a conviction in Johnson
County."

Colonel Iams, a veteran of the War Between the States on the
Union side, was a garrulous, flamboyant character, overflowing

with schemes and ideas for the continuing and exclusive use of the free range by the Association. Some had been tried. They had failed, as in the present instance. But if redress could not be had by hailing rustlers into court, there was another way in which range thievery could be put down. If stock detectives were instructed to use their guns instead of spending their time gathering evidence and making arrests, rustling would quickly lose its attractiveness.

Whether this was another one of Iams' ideas, or suggested by someone else, it had his support when put into practice. Within a month, two men were murdered in Johnson County. Neither man was a rustler, but they were friendly with men who were. There were no arrests; no official investigations. But Fred G. S. Hesse, an Englishman and manager of what was left of Moreton Frewen's old 76 spread and owner of the 28 ranch, both on Crazy Woman Creek, was suspected of knowing who the killers were. This may have had no more relevance than that he was a widely hated man.

The two killings and a number of instances in which men were fired at from ambush, as the Wyoming Stock Growers' Association cracked down on suspected cow thieves, did not have the expected effect; instead, rustling increased. Jack Flagg speaks of a herd of two hundred and fifty head of cattle being spirited across eastern Wyoming in a single operation and sold in Dakota. Whether true or not, it was evident that the gulf between the big owners and the small fry had deepened.

The Association's star detective was an efficient, saturnine, handsome individual who went by the name of Frank M. Canton in Wyoming. His honest name was Joe Horner. Back in the seventies he had left Texas in a hurry for reasons too obvious to call for recital here. In Wyoming, in 1878, he went to work for the Association as a range detective, an arrangement that was not terminated until 1892. However, in 1882 he got himself elected sheriff of Johnson County and, unsuspected, served in that dual capacity until 1886.

Before, during and after his career in Wyoming, Frank Canton was a merciless, congenital, emotionless killer. For pay, he murdered eight—very likely ten men. When a compiler of one of the so-called "galleries of gunfighters" turns the spotlight on Wyoming, the celebrated Tom Horn, of a somewhat later day, is given the full treatment. Little attention is given to Frank Canton. Perhaps that is because there was nothing glamorous about Canton. Even Jesse James was kind to his mother.

Although the figures compiled by various spring roundups of 1889 revealed a better-than-average calf crop, there was a feeling of unease on the range. Far to the west in the Lost Cabin country Association detectives swooped down on a supposed rustler camp. Men were wounded on both sides. A score of yearlings were recovered. The alleged rustlers went to court, presented a bill of sale showing them to be the legal owners of the cattle, and got a writ for their return. Which, needless to say, was never done, the Association lawyers branding the bill of sale as a fake. The Association had taken a stand on controlling the range and it was not retreating an inch. It was in that spirit that Albert J. Bothwell, the cattle king, and five of his neighbors on the Sweetwater took the law into their own hands and perpetrated the crime that history has properly labeled "the Crime on the Sweetwater"—in other words, the lynching of Ella Watson, a brushwood tart of no consequence, and her ex-paramour James Averell.

Bothwell was a member of the inner circle of the Wyoming Stock Growers' Association. Tom Sun, his neighbor below him at the Devil's Gate, a Frenchman by birth, was a Wyoming pioneer, dating back to fur trade days. He was the first stockman to import Oregon horses and cattle into the Territory. His sprawling Hub-and-Spoke spread was known throughout Wyoming. He was a hard, ruthless man where his interests were threatened. With Bothwell, John Durbin, Ernest McLain, R. B. Connor and R. M. Gailbraith, he claimed sixty miles of range along the Sweetwater. Between them they didn't *own* more than a section or two. They were not interested in *owning* the land; they just wanted to have the exclusive use of it—without cost.

These six men were all members in good standing of the Association. They met together at Bothwell's ranch on the morning of July 20 to reach a decision on a matter they had previously discussed on several occasions. A seventh man was present, George B. Henderson, manager of John Clay's big 71 Quarter Circle, with its headquarters some distance upriver at the Three Crossings of the Sweetwater. Henderson was present as a guarantee of the unity of the big spreads along the river. It had been expected that Clay himself would be there, but Clay, apprehensive of the action to be taken, had absented himself by remaining in Cheyenne and had sent Henderson in his stead. If Clay, shrewd man that he was, figured that by not appearing personally he could not be charged as a party to the conspiracy being hatched if something went wrong, he was grossly mistaken. By picking up the pieces of the bankrupt Swan Land and Cattle Company and putting them back together again, he had made himself a very rich man. In sending Henderson to the Bothwell ranch to represent him, either with or without instructions, he was putting a stain on his reputation that was never to be completely erased.

Since he was not among those present at Bothwell's place that hot, sunny July morning, his version of what took place of necessity had to be a secondhand account. According to Clay, the assembled owners had reached a decision by the time they sat down to their noonday dinner. They were to deliver an ultimatum to Averell and Ella that afternoon, giving them the choice of getting out of the Sweetwater Valley while they still had their health or being forcibly ejected.

There is nothing in the accumulated evidence to suggest that such was the case. Shortly after dinner Henderson left and returned to the Three Crossings; half an hour later, with Bothwell, grim and sadistic, doing the driving, he, Tom Sun, John Durbin and Rob Connor got into a buckboard and set off down the river. McLain and Gailbraith followed close behind in the saddle. All were armed with rifles. The grim business on which they were now embarked was the culmination of three years of strife, dating back to the time when Jim Averell, despite the warnings and threats of Albert Bothwell, had taken up a homestead on the Sweetwater. It was three miles east of Independence Rock, the famous landmark christened "the register of the desert" by Father Jean De Smet, on which thousands of Oregon-bound emigrants had scratched their names.

Averell was thirty-three, a handsome, manly looking ex-soldier, having served several hitches in the army. In addition to his other qualifications, he was well educated, intelligent and foolishly reckless in his condemnation of his powerful neighbors.

At the point where the Rawlins-Lander stage line crossed the old Oregon Trail, he had established what in Western terms was known as a road ranch, where he sold whisky, groceries and such other supplies as cowboys fancied they needed. In three years the road ranch had developed into a profitable business. Too profitable, in the opinion of Tom Sun and Bothwell. They branded the place a hangout for rustlers. Undoubtedly some of the men who patronized it were rustlers. It was equally true that some of the cowboys who spent an hour or two under Averell's roof were employed on the big spreads. As much as they would have liked to do it, Bothwell and the other owners did not dare to forbid their riders the privilege of resorting there.

Although Bothwell did a lot of huffing and puffing about mavericking and rustling, his real gripe was that Jim Averell, despite warnings, had had the effrontery to take up a homestead in what every cattleman along the Sweetwater knew was the Bothwell pasture. If one man was permitted to invade the valley, it wouldn't be long before a second man and a third, and so on, would be moving in. Tom Sun and the others found it a convincing argument and they agreed that Averell would have to be run out. But he refused to scare. He wrote letters to various newspapers complaining about what was being done to him. Only the *Casper Weekly Mail* was courageous enough to publish his blast condemning the "range hogs who by threats of bodily harm and other forms of intimidation are preventing settlers from locating along the Sweetwater."

In particular, Averell closed his road ranch and rode down to Rawlins, fifty miles to the south, for the winter. The town was noisy and crowded with cowboys out of work. In one of the Rawlins' brothels Averell renewed his acquaintance with a plump but very attractive corn-bred strumpet of twenty-seven from Kansas named Ella Watson. Dismissing love as a possible explanation, one wonders what form of persuasion he used to induce her to return to the Sweetwater and set up housekeeping with him.

Ella's presence enlived the road ranch and improved business. If she was infatuated with Averell, as reasonable an explana-

tion as any, it did not last long. In the spring of 1888 she filed on
a homestead of her own on Horse Creek, a trickle of running
water a mile west of Averell's ranch. She had a one-room cabin
built and a small pasture fenced off. Witnesses later testified that
they had often seen as many as six or eight yearlings in her pasture
—never more—branded EK. It was an unregistered brand, the
Carbon County brand committee having rejected her application.

The story was soon widespread that her cattle were yearlings
that cowboys had stolen and exchanged for the privilege of sharing her bed for an hour. Maybe so. But tales of the number of
cattle she was receiving grew. If they were not to be seen in her
pasture, it was alleged, it was because she was passing them on to
her former paramour, Jim Averell, the "head of a gigantic rustling
ring."

These tales were without foundation. No evidence was produced then or thereafter that Averell was a rustler. Bothwell, intent on blackening the man's reputation and driving him out of
the Sweetwater Valley, gave such stories a wide circulation. He
was aware of the shoddy nature of the tales he spread. So were the
other owners. The beef roundup figure was the best evidence in
the world that they were not being menaced by any organized
rustling ring.

"Usually it takes an unexpected act of violence to whip into
sudden flame a long-smoldering situation such as prevailed on the
Sweetwater. But there is nothing in the record to indicate that
such was the case in this instance," unless, as this writer has suggested in a previous accounting of what occurred on July 20,
1889,[1] "it was a manifestation of the growing unease among the
big stock interests over the worsening conflict in Johnson County
that was to culminate in the so-called 'Johnson County War.' "

According to John Clay, the purpose of the party that set out
from Bothwell's ranch that hot, sunny afternoon was to deliver
an ultimatum to Averell and Ella Watson: clear out of the country or get hurt.[2] Fortunately there were witnesses—prejudiced, it
must be admitted—but they risked their necks to tell what they
had seen. Bothwell and his associates carried no ultimatum; it was
a lynch party from the start. The Association's puppet press failed

miserably in its attempt to put a better face on the sadistic expedition.

Accompanied by John DeCorey, described as a cowboy in her employ (which damaging admission indicates that she had work for such a man to do), Ella had walked down to the river where a small band of Shoshone Indians were camped, adjacent to where the trail crossed the Sweetwater, to buy a pair of beaded moccasins. As Ella and DeCorey were returning, the lynch party drove past them. No words were exchanged, but when she and DeCorey reached her cabin they found the six men waiting for them.

Gene Crowder, a fourteen-year-old range waif who had attached himself to Jim Averell, was there. Subsequently, at the coroner's inquest, he became an important witness.

"I was at Ella's trying to catch up a pony when they [the lynchers] rode up," he testified. "John Durbin took down the wire gate and drove the cattle out of the pasture [he doesn't say how many], while McLain and Connor kept Ella from going to the house. After a while they told her to get into the wagon and she asked them where they were going. They told her to Rawlins. She wanted to go to the house and change her clothes, but they would not let her and made her get into the wagon. Bothwell told her he would rope and drag her if she did not get in.

"She got in and we all started toward Jim's. I tried to ride around the cattle and get ahead, but Bothwell took hold of my pony's bridle and made me stay with them."

The lynch party went on to the road ranch and caught Averell at his second gate as he was hitching a team preparatory to leaving for Casper for supplies. They told him they had a warrant for his arrest. When he asked to see it, they patted their rifles and told him that was warrant enough. They made him get in the buck board with Ella and then drove off in the direction of Independence Rock.

"I started to follow them," DeCorey testified at the inquest, "but Bothwell pointed his rifle at me and ordered me to go to the house and stay there."

As soon as the lynchers were out of sight, DeCorey and young Crowder spurred quickly to the store and found four or five men lounging there, cowboys by profession. With the exception of one,

Frank Buchanan, their reputations were not of the best. Buchanan had bucked cattle for John Clay and Tom Sun and was rated a reliable man, but reckless and foolishly brave. He proved it by leaping into the saddle and taking off after the lynchers (when DeCorey and the boy had told their story), armed with only a pistol.

From a distance he saw the buckboard swing around the western end of Independence Rock, cross at the ford and continue up the bed of the river for a mile or more. He lost sight of the party when it turned up Spring Creek Canyon.

At this time of the year Spring Creek was dry, but the creek bed was clogged with high brush and gigantic boulders. Buchanan got down from the saddle and after tethering his horse, continued up the canyon on foot, hearing angry voices somewhere ahead of him. Using the boulders and brush for cover, he advanced until he caught sight of the lynch party and its victims. Lariats had been thrown over the limb of a scrub pine that projected out over the floor of the canyon from a limestone ledge.

"Bothwell had a rope around Jim's neck," Buchanan testified, "and had the end tied to a tree. He told him [Averell] to be game and jump off. McLain was trying to put a rope around Ella's neck, but she was jerking her head so that he did not succeed at that time.

"I opened fire on them, but do not know whether I hit anyone or not. They began shooting at me. I unloaded my revolver twice but had to run as they were shooting at me with Winchesters. I ran to my horse and rode to the ranch [Averell's] and told them Jim and Ella had been hanged, and then I started for Casper to get the sheriff."

None of the idlers to whom he told his news volunteered to accompany him. In fact, he was no sooner gone than they fled, evidently fearing that they might be marked for extermination.

It was a good fifty miles to Casper. In his excitement Buchanan lost the trail during the night and it was three o'clock in the morning when he pounded on the door of Ted Healy's homestead shack. He was still twenty-five miles from Casper. Healy pulled on his britches and agreed to go for the sheriff. After giving his horse several hours in which to recuperate, Buchanan turned back to Averell's place. By the time he arrived, the sun was an hour high. He found DeCorey, young Crowder and Ralph Cole, one of Averell's friends, there. As they waited out the day for the sheriff and coroner, Buchanan and Cole built a rough pine box in which to bury one of the victims and began putting a second box together.

They had a long wait. Healy did not reach Casper until Sunday noon. Very few Casperites had ever heard of Ella Watson. But whatever she was, she was a woman, and word that she had been lynched was enough to unleash an outpouring of wrath.

Carbon County Undersheriff Phil Watson (not related to Ella), who made his headquarters in Casper, began organizing a posse, deputizing a number of men including Dr. Joe Benson, the acting coroner, who swore in his own coroner's jury. It is irrelevant that several members of the posse, including Watson himself, were suspected of being connected with a horse thief ring; when they set out from Casper at daybreak on Monday morning, they were unconsciously uplifted by the feeling that they were unselfishly engaged in looking after the people's business.

The telegraph wires between Rawlins and Cheyenne were already clicking with what purported to be a "reliable" account of the execution of the "cattle thieves who had terrorized the Sweetwater Valley for years and were guilty of numerous murders." The author of this "reliable" story was undoubtedly George Henderson, John Clay's ranch superintendent, who had reached Rawlins and was alarmed by the public reaction to the lynching of Averell and Ella. Secretary Iams must have shared his concern, for he saw to it that the obedient Cheyenne *Leader* spread the "true" story across its front page in its next edition. He also wired Henderson to proceed to Cheyenne at once.

It was past Monday midnight when Sheriff Watson and his posse reached Averell's road ranch. After an hour had been spent rustling up something to eat, Buchanan suggested that they remain where they were until daylight. Watson wouldn't hear of it. With several men carrying lanterns to light the way, the whole party set out for the scene of the lynching.

"It was breaking day when the posse, directed by Frank Buchanan, caught sight of the two bodies swaying lifelessly in the dawn breeze. It was now the morning of July 23. For thirty hours or more, under a blazing sun, Jim and Ella had been hanging there, and their bloated, blackened faces were almost unrecognizable. The ledge from which they had been pushed off had allowed them only a drop of two feet, insufficient to break their necks, which meant that they had slowly strangled to death." [3] [4] [5]

The bodies were cut down and taken to Averell's place, where the coroner held an inquest. On the evidence given by Frank Buchanan, John DeCorey and the Crowder boy, a verdict was rendered to the effect that "the deceased man and woman, James Averell and Ella Watson, came to their deaths by being hanged by the neck at the hands of A. J. Bothwell, Tom Sun, John Durbin, R. M. Gailbraith, Bob Connor and Ernest McLain."

"The next morning two graves were dug a short distance from the Averell building," says Mokler. "Although the graves were quite shallow, it is said there was at least twelve inches of water in them when the bodies were interred, the water having seeped through from the river, which was about on a level with the burial spot."

In the meantime, Iams, Henderson and their lackey, Ed Towse of the *Leader,* had metamorphized Ella Watson, "against whom," the valiant *Carbon County Journal* dared to say, "there is no evidence that she was anything more than a common prostitute," into Cattle Kate Maxwell, the bandit queen who was wanted in half a dozen Western states. If you could believe what you read, "Ella Watson" was only an alias for this terrible female, this former Chicago dance-hall Jezebel who wore diamonds, owned race horses, committed numerous robberies, murdered several husbands and ruled "the most formidable gang of cattle rustlers and horse thieves the West had ever known."

Who could believe such sensational, pulp-paper trash? Many people did. Out-of-state newspapers embellished and reprinted it. Even the *National Police Gazette* took a whack at it. You can be sure that newspaper artists pictured her as ravishingly beautiful and titillated masculine readers by showing her dashing off a glass of champagne and showing a lot of leg. This mythical, nonexistent creature who was spawned in the editorial room of the Cheyenne *Leader* achieved the purpose for which she was created. People were not excited about the killing of Jim Averell; it was the lynching of the woman that had them aroused. If her reputation could be blackened to the point where the feeling would be that "she got only what she had coming to her," the clamor would end. And it largely did.

By methods that do not meet the eye, a second inquest into the double lynching was held, and the verdict this time was that the deceased had come to their death "at the hands of parties unknown."

Warrants had been served on Bothwell and his accomplices and they underwent a preliminary arraignment at Rawlins. The hearing was a travesty on legal procedure; it was held in a hotel room, not in court; no witnesses were called; and although the charge was murder in the first degree, and not subject to bail, the defendants were admitted to bail in the trifling (to men of their means) sum of $5,000 each and were permitted to sign one another's bonds. Needless to say, the presiding Judge, Samuel T. Corn, was a creature of the Wyoming Stock Growers' Association.

The grand jury of Carbon County convened in Rawlins on October 14. First on the docket was the case of the Territory of Wyoming vs. Albert J. Bothwell, Ernest McLain, Robert B. Connor, Tom Sun, Robert M. Gailbraith and John Durbin, with Judge Corn presiding. The Association had been busy in their behalf. Messrs. Corlett, Lacey and Riner, its biggest legal guns, were on hand to see that everything went according to plan. They were not needed; not a member of the sixteen-man jury but knew before he took his seat what the verdict would be. That it would be acquittal became apparent when the prosecuting attorney began calling his witnesses and discovered that they had either died or disappeared. Delivering himself of some pious twaddle, Corn charged the jury, which retired briefly. After some "due deliberation" it returned to inform the court that it had not found a true bill against the defendants, whereupon Judge Corn ruled:

"The grand jury at the present term of this court, having failed to find a true bill indictment against the defendants, or either of them, it is ordered by the court that each of them, and their bonds be discharged."

Only the Wyoming Stock Growers' Association could have

thwarted justice in that highhanded fashion. It had nothing to say about the missing witnesses, but others did. Says Mokler:

"Buchanan, the material witness for the prosecution, who was under a five-hundred-dollar bond to appear, was 'induced' to leave the country. He came to Casper in September and slept in a livery stable for two nights, then mysteriously disappeared and has never again been seen by anyone here. . . . John DeCorey and Ralph Cole also mysteriously disappeared, and Gene Crowder, the fourteen-year-old boy, died of Bright's disease before the case came to a hearing." According to Asa Mercer, the fighting editor and author of *The Banditti of the Plains*, "He [Crowder] was taken in charge by the cattlemen. He lingered some weeks and died—rumor strongly insisting at the hands of his protectors by the administration of a slow poison."

Of Ralph Cole, Mokler says: "Cole left the Averell ranch the night after the hanging, and he was followed by George Henderson. . . . The next day, while trying to make his way to a station on the Union Pacific Railroad, he was overtaken by Henderson, who shot him, and the body was burned to ashes." In corroboration, Mercer says: "He [Cole] was hunted like a wild beast, and the supposition is that he sleeps in some lonely mountain gorge." About John DeCorey, the fourth missing witness, this writer has said: "DeCorey was seen in Steamboat Springs, Colorado, two weeks after the lynching. No trace of him was found after that. If the law had not been under the complete domination of the rich, vested interests, some legal effort would have been made to determine the fate and whereabouts of the missing witnesses. But nothing was done."

Of the several men involved in the lynching of Jim Averell and Ella Watson, George Henderson was the first to die. He was shot and killed several months later in a dispute with a cowboy over wages. "As proof of the bitterness that remained over the lynching, his killing was regarded as a salutary act of retributive justice."

Time has erased the landmarks connected with the tragedy on the Sweetwater. Averell's buildings were soon torn down and the lumber carted away to be used a second time. Bothwell put skids under Ella's cabin and dragged it across country to be used for years as an icehouse. A succession of dry years long ago killed off the sickly pines in Spring Creek Canyon. Not only have the graves in which Averell and Ella were buried been lost, so have most of the memories of her been eroded by the ghostly image of Cattle Kate Maxwell.[6]

XXIV

The Johnson County Insurrection

When Wyoming achieved statehood in 1890, it changed very little. The cattlemen who had controlled the Territorial government took control of the State government. The best the small fry could do was to elect four men to the Assembly. Joseph M. Carey and Francis E. Warren, both pillars of the Wyoming Stock Growers' Association, were elevated to the U.S. Senate. Amos W. Barber, a bumbling sort of man of no consequence and a tool of the Association, became Acting Governor.

The ruling clique in Cheyenne showed its muscle by revamping the powerful State Livestock Commission. It did away with out-of-state inspectors and reduced the board to three permanent members, all subservient to the Association. When the fall shipping season arrived, the board instructed its inspectors at the shipping points to seize all cattle shipped by suspected rustlers, sell them and impound the proceeds of such sales. Where a bill of sale was offered in proof of ownership, it was to be disregarded and the possessor of it directed to come to Cheyenne and present his evidence to the board. In other words, he had the privilege of proving that he was not a thief. Knowing the cards were stacked against him, no shipper of seized cattle appeared before the board seeking relief or perhaps justice would be a better word.

In all, about five carloads of cattle were seized that fall. The proceeds, amounting to five thousand dollars or more, were impounded, of which very little was recovered by the rightful owners. Nothing the Wyoming Stock Growers' Association had ever done so inflamed public opinion. Among its own members there were those who disapproved. But they were silent, as perforce they had to be. There were other cattlemen, not Association men, and by no stretch of the imagination to be classed as rustlers, who came to the support of neighbors who had felt the iron heel of the Cheyenne ring. More than any other one thing, this seizure and sale of a man's cattle, on the suspicion that he was a rustler, was responsible for what we know as the Johnson County War of 1892. That was still some months away; the almost immediate reaction was an outbreak of rustling such as Wyoming had never known. It was more than range thievery undertaken for gain; it was rebellion; the oppressed striking back at its oppressors.

"On account of the Burlington Railroad building from Alliance, Nebraska, to Billings, Montana, there was an immense demand for beef from the various contractors to feed their men, and a good deal of the supply came from cowpunchers whose herds of cattle were visionary," complains John Clay in his remarkable *My Life on the Range* (remarkable chiefly for its perversions of the facts). "The owners supplied the beef, but got no pay for it. It was almost impossible to detect this class of thieving, and as the sheriffs of the different counties were elected by popular vote, their sympathies, to say the least of it, were with the rustlers. The reign of law was consigned to the ice chest. It was frozen up.

"This was the state of affairs that faced Wyoming cattleowners in 1891, for about that year the evil was hydra-headed. Consequently there were numerous meetings during the fall and winter that followed. The men who took the leading part in this class of work Maj. Wolcott [Frank Wolcott, manager of the VR Ranch owned by the Tolland Company, on a tributary of the North Platte in Converse County], Ex-Gov. Baxter [ex-Territorial governor and owner of the Western Union Beef Company] and H. B. Iams, secretary of the livestock board. [Also secretary of the Wyoming Stock Growers' Association.] They were backed by every large cattleman in the state, and behind them they had the moral influence of the two Senators, Warren and Carey. The acting governor, Dr. Barber, was also friendly." [1]

Add the name of William C. Irvine, manager of the Converse Cattle Company and the Ogallala Land and Cattle Company, member of the Livestock Commission, whose ranching interests were in the Cheyenne River country, and you have the tight little inner circle of men who conceived and were responsible for what Asa Mercer was to label "The Johnson County Invasion."

Early in December, Buffalo was aroused by two murders that occurred within a few miles of town. In fact in both instances the two men were on their way home from Buffalo when they were gunned down. The town had experienced a double murder before this, but this time they came back to back. In neither instance was the slayer, or slayers, taken into custody and brought to trial. Which, in view of the fact that there was scarcely a person in that part of Johnson County who was in any doubt as to who the killers were. The chief suspect was Frank Canton, the stock association detective and informer.

The first man to be struck down was young Orley E. Jones, popularly known as Ranger Jones, cowboy and broncobuster who, when he was not otherwise engaged, may have swung the wide loop. He had taken up a homestead on the Red Fork of the Powder next to his brother Johnnie. Behind a two-horse team he had driven into Buffalo in a buckboard to purchase some finishing lumber and flooring for the cabin he was building for his bride-to-be. But at that time of the year, a young, unattached cowpuncher could enjoy himself in Buffalo. It was not until November 29 that he started home. He got no farther than the low ridge south and west of town when he was gunned down.

There was a widely held theory about what led to the killing of Ranger Jones. He and Fred Hesse, the arrogant Englishman who was a power on the North Fork, had been trading accusations long-distance for several years. A few evenings back, while making the rounds of the Buffalo saloons with a bunch of cowboy cronies, young Jones and Hesse had come face to face, and Ranger had grievously humiliated the man. Without a shred of evidence to justify the conjecture, many people leaped to the conclusion that Hesse had retaliated by hiring Frank Canton to kill Ranger Jones.

However that may have been, there were no arrests, no indictments. His frozen body had not yet been found when Buffalo was
rocked by the killing of John A. Tisdale, a small and prosperous
rancher with a spread at the head of the Red Fork.

There were numerous Tisdales in Johnson County. John A.
Tisdale was the older brother of Al Allison Tisdale, a partner in
Jack Flagg's Hat outfit and of dubious reputation, and the father
of two young children, Martin and John, Jr. He was unrelated to
the Tisdale brothers, J. N. and Robert, Canadians, the wealthy
owners of a big spread on the South Fork of Powder River, who
were firmly aligned with the Wyoming Stock Growers' Association.

Had John Tisdale stuck to his knitting and refrained from
aligning himself with his less fortunate neighbors in their quarrel
with the Cheyenne overlords, he would not have warranted more
than passing mention in this narrative. But he was outspoken in
his condemnation of the injustice to which the farmer-stockman
homesteader was subjected. It cost him his life. Based on the evidence, that conclusion is unescapable; he was fomenting too much
trouble and he had to be stopped.

Tisdale drove into Buffalo on November 29 to buy his winter
supplies and toys and gifts for his children and his wife. The men
with whom he spoke that afternoon and the following morning
agreed that they found him depressed and gloomy; several remembered him saying he was afraid something might happen to him
before he reached home. That something had shaken him was evident by the amount of drinking he did that afternoon. He was not
normally a drinking man. On his way to town, had he been threatened or warned that his life was in danger? How else explain his
strange conduct?

There were no neutrals in the struggle going on in Johnson
County. It was well known that some of Buffalo's leading businessmen were on the Association's side of the fence. They included some of the men Tisdale spoke with that day.

He left town in the afternoon of November 30. For some unknown reason, unless it was fear, he turned in at the Cross H, only
six miles from Buffalo, and spent the night there. He was on his
way again in the morning and got as far as Haywood's Gulch, an-

other two miles, when a hidden assassin killed him, led the team, one horse of which he had wounded, off the road and then shot the animals. Taking his time, he walked to his horse, a big sorrel with white stockings on its hind feet, and turned into the horse trail which led along a ridge that was a short cut to town. Charlie Basch, on his way into Buffalo on business, saw the man. He recognized the horse, and he recognized the rider. It was Frank M. Canton.[2]

It took Charlie Basch a long time to screw up enough courage to tell what he had seen, and stick to it. At the inquest into the death of John Tisdale, he testified that he had been mistaken in previously saying he had recognized the horse and rider. Under oath, he swore that he didn't have any idea who the man was. Being under heavy suspicion, Canton demanded a hearing and "proved" he had not been out of town on December 1. Weeks later, Basch got around to telling the truth. But it was too late. Canton and Hesse had made a hurried exit from Buffalo and sought sanctuary in Cheyenne.

It must be said for the Wyoming Stock Growers' Association that, whatever the circumstances, it always managed to look out for its own. Over the years, in control of the law, it had pursued its arrogant ways and won many minor victories, but it had yet to win the big battle—the elimination of the rustler.

Rustler, in Association parlance, applied not only to actual cow thieves but to all those who supported, or otherwise abetted them. In other words, if anyone opposed the Wyoming Stock Growers' Association, he was *per se* a rustler. That, it developed, included a great many people.

In Cheyenne, as 1891 drew to a close, a little group of men, high up in the inner councils of the Association, solemnly discussed a matter they had had before them for days. What they were considering was an armed invasion of Johnson County: the striking force to be composed of Association members, employees, and by half a hundred Texas mercenaries. The expedition was not to waste its time taking prisoners; proven and suspected rustlers were to be shot on sight.

Secretary Iams had a list of seventy men marked for execution. He assured his fellow conspirators that there would be no interference by the several hundred troops stationed at Fort McKinney, adjacent to Buffalo, which indicates that he had discussed the matter with Senators Carey and Warren. However that may have been, the conferees unanimously agreed that immediately following the annual spring meeting of the Association, the march into Johnson County would get under way.

Whether this hare-brained, crackpot undertaking originated with Major Frank Wolcott, a notorious hothead, or with William C. Irvine, who had an equally short fuse, is of no consequence; it is enough to say that this little group of willful men had committed the Wyoming Stock Growers' Association to the costliest, most disastrous move it ever made. It was doomed to failure before it got started. Looking back over the years, one must wonder how successful, wealthy men who had made their way to the top in the past ten years, could have loaned themselves to such an undertaking. By no stretching of the imagination was it a war; in the end, all it accomplished was to make a martyred hero of an unknown cowpuncher named Nate Champion and to elevate Asa Shinn Mercer, the ambivalent and persecuted editor-publisher of the *Northwestern Livestock Journal,* to enduring fame as the author of the vitriolic *The Banditti of the Plains,* a scathing account of the Johnson County invasion.

Preparations began at once. In January, R. S. Van Tassel, high up in Association councils, was sent to Colorado to buy horses. He was a good judge of horseflesh. In and around Longmont he found a number of animals that measured up to his needs. In the meantime, Tom Smith, an Association detective, had been dispatched to Texas to recruit a number of gunmen. A Texan himself, Smith went home to Lamar County and in a week or more succeeded in signing up twenty-two young toughs, among them the notorious Texas Kid. They were to be paid five dollars a day and expenses, with a bonus of fifty dollars for every man they killed. They were promised that when they arrived in Wyoming they would be deputized and armed with blank warrants, so that by writing in the dead man's name they could claim he was shot down while resisting arrest. The promises were not kept; the Texans were not deputized and saw no warrants. Not that it mattered in the slightest to them.

Secretary Iams had taken himself to Idaho to recruit a few mercenaries on his own account. The only success he had was in Owyhee County, where he succeeded in getting George Dunning, a tough young cowpuncher who had been making trouble for the Owyhee Stock Association, to join up. Iams was to regret the day he laid eyes on the man, for Dunning accepted for the sole purpose of warning the rustlers of their danger and doing what he could to defeat the cattle kings.

Plans for the invasion had been completed without a hitch. The horses had arrived from Colorado and been branded; wagons had been purchased for the transportation of baggage, supplies and a small cannon, on loan from nearby Fort D. A. Russell. Major Frank Wolcott had been appointed field commander. He was now in Denver awaiting the arrival there of Tom Smith and the Texas men. The annual spring meeting of the Association was in session, with a heavy attendance. The need for the utmost secrecy had been impressed on the members. Although they weren't talking, secrecy was impossible. The heavy sale of guns and ammunition, and the activity in the yards of the Colorado Southern Railroad were evidence enough that something of major importance was about to occur.

The early afternoon train from Denver rolled into Cheyenne on time on April 5, 1892. Attached to it was a Pullman with all blinds down. In the car were Wolcott and the twenty-two Texans. The Pullman was shunted to another track and coupled onto the "Invasion Special," consisting of three stock cars in which the horses were loaded, and a flat car on which three new Studebaker wagons had been anchored. Supplies and baggage were put aboard a fifth car. The Pullman, with its human freight, brought up the rear. In little groups of twos and threes the cattlemen sauntered down from the Cheyenne Club and climbed aboard. All this activity alerted the town, and when the Special pulled out at five-thirty and took the main line of the Colorado Southern to the north, it was obvious to the group gathered on the depot platform that something of the gravest importance was taking place.

By way of the Colorado Southern and the Fremont, Elkhorn and Missouri Valley Railroad, the Special was bound for Casper, a hundred and fifty miles to the northwest, where the march of a hundred and twenty-five miles on horseback to Buffalo was to begin. It was the intention of the invaders on reaching Buffalo to seize the courthouse, take possession of any arms the local militia might have, and then proceed with the gruesome job of exterminating the men that had been marked for destruction.

There were fifty-two men aboard the Special when it steamed out of Cheyenne. Nineteen were cattlemen. Five Association employees, among them Frank Canton, six so-called noncombatants, including a doctor, three teamsters and two newspaper correspondents (Sam T. Clover of the Chicago *Herald* and the ubiquitous Ed Towse, now city editor of the Cheyenne *Sun*); twenty-two mercenaries (twenty-one from Texas and George Dunning from Idaho) completed the roster.

Dissension broke out early in the evening when Major Wolcott caught Canton rummaging through the baggage car and ordered him out. Smith and the Texans took Canton's side of the argument. Wolcott sulked, and it removed the last hope of success.

In the pre-dawn darkness of April 6 the Invaders reached Casper and made camp outside of town. The saddle stock had been loosely picketed. At breakfast time it was discovered that many had broken away. Several hours were lost in rounding them up and the morning was half gone before the expedition got under way. The weather was cold and miserable. The frost was coming out of the ground and the road was a strip of yellow gumbo in which the horses slithered and the wagons got stuck. Wolcott ordered the telegraph line cut, isolating Buffalo from the outside world.

For several days the Invaders disappeared in the infinity of the plains, but wild tales of men being shot or hanged and homes burned swept the state. Gillette reported that a stagecoach driver claimed he had seen two wagonloads of wounded men being taken to the hospital at Fort McKinney.

It was five o'clock in the afternoon of April 8 when the Invaders reached the Tisdale brothers' ranch, the intention being to spend the night there and recuperate. These plans went by the board when Mike Shonsey (Association spy and informer) arrived with word that fourteen rustlers, led by Nate Champion, were holed up at Johnny Nolan's abandoned K C Ranch. Wolcott was all for pushing on at once and blasting hell out of Nate Champion and his gang before they took alarm and fled. Again there was dissension; Fred Hesse, Canton and some others were for sticking to the original plan to march directly to Buffalo. Wolcott had his way about it, and facing up to a bitter wind and blinding snow, they spent the night covering the fifteen miles to the K C. The Major got lost in the storm and took shelter in a haystack.

Mike Shonsey and two of the Texans had been sent ahead to reconnoiter the house. They rejoined the column with the information that the rustlers were still there, playing a fiddle and having a good time. But the fourteen men of his original story had dwindled to four: Champion, his close friend Nick Ray, and two out-of-work cowboys who had spent the winter trapping; by name, Ben Jones and Bill Walker.

When Wolcott rejoined his forces, he ordered his men to keep to the brush along the looping Middle Fork until they had the house surrounded, keep themselves concealed and await developments. They had only two buildings to watch: the cabin and a log stable, seventy-five yards to the rear.

The first man to step out of the cabin was Ben Jones. He started for the creek, carrying a tin bucket to get water for breakfast. He was captured without outcry. Sometime later Bill Walker came out to see what had become of his friend Jones. The moment he turned the corner of the stable, he, too, was captured. Not a shot had been fired, but when Nick Ray opened the cabin door and walked out ten or a dozen steps, looking about suspiciously, the Texas Kid took aim and shot him, allegedly on Wolcott's order. Ray staggered back toward the door. Half a dozen rifles cracked from different directions and he fell forward on his face. Champion ran out and dragged his dying partner inside.[3]

Nate Champion and Nick Ray would have been the last persons in the world to deny that they had done some rustling over the years. Both had been connected with Jack Flagg's Hat outfit. But there is nothing in the record to indicate that they were small or mean or ever betrayed a friend. If Nate Champion had been made governor or left a million dollars at his death, he would have been forgotten long ago. As it is, he will be remembered as long as there is a Wyoming.

On the pages of a small bloodstained notebook, he wrote the story of his last hours in the K C cabin. It is not a saga of despair —just a simple account of how a brave man died. It has become a classic. Frank Canton picked it up from Champion's dead body, and before handing it over to Major Wolcott, read it aloud to the group that paused to listen. No one will ever know why Wolcott didn't destroy it. Perhaps in the dim recesses of his mind he realized that it should be preserved. When he turned the notebook over to Sam Clover, the correspondent of the Chicago *Herald*, he must have known that he was practically guaranteeing its publication.

Incorporated in Clover's despatches from the West, it appeared in full on April 16, 1892:

"Me and Nick was getting breakfast when the attack took place. Two men was with us—Bill Jones and another man. The old man went after water and did not come back. His friend went to see what was the matter and he did not come back. Nick started out and I told him to look out, that I thought there was someone at the stable would not let them come back.

"Nick is shot but not dead yet. He is awful sick. I must go and wait on him.

"It is now about two hours since the first shot. Nick is still alive.

"They are still shooting and are all around the house. Boys, there is bullets coming in like hail.

"Them fellows is in such shape that I can't get at them. They are shooting from the stable and river and back of the house.

"Nick is dead. He died about 9 o'clock. I see a smoke down at the stable. I think they have fired it. I don't think they intend to let me get away this time."

There was a lull of several hours in the fighting, the attackers having decided that they were wasting ammunition to no purpose and that burning the house was the only way in which Champion could be driven out. Several men were sent to a nearby ranch for a load of hay. When they returned without having found any, the leaders of the expedition could not decide on what to do next. Champion was writing again:

"It is now about noon. There is someone at the stable yet.

They are throwing a rope at the door and dragging it back. I guess it is to draw me out. I wish that duck [man] would go further so I can get a shot at him.

"Boys, I don't know what they have done with them two fellows that stayed here last night.

"Boys, I feel pretty lonesome just now. I wish there was someone here with me so we could watch all sides at once. They may fool around until I get a good shot before they leave."

Champion does not appear to have had any idea of the size of the party that had him pinned down, nor had anyone come close enough to be recognized. The attackers drew back several hundred yards and called in the men that were guarding the road against a chance visitor as they ate dinner. Leaving the road unguarded was a costly mistake, for as they dined, a horseman and a lad of seventeen, driving a team drawing the running gear of a wagon, came down the slight slope to the west, obviously making for the bridge over the Middle Fork, a mile or two to the southeast.

The man was Jack Flagg; the boy, his stepson Alonzo Taylor. Flagg had left his ranch on the Red Fork, eighteen miles to the west that morning, bound for the Democratic convention at Douglas. All unknowing, he had ridden right into the hands of the Invaders. Of all the prizes they hoped to bag, Jack Flagg was Number One.

Too late, someone fired a shot that missed. One shot was all the warning Flagg needed. He called to the boy to unhitch one of his horses and flee, while he (Flagg) seized his rifle and held off a group of pursuers. Miraculously, Flagg and the boy escaped. The political convention forgotten, they made tracks for Buffalo, not aware that Terence Smith, a Middle Fork rancher, had heard the shooting and was spreading the news as he raced for Buffalo.

Champion proved that he didn't know that it was his friend Jack Flagg who had passed. He wrote:

"It is about 3 o'clock now. There was a man in a buckboard and one on horseback just passed. They [the Invaders] fired on them as they went by. I don't know if they killed them or not. I seen lots of men come out on horses on the other side of the river and take after them.

"I shot at a man in the stable just now. Don't know if I got him or not. I must go look out again. It don't look as if there is much show of my getting away. I see twelve or fifteen men. One looks like [name scratched out]. I don't know whether it is or not. I hope they did not catch them fellows that run over the bridge toward Smith's."

And later: "They are shooting at the house now. If I had a pair of glasses I believe I would know some of those men. They are coming back. I've got to look out."

Then with evening approaching:

"Well, they have just got through shelling the house again like hail. I heard them splitting wood. I guess they are going to fire the house tonight. I think I will make a break when night comes, if alive.

"Shooting again. I think they will fire the house this time.

"It's not night yet. The house is all fired. Goodbye, boys, if I never see you again."

Wolcott, making use of the wagon Flagg had left behind, had it wheeled to the rear of the stable, where it was filled with pitch pine faggots and what hay could be scraped up. The wagon was then pushed up against the house and a match applied. The roof caught fire almost at once, and soon the whole building was in flames. Champion waited as long as he dared and then made his break. He didn't get more than fifty yards when life was blasted out of him.

Knowing that news of their presence was by now far ahead of them, the Invaders got away from the K C at once and cut across country until they struck the main road into Buffalo. Stopping only briefly to change horses, they reached the T A ranch fourteen miles from Buffalo. They were about to continue their march when an accident occurred. Mounting a strange horse, one of the Texans, Jim Dudley, dropped his rifle. The gun went off, the slug shattering his left knee. Charlie Ford, manager of the T A, volunteered to take the injured man to the hospital at Fort McKinney. There, a few days later, he died of blood poisoning.

The march from the T A had been resumed but had gone only a short distance when a messenger from Buffalo on a lathered horse informed them that the town was in an uproar and that several hundred armed men were marching south to meet them. Irvine and Wolcott conferred briefly and decided to turn back to the T A and fort up there until the situation could be studied. When morning came, they found the T A besieged by several hundred armed and determined men. The arrogance and smugness ran out of the leaders of the Invaders like air out of a pricked balloon.

Sheriff Red Angus and a posse had made a hurried ride to the K C. When Angus got back and reported what he had found—the burned cabin, the incinerated remains of Nick Ray and Nate Champion's bullet-riddled body—it was greeted with cries of outrage and a burst of scattered rifle fire that relieved the feelings of the Johnson County men.

The T A buildings were well situated to withstand an attack: the ranch house, built of twelve-inch squared logs, being impervious to rifle fire.

Throughout Monday, April 11, reinforcements joined the besiegers, arriving by twos and threes from distant ranches, convinced that the Invaders meant to "drive them from their homes, seize their small herds, and repossess their homesteads by fire and sword." [4] At best they were only a leaderless, armed mob. But such moments have a way of producing hitherto unrecognized leaders. The Johnson County men turned to Eli Snider, a respected pioneer and rancher-businessman, and giant, bearded Rap Brown, the manager of the Buffalo flouring mill. They couldn't have made a better choice; Snider established headquarters at the Covington ranch between the T A and town. Rap Brown became field commander. During the morning he captured the three supply wagons of the Invaders, containing their store of ammunition, dynamite and food.[5] It meant that the position of the men trapped at the T A would soon become desperate. Not only would they have to husband what ammunition they had, but in a day or two they would be going hungry.

Wolcott, obviously convinced that the "rustlers" would attempt to rush the house, had done what he could to hold them off. Logs had been piled against the windows, leaving only loopholes at the top. During the night of April 11, he had a trench dug outside the doors from which an advancing enemy could be picked off. It was a wasted effort; what the besieged needed was help—and quickly. In the pre-dawn darkness Wolcott and Irvine had got a messenger through the lines bound for Gilette, a hundred miles to the east, from where the telegraph to Cheyenne was still functioning. He carried an urgent message to Governor Barber ordering him to have the troops from Fort McKinney marched to their rescue.

As Tuesday, with its long hours of rattling gunfire, passed, Wolcott and Irvine had no way of knowing whether their messenger had got through or not. As a further annoyance another one of the Texans dropped his cocked revolver and was shot in the thigh, a wound from which he died several days later. Far away in Washington, Senators Carey and Warren, acting on Governor Barber's urgent request, were closeted with Secretary of War Elkins and finally with President Harrison. At a few minutes after midnight Colonel Van Horn, the commandant at Fort McKinney, received an order from Grant to march to the scene of the "insurrection" and take the Invaders into custody. Sometime after 2 A.M. of the freezing morning of April 13, Colonel Van Horn and three Troops of the 6th Cavalry clattered out of McKinney. On reaching the T A, he conferred with Sheriff Red Angus and Rap Brown. They were willing that he arrest the besieged men, insisting, however, that the prisoners be later turned over to the civilian authorities of Johnson County. Van Horn assured them that would be done.

Of course—and through no fault of his own—that promise was never fulfilled. With the Republican High Command in Washington calling the play, the promise of a post commander in Wyoming was immaterial. What followed was just comic opera.

The "prisoners" were taken under military escort to Fort D. A. Russell and later moved to Laramie and lodged in the State Penitentiary, in a wing of their own and treated as guests. Weeks dragged by as defense attorneys sparred for time. It was costing a huge sum of money to keep the prisoners. Johnson County was broke. It was happy to agree to a change of venue and have the prisoners freed without bail on their own recognizance. The action moved to Keefe Hall, an auditorium in Cheyenne. As the defendants waited for a trial date to be set, they moved about town at will, carrying arms and patronizing saloons. Even the town half-wits could foresee how the farce would end.

Finally on January 2, 1893, the trial of the Invaders got under way. Weeks had been spent impaneling a jury. Both sides were anxious for a dismissal, but Judge Van Deventer for the defense demanded a directed verdict of acquittal, which would make a second trial of his clients impossible. County Prosecutor Bennett acceded and the court threw up its hands in disgust and the cases were dismissed.

Cheyenne, wearied of the whole dull mess, heaved a sigh of relief. Nine months had passed since the Invasion Special had made its way north. The Association was still in the driver's seat. There were some who said it hadn't learned a thing. But maybe it had; at least in its controlled press men formerly classed together as rustlers were being referred to as "citizens."

Notes

CHAPTER I

1. See Frederick R. Bechdolt's *Tales of the Old-Timers.*
2. Lawrence Sullivan Ross, inducted as Governor of Texas in January, 1887.
3. Nocona was the Indian husband of Cynthia Ann Parker and the father of her two children. The importance of the Pease River battle was somewhat dimmed by its emotional impact when Sul Ross found a "white squaw" among his captives who proved to be the long-lost Cynthia Ann.
4. Charles Goodnight stated that he saw Peta Nocona several years after the Pease River fight.

CHAPTER II

1. Son of Peta Nocona and Cynthia Ann Parker.
2. Citation from *Red River Valley,* Harry Sinclair Drago, 1926.

CHAPTER III

1. J. Evetts Haley cited: *Charles Goodnight, Cowman and Plainsman.*
2. With New Orleans in Union hands after its ironclads had closed the Mississippi, it became a lively market for contraband Texas beef, even though it meant trading with the enemy.
3. For a detailed account of the Horsehead Crossing drive, see J. Evetts Haley, *Charles Goodnight, Cowman and Plainsman* and *The No-Gun Man of Texas* by Laura V. Hamner.

CHAPTER IV

1. See the modern two-volume edition of *The Trail Drivers of Texas*, published by the Argosy-Antiquarian Press, New York, 1963.
2. See *The Trail Drivers of Texas*, pp. 908-1013; J. Frank Dobie, *Country Gentleman*, March, 1927.
3. There are accounts of Loving's death in which Goodnight is said to have assisted in the amputation of his partner's arm, which may be dismissed as fiction.
4. From the *Goodnight Recollections* compiled by the Panhandle-Plains Historical Society, Canyon, Texas.
5. Cited from Frank Howell's letter to Mrs. Laura Cahoon. Keleher, *Violence in Lincoln County*, p. 59.
6. Letter of Major F. C. Godfroy, Agent for the Mescalero Apaches, to Secretary of the Interior Carl Schurz.

CHAPTER V

1. Thomas Benton Catron, for whom Catron County is named, graduated from the University of Missouri in 1860 and was studying law when the War Between the States erupted. He declared for the Confederacy and served throughout the struggle. When he arrived in New Mexico in 1866, he was far from affluent. At his death in 1921 he was one of the wealthiest men in the State. In Territorial days he held a succession of important political offices. His connection with Murphy and Dolan cannot be doubted, for he financed the original firm of L. G. Murphy and Co.
2. Murphy was in failing health when he withdrew from the firm and took up residence at his Carrizozo ranch. Ten months later he advertised the ranch, with its 800 square miles of range, for sale. Catron bought it and operated it for four years before selling it. Murphy died in Santa Fe on October 20, 1878.
3. For a detailed account of the legal maneuvering in the Emil Fritz case, see Keleher, *Violence in Lincoln County*.
4. Evans, Baker, Hill and Davis were rescued from the Lincoln jail by a force of some thirty armed men. The door had been conveniently left unlocked.

CHAPTER VI

1. The Kid had once worked for Chisum and they had fallen out over wages he claimed were due him. In the days of his outlawry he stole enough Jingle-Bob to square that account many times over.
2. According to Roberts, he acquired the name of "Buckshot" when he survived a blast of buckshot fired at him by a McLennan County (Texas) sheriff.
3. Cited from various sources.

4. From this same room the Kid was to make his spectacular escape on April 28, 1881.

CHAPTER VII

1. Like Murphy, Dolan and Riley, William Brady was born in Ireland and emigrated to the United States when a young man. He served throughout the War Between the States with several New Mexico volunteer regiments. For bravery in action, he was promoted to the rank of major in 1865.

2. George W. Peppin arrived in New Mexico with the so-called California Column in Civil War days, and at the conclusion of the war remained in Mesilla, where he was probably on intimate terms with John Kinney and his outlaw gang.

3. Cited from Keleher, *Violence in Lincoln County,* pp. 140-141.

CHAPTER VIII

1. There is reliable evidence that the troops had not left town when the looting got under way; in fact, they participated in it.

2. Mrs. McSween was also executrix of the Tunstall estate, but the assets had been so scattered and destroyed that she was able to recover less than $2,000.

3. In his *Story of the American Railroads,* Stewart Holbrook tells how young Edward Gillette, one day to become famous as locating engineer for the Santa Fe, Burlington, and Denver and Rio Grande, arrived in Santa Fe ahead of his chief and the other members of his party dead broke and how he appealed to Governor Wallace for eating and sleeping money, which Wallace provided. It was no little favor, considering that Wallace's salary as governor was a munificent $2,500 a year.

CHAPTER IX

1. For the history of Colorado River steamboating, see Harry Sinclair Drago's *The Steamboaters.*

2. When Charles E. Perkins erected his store in 1879, he built it to serve the dual purpose of providing a place for his business and as a fort against Apache attacks. Its stone walls were two feet thick and its windows loopholed for gunfire.

3. Cited from *Arizona's Dark and Bloody Ground,* Earle R. Forrest, p. 28.

4. Jim Stinson quoted in an interview in the *Arizona Republican,* November, 1930.

5. Although the two factions are often referred to as the sheepmen and the cattlemen, that is not accurate, for there were men associated with the Tewksburys, such as Jim Roberts, George Newton, John Rhodes and others who by no stretch of the imagination could be identified as sheepmen.

CHAPTER X

1. In addition to the three boys, Tewksbury's Indian wife presented him with a daughter. She was not with her father and brothers when they came to Arizona and her name does not appear in any of the tales about the Pleasant Valley War, but she is said to have arrived in Globe some years later and that Jim Tewksbury died in her home there.
2. A skull and rusted rifle were found several years later. Folklore has it that the rifle was identified as Mark Blevans'—which is to be doubted.
3. Long after he disappeared from Arizona, Tom Tucker served as under-sheriff at Santa Fe, New Mexico, and died a natural death in Texas many years later.
4. In 1887 most of Tonto Basin and all of the Pleasant Valley country were a part of the original Yavapai County. Huge pieces have since been sliced off and are now part of Coconino and Gila counties.

CHAPTER XI

1. Arizona's first Territorial Government was set up at Navajo Springs by Governor J. B. Goodwin on December 29, 1863, but was soon removed to Prescott.
2. Owens served for three years as sheriff of Apache County, in the course of which he killed at least three rustlers and secured convictions against sixteen others. He later served as a detective for the Santa Fe Railroad and finally as an express messenger for Wells, Fargo. His last years were spent as a businessman at Seligman, Arizona, where he died in 1918.
3. John Blevans dropped out of sight after serving his time in the Yuma Penitentiary and led a peaceful life. He died in 1928 in an automobile accident near Phoenix with his granddaughter.
4. Harry Middleton was not related to William Middleton at whose ranch the first big battle of the Pleasant Valley War occurred.
5. Sheriff Glenn Reynolds and a deputy were killed by a group of Apache prisoners whom they were taking to the penitentiary at Yuma, November 2, 1889.

CHAPTER XII

1. Ed and Jim Tewksbury had lodged that charge against him and then dropped it.
2. Stott had come to Holbrook expecting to find employment with the Aztec Land and Cattle Company, which he had been more or less promised by his home-town neighbor, Governor Thomas Talbot, of Massachusetts, who was financially interested in the company. But other stockholders had sent so many young men West with similar promises that the Hash Knife was turning men away.

3. In addition to his livery business, Sam Brown had money invested in sheep and may have been a silent partner in the firm of Daggs Brothers.

4. Why Stott's parents took no legal action to reclaim his property or bring his slayers to justice may have been due to the fact that it couldn't have been done without reviving the old story that the boy had bought rustled stock, a charge that he had vehemently denied.

CHAPTER XIII

1. Rhodes was Ed Tewksbury's brother-in-law, having married John Tewksbury's widow, Mary Crigler Tewksbury, who was credited with preventing the hogs from devouring his body.

2. S. W. Young was not a feudist. As a neutral he was a stabilizing influence on the fragile peace that came to Pleasant Valley.

3. For forty years Miss Ola Young, S. W. Young's daughter, was postmistress. Her tiny office, six by six feet, is said to have been the smallest in the United States.

CHAPTER XIV

1. Cited from Albert Pike, *Narrative of a Journey in the Prairie*, Arkansas Historical Association.

2. U.S. Senator James Wadsworth, Jr., was her nephew. He was placed in charge of Mrs. Adair's holdings in 1911 and played an important role in settling her estate.

3. For the record, the first white females in the Panhandle were the strumpets in what was appropriately called "Hide Town," the huddle of tents and picket shacks a mile below the military reservation line at Fort Elliott, which became Mobeetie. It was there that the notorious Doc Holliday, the gambler, and his inamorata, Big Nose Kate Fisher, plied their respective trades, and where Bat Masterson shot and killed the army's bad boy, Sergeant Flynn, and was himself wounded in the shoot-out.

4. Cited from *A History of the JA Ranch*, by Harley True Burton.

CHAPTER XV

1. See *Microbe Hunters*, by Paul De Kruif.

2. Letter published in *Fort Griffin Echo*.

3. Cited from J. Evetts Haley, *Charles Goodnight, Cowman and Plainsman*.

4. Unpublished letter to Martin S. Garettson, Secretary American Bison Society.

5. See Harry Sinclair Drago, *Red River Valley*.

6. Ibid.

7. Cited from J. Evetts Haley, *Charles Goodnight, Cowman and Plainsman*.

8. Unpublished letter to Martin S. Garettson, Secretary American Bison Society.

CHAPTER XVI

1. Cited from the Galveston *News*.
2. Cited from *Charles Goodnight, Cowman and Plainsman,* by J. Evetts Haley.
3. Cited from *Life and Times of Timothy Dwight Hobart,* by L. F. Sheffy.
4. Ibid.
5. Ibid.

CHAPTER XVII

1. Cited from *The Trail Drivers of Texas,* Vol. 1.
2. They included Albert Sidney Johnston, Robert E. Lee, Fitzhugh Lee, J. E. B. (Beauty) Smith, William J. Hardee, Earl Van Dorn, Theodore O'Hara, John B. Hood, Edmund Kirby Smith. There was one among them who was to fight for the Union—George H. Thomas, the "Rock of Chickamauga."
3. Mary Custis Lee was the great-granddaughter of Martha Washington.
4. Cited from "Red River Station," Glen O. Wilson, *Southwestern Historical Quarterly,* January 1958.

CHAPTER XVIII

1. Stuart relates that on their way north they discovered in the lower end of Salt River a tract of four or five acres with a coating of salt that was from four to five inches thick. They filled a barrel with salt, which they disposed of at a fancy price on reaching the Beaverhead. This salt bed was worked for years by the Mormons.
2. Stuart married a Snake Indian girl named Auboney, on May 2, 1862. It was a legal marriage and lasted until her death in 1887. He had nine children by Auboney, of whom three daughters survived her. Mary, next to the youngest, became the wife of Teddy Blue (E. C. Abbott), the well-known cowboy and friend of Charlie Russell, the famous Western painter.
3. Cited from *Gold Camp,* by Larry Barsness.
4. Although Red Yeager's identity as Erastus Yeager was not established until several years later, and that he hailed from West Liberty, Iowa, no one was as surprised as the Stuart brothers, for the three of them had been boys together in Iowa.

CHAPTER XIX

1. Cited from *Wyoming Cattle Trails,* by John K. Rollinson.
2. Cited from *Forty Years on the Frontier,* by Granville Stuart.
3. During his years on the D-S, Stuart accumulated a library of 3,000 volumes, to which his cowboys always had access. How different the D-S was from

other spreads can be judged from Teddy Blue's exclamation when he sat down to supper at the end of his first day on the ranch and saw what was on the table. "Jesus Christ," he demanded, "is this the way you fellows live? Hot bread three times a day!"

4. The series of prairie fires to which Stuart refers, burning out of control, dropped ashes on Miles City, one hundred and thirty miles to the southeast.

5. Cited from *Forty Years on the Frontier*, by Granville Stuart.

6. Ibid.

CHAPTER XX

1. A year later Billings became the great shipping point for cattle from the ranges to the north and proudly advertised itself as the Cowboy Capital of Montana.

2. When the ownership of the D-S changed hands, Stuart and Con Kohrs became the sole owners under the title of the Pioneer Cattle Company, capitalizing the firm for a million dollars. Kohrs' favorite story about Stuart was that he (Stuart) had brought a bagful of books along on a drive to Billings for the entertainment of the crew. "The boys were doing so much reading and so little work that when we reached the Yellowstone I threw the bag into the river. You might say I started the first circulating library in Montana."

3. Cited from *Forty Years on the Frontier*, by Granville Stuart.

CHAPTER XXI

1. For the complete treaty, see Dr. C. G. Coutant's *History of Wyoming*, Vol. 11, pp. 605-614.

2. Save for some correction of the southern boundary with Colorado and Utah, the original lines were what they are today.

3. The so-called "pilgrim cattle" were cattle that were shipped west from Midwest feed lots and were of Holstein, Guernsey and other barnyard strains. They were such poor foragers and so susceptible to disease that the experiment of putting them on the open range was quickly discontinued.

4. See Helena Huntington Smith's *The War on Powder River*, a brilliant and informative account of the Johnson County War.

CHAPTER XXII

1. Gene M. Gressley in *Bankers and Cattlemen* lists half a hundred American investors in the range cattle industry, along with their addresses and principal business. See Chapter 3.

2. U.S. Attorney, Governor and U.S. Senator, Carey Avenue in Cheyenne was named in his honor.

3. See Gressley, *Bankers and Cattlemen,* for a detailed account of the promotional pamphlets and guides issued by the railroads and stockmen's associations.

4. Cited from Helena Huntington Smith, *The War on Powder River,* Chapter 6.

5. First published in 1923. Reprinted by Argonaut Press, N.Y., 1966. Early history of Casper, Wyoming, and Natrona County.

CHAPTER XXIII

1. Cited from *Notorious Ladies of the Frontier,* pp. 226-228.

2. See *My Life on the Range,* John Clay, Jr., Chapter 22. A biased account.

3. Cited from *Notorious Ladies of the Frontier,* by Harry Sinclair Drago.

4. Cited from *The War on Powder River,* by Helena Huntington Smith, Chapter 18.

5. When she was hanged, Ella was wearing the moccasins she had purchased that afternoon. They had fallen off her feet as she was swung up and lay unnoticed on the ledge for several days, when they were picked up by E. C. Jameson and his wife and carried away to be exhibited as souvenirs.

6. It may be of interest to the reader to know that Bothwell retired from the range cattle business some years later and moved to California, where he died; Bob Connor left Wyoming for his old Eastern home at Mauch Chunk, Pennsylvania; Gailbraith went to Little Rock, Arkansas, and engaged in the banking business and died a wealthy man; McLain removed to Canada, while Tom Sun lived out his life on the Sweetwater.

CHAPTER XXIV

1. What Clay really meant was that the Republican political machine represented an investment of $25,000,000, and was therefore sacrosanct.

2. For a detailed account of the killing of John Tisdale, see Helena Huntington Smith's *The War on Powder River,* Chapters 23 and 24.

3. Irvine, using a pair of glasses, recognized him. It could not have been long after that when Wolcott and he realized that Nate Champion was alone in the house.

4. Cited from *The War on Powder River,* p. 214.

5. Ibid.

Bibliography

Abbott, E. C. (Teddy Blue), and Helena Huntington Smith, *We Pointed Them North*. Norman, University of Oklahoma Press, 1955.

Adair, Cornelia, *My Diary—August 30 to November 5, 1874*. Bath, England, Tyson and Company, 1918.

Adams, Ramon F., *The Rampaging Herd*. Norman, University of Oklahoma Press, 1959.

Athearn, Robert G., *High Country Empire*. New York, McGraw-Hill Book Company, 1960.

——, *Westward the Briton*. New York, Charles Scribner's Sons, 1953.

Atherton, Louis, *The Cattle Kings*. Bloomington, Indiana University Press, 1961.

Barnes, Will C., and William MacLeod Raine, *Cattle*. Garden City, Doubleday, 1930.

Barsness, Larry, *Gold Camp*. New York, Hastings House, 1961.

Bechdolt, Frederick R., *Tales of the Old-Timers*. New York, The Century Company, 1924.

Brisbin, Gen. James S., *The Beef Bonanza, or How to Get Rich on the Plains*. Philadelphia, Lippincott, 1881.

Burt, Struthers, *Powder River*. New York, Farrar and Rinehart, 1938.

Burton, Harley True, *A History of the JA Ranch*. Austin, The Von Boeckman-Jones Company, 1928.

Canton, Frank M., *Frontier Trails*, edited by Edward Everett Dale. Boston, Houghton Mifflin, 1930.

Carter, Captain Robert G., *The Old Sergeant's Story: Winning of the West*. New York, Hitchcock, 1926.

Chisholm, James, *South Pass: 1868,* edited by Lulu Homsher. Lincoln, University of Nebraska Press, 1960.

Chittenden, Hiram Martin, *History of Early Steamboat Navigation on the Missouri River.* Minneapolis, Ross and Haines, 1962 (Reprint).

Clay, John, Jr., *My Life on the Range.* Norman, University of Oklahoma Press, 1962 (Reprint).

Clover, Sam T., *On Special Assignment.* Boston, The Lothrop Company, 1903.

Coutant, C. G., *History of Wyoming.* New York, Argonaut Press, 1966 (Reprint).

Cox, James, *Historical and Biographical Record of the Cattle Industry.* St. Louis, Woodward and Tiernan Ptg. Co., 1895.

Cunningham, Eugene, *Triggernometry.* New York, Press of the Pioneers, 1934.

Dale, Edward Everett, *The Range Cattle Industry.* Norman, University of Oklahoma Press, 1930.

Dimsdale, Thomas J., *The Vigilantes of Montana.* Missoula, 1946 (One of many reprints).

Dobie, J. Frank, *The Longhorns.* Boston, Little, Brown, 1941.

———, *The Mustangs.* Boston, Little, Brown, 1952.

Dodge, Colonel Richard I., *Thirty-three Years Among Our Wild Indians.* Hartford, Worthington and Company, 1883.

Drago, Harry Sinclair, *Wild, Woolly and Wicked.* New York, Potter, 1960.

———, *Great American Cattle Trails.* New York, Dodd, Mead, 1963.

———, *Roads to Empire.* New York, Dodd, Mead, 1968.

Dykes, J. C., *The Bibliography of a Legend.* Albuquerque, University of New Mexico Press, 1956.

Fletcher, Robert H., *Free Grass to Fences: The Montana Cattle Range Story.* New York, University Publishers, 1960.

Frink, Maurice, *Cow Country Cavalcade: Eighty Years of the Wyoming Stock Growers' Association.* Denver, Old West Publishing Co., 1954.

Gard, Wayne, *The Great Buffalo Hunt.* New York, Knopf, 1959.

———, *Frontier Justice.* Norman, University of Oklahoma Press, 1949.

Garrett, Pat F., *The Authentic Life of Billy the Kid.* Santa Fe. Published by author. Numerous reprints.

Greene, A. C., *A Personal Country.* New York Knopf, 1969.

Haley, J. Evetts, *Charles Goodnight, Cowman and Plainsman.* Boston, Houghton Mifflin, 1936.

Hebard, Grace Raymond, and E. A. Brininstool, *The Bozeman Trail.* Glendale, Arthur H. Clark Co., 1936.

Hough, Emerson, *Story of the Outlaw.* New York, Grosset & Dunlap, 1923.

Howard, Joseph Kinsey, *Montana, High, Wide and Handsome.* New Haven, Yale University Press, 1943.

Keleher, William A., *Turmoil in New Mexico.* Albuquerque, University of New Mexico Press, 1952.

————, *Violence in Lincoln County*. Albuquerque, University of New Mexico Press, 1957.

Kennedy, Michael, *Cowboys and Cattlemen*. New York, Hastings House, 1964.

Langford, N. P., *Vigilante Days*. Missoula. A reprint, 1957.

McCarty, John L., *Maverick Town, the Story of Old Tascosa*. Norman, University of Oklahoma Press, 1946.

McFarling, Lloyd, *Exploring the Northern Plains*. Caldwell, Caxton Printers, 1955.

Marcy, Col. R. B., *Thirty Years of Army Life on the Border*. New York, Harper Brothers, 1866.

Mercer, Asa Shinn, *The Banditti of the Plains: the Crowning Infamy of the Ages*. Norman, University of Oklahoma Press (a reprint), 1954.

Mokler, Alfred James, *History of Natrona County, Wyoming*. Chicago, Lakeside Press, 1923.

Monaghan, Jay, *Last of the Bad Men (Tom Horn)*. Indianapolis, Bobbs-Merrill, 1946.

Pelzer, Louis, *The Cattlemen's Frontier*. Glendale, Arthur H. Clark Co., 1936.

Raine, William McLeod, *Famous Sheriffs and Western Outlaws*. New York, New Home Library (a reprint), 1944.

Richthofen, Walter, Baron von, *Cattle Raising on the Plains of North America*. New York, D. Appleton, 1885.

Rollinson, John K., *Wyoming Cattle Trails*. Caldwell, Caxton Printers, 1948.

Sandoz, Mari, *The Cattlemen*. New York, Hastings House, 1958.

Sheffy, Lester F., *The Life and Times of Timothy Dwight Hobart*. Canyon (Texas), The Plains-Panhandle Society, 1950.

Smith, Helena Huntington, *The War on Powder River*. New York, McGraw-Hill Book Company, 1966.

Spring, Agnes Wright, *Seventy Years: a Panoramic History of the Wyoming Stock Growers' Association*. Cheyenne. Sponsored by the Association, 1942.

Strahorn, Robert E., *Handbook of Wyoming and Guide to the Black Hills and Big Horn Regions*. Very likely paid for and distributed by the Union Pacific Railroad. Circa 1877.

Stuart, Granville, *Forty Years on the Frontier*. Edited by Paul C. Phillips. Glendale, Arthur H. Clark Co., 1925.

Vestal, Stanley, *The Old Santa Fe Trail*. Boston, Houghton Mifflin, 1939.

Webb, Walter Prescott, *The Great Plains*. Springfield, Mass., Ginn and Co., 1921.

Index